A Book Of

INDUSTRIAL RELATIONS AND LABOUR LAW

For
BBA Semester - IV
As Per Revised Syllabus
Effective from June 2014

Prof. Sharad D. Geet
M.A. (Eco.), M.Com., LL.B., D.C.L.

Mrs. Asmita A. Deshpande
B.Com., M.B.A.

N2387

BBA : Industrial Relations and Labour Law ISBN 978-93-5164-248-0

Second Edition : January 2016
© : Authors

The text of this publication, or any part thereof, should not be reproduced or transmitted in any form or stored in any computer storage system or device for distribution including photocopy, recording, taping or information retrieval system or reproduced on any disc, tape, perforated media or other information storage device etc., without the written permission of Authors with whom the rights are reserved. Breach of this condition is liable for legal action.

Every effort has been made to avoid errors or omissions in this publication. In spite of this, errors may have crept in. Any mistake, error or discrepancy so noted and shall be brought to our notice shall be taken care of in the next edition. It is notified that neither the publisher nor the authors or seller shall be responsible for any damage or loss of action to any one, of any kind, in any manner, therefrom.

Published By :
NIRALI PRAKASHAN
Abhyudaya Pragati, 1312, Shivaji Nagar,
Off J.M. Road, PUNE – 411005
Tel - (020) 25512336/37/39, Fax - (020) 25511379
Email : niralipune@pragationline.com

Printed By :
Repro Knowledgecast Limited,
Thane

☞ DISTRIBUTION CENTRES

PUNE
Nirali Prakashan : 119, Budhwar Peth, Jogeshwari Mandir Lane, Pune 411002, Maharashtra
Tel : (020) 2445 2044, 66022708, Fax : (020) 2445 1538
Email : bookorder@pragationline.com, niralilocal@pragationline.com

Nirali Prakashan : S. No. 28/27, Dhyari, Near Pari Company, Pune 411041
Tel : (020) 24690204 Fax : (020) 24690316
Email : dhyari@pragationline.com, bookorder@pragationline.com

MUMBAI
Nirali Prakashan : 385, S.V.P. Road, Rasdhara Co-op. Hsg. Society Ltd.,
Girgaum, Mumbai 400004, Maharashtra
Tel : (022) 2385 6339 / 2386 9976, Fax : (022) 2386 9976
Email : niralimumbai@pragationline.com

☞ DISTRIBUTION BRANCHES

JALGAON
Nirali Prakashan : 34, V. V. Golani Market, Navi Peth, Jalgaon 425001,
Maharashtra, Tel : (0257) 222 0395, Mob : 94234 91860

KOLHAPUR
Nirali Prakashan : New Mahadvar Road, Kedar Plaza, 1st Floor Opp. IDBI Bank
Kolhapur 416 012, Maharashtra. Mob : 9850046155

NAGPUR
Pratibha Book Distributors : Above Maratha Mandir, Shop No. 3, First Floor,
Rani Jhanshi Square, Sitabuldi, Nagpur 440012, Maharashtra
Tel : (0712) 254 7129

DELHI
Nirali Prakashan : 4593/21, Basement, Aggarwal Lane 15, Ansari Road, Daryaganj
Near Times of India Building, New Delhi 110002
Mob : 08505972553

BENGALURU
Pragati Book House : House No. 1, Sanjeevappa Lane, Avenue Road Cross,
Opp. Rice Church, Bengaluru – 560002.
Tel : (080) 64513344, 64513355,Mob : 9880582331, 9845021552
Email:bharatsavla@yahoo.com

CHENNAI
Pragati Books : 9/1, Montieth Road, Behind Taas Mahal, Egmore,
Chennai 600008 Tamil Nadu, Tel : (044) 6518 3535,
Mob : 94440 01782 / 98450 21552 / 98805 82331,
Email : bharatsavla@yahoo.com

niralipune@pragationline.com | www.pragationline.com
Also find us on ▮ www.facebook.com/niralibooks

Preface ...

We are earnestly happy to present to the B.B.A. students of the Savitribai Phule Pune University, this Text Book on 'Industrial Relations and Labour Law'. This book is written according to the syllabus prescribed by the Savitribai Phule Pune University for B.B.A. - Semester IV.

Our book on 'Business Law' for B.B.A. - Semester III has been well received by the student and teacher community alike. We hope that they will receive this book also with the same enthusiasm.

We are sure that this book will be of immense use to the students of B.B.A. from the viewpoint of their examination and will help them to enhance their knowledge of the Acts prescribed for the examination.

We are very much thankful to Dr. K. R. Shimpi, Principal, Sir. Dr. M. S. Gosavi Institute of Business Studies, Nashik for encouraging us to write this book by giving valuable suggestions.

We express our sincere thanks to Shri. Dineshbhai Furia, Shri. Jignesh Furia, Mr. Malik Shaikh, Mr. Amol Mahabal, Mr. Prasad Chintakindi and the entire staff of Nirali Prakashan, Pune, who have taken pains and keen interest in publishing this book.

Inspite of sincere efforts, some errors might have crept in the book. We hope that we shall be excused for the same.

We shall consider our labour amply rewarded if this book is appreciated by those for whom it is meant.

We extend our good wishes to all students, teachers, and readers with a genuine hope that they will receive this book with great enthusiasm.

PUNE
November 2014

Prof. S. D. Geet
Mrs. Asmita A. Deshpande

Syllabus ...

Unit 1 : Introduction to Industrial Relations
- Meaning, Definition, Importance, Scope of Industrial Relations and Factors in Industrial Relations
- Approaches towards the study of Industrial Relations (Psychological Approach, Sociological Approach, Socio Ethical Approach, Gandhian Approach, Industrial Relations Approach and HR Approach)
- Evolution of Industrial Relations
- Trade Unions : concept, functions, TU Movement in India

Unit 2 : Industrial Disputes, Collective Bargaining and Workers Participation in Management :
- Meaning, definition and Causes of Industrial Disputes
- Model Grievance Procedure
- **Types of Conflict Resolution** : Negotiation, Investigation, Mediation, Conciliation, arbitration and Adjudication.
  Works Committee, Conciliation Officer, Board of Conciliation, Court of Enquiry, Labour Court, Industrial Tribunal and National Tribunal.
- Collective Bargaining - Meaning, Characteristics, Importance, Process, Pre-requisites and Types
- **Employee Engagement :** Concept, Importance and Employee Engagement in India
- **Workers Participation in Management (WPM) :** Meaning, Pre-Requisites, Advantages and Disadvantages, Levels and Types Labour Laws

Unit 3 : The Industrial Disputes Act, 1946 and The Factories Act 1948 :
The Industrial Disputes Act, 1946 -
- Definitions, Authorities under the Act, Power and Duties of Authorities, Strike and lockout, Lay-off, retrenchment, closure and dismissal, Grievance Redressal Machinery, Penalties

The Factories Act, 1948 -
- Definitions, Authorities, Provisions regarding Safety, Provisions regarding Health, Provisions regarding Welfare, Provisions regarding Leave with Wages, Provisions regarding Working hours of adults, Penalties.

Unit 4 : The Payment of Wages Act, 1936 and
The Minimum Wages Act, 1948 :
The Payment of Wages Act, 1936 -
- Definitions, Provisions, Penalties

  The Minimum Wages Act, 1948 -
- Definitions, Provisions, Penalties

Unit 5 : Trade Union Laws :
- The Trade Union Act 1926 : Definitions, authorities and all provisions.
- Maharashtra Recognition of Trade Union and Prevention of Unfair Labour Practices Act, 1971 : Definition, authorities and all provisions under the Act.

***

Contents ...

1. **Introduction to Industrial Relations** — 1.1 – 1.24

2. **Industrial Disputes, Collective Bargaining and Workers Participation in Management** — 2.1 – 2.38

3. **The Industrial Disputes Act, 1946 and the Factories Act 1948** — 3.1 – 3.102

4. **The Payment of Wages Act, 1936 and The Minimum Wages Act, 1948** — 4.1 – 4.40

5. **Trade Union Laws** — 5.1 – 5.42

- **Question Paper: April 2015** — P.1 – P.1

Publisher's Note

Inspite of our best efforts, care and caution, errors might have crept in. The publication is being sold on the condition and understanding that the information given in this book is merely for guidance and reference. It must not be taken as having authority of, or binding in any way on the author, publisher, sellers etc. who do not owe any responsibility for any damage or loss to any person, who may or may not be a purchaser of this publication on account of any action taken on the basis of this publication. However, if any discrepancies, omissions, errors etc. are noticed, kindly bring the same to our notice, so that we can take necessary steps to correct them in the next edition.

***

Chapter 1...

Introduction to Industrial Relations

Contents ...

1.1 Introduction
1.2 Meaning and Definitions of Industrial Relations
1.3 Nature and Characteristics or Features of Industrial Relations
1.4 Scope of Industrial Relations
1.5 Objectives and Importance of Industrial Relations
1.6 Measures for the Development of Good Industrial Relations/Factors in Industrial Relations
1.7 Evolution of Industrial Relations in India
1.8 Approaches towards the Study of Industrial Relations
1.9 Definitions and Nature of a Trade Union
1.10 Growth of Trade Unions
    1.10.1 Growth of National Level Federations of Trade Unions
1.11 Objectives and Functions of Trade Unions
- Questions for Discussion
- Questions from Previous Pune University BBA Examinations

1.1 Introduction

An industry is a social world in miniature. Industries not only help in producing goods and services but they also provide employment to the people. Different categories of human elements are directly or indirectly involved in industries. Industrial relations play a very vital role in increasing industrial activities. In fact, the economic activity is the central field of industrial relations. The economic system and also labour legislation of a country, besides other factors, affect the industrial relations. A man has to struggle constantly for the purpose of satisfaction of his material wants. No doubt, the industrial revolutions are important for the development of industries. But they create imbalance as they prejudicially affect the rights and interests of the people in different sectors who work in the industries. This results in inequitable distribution of income and wealth. It is so because the means of production are controlled and utilised by the dominant sectors for the maximising the benefit of the people working in the dominant sectors and labour is exploited. This leads to imbalance and disorder in industrial relations. If industrial relations are not smooth, industries cannot develop properly. Economic development is closely related to smooth and good industrial relations and industrial peace. Therefore, industrial relations are not merely a matter between employers and employees. Hence, all the efforts must be done to maintain good and smooth industrial relations.

In an industrial sector of a country, the element of labour goes to constitute one of the most important and basic components; whereas the principal component of a given organisation is invariably its human resource or, people at work. From a country's point of view, human resources are the sum total or aggregate of knowledge, skills, creative abilities, talents, aptitudes as obtaining in its population, in a given point in time. While from the viewpoint of the individual enterprise, its human resources represent the total of the inherent qualities and abilities, acquired knowledge and skills as exemplified in the talents and aptitudes of the employees of that enterprise. Thus, human factor is very crucial for any organisation. In fact, it is the human resource which is of paramount importance in the success of any enterprise, simply because the bulk of problems of any organisational setting are related to human rather than physical, technical or economic nature. The failure to recognise and to utilise this effectively causes immense loss not only to the given enterprise but also to the nation concerned, as a whole.

It goes without saying that maintaining healthy industrial relations is the *minimum prerequisite* for ensuring a proper and smooth working and development of the enterprises concerned. Before we examine the various aspects of 'Industrial Relations,' let us first understand the meaning of the concept of 'Industrial Relations.'

1.2 Meaning and Definitions of 'Industrial Relations'

Today, industrial activity is continuously expanding and will continue to do so in the future. Based on their individual experiences, the people in the industrial field discuss the various aspects relating to human resources, production and productivity, industrial relations, peace, unrest, etc.

Hence, we find different approaches to the same aspect. The concept of 'industrial relations' is also not an exception to this. We find that there are as many as definitions of it as are the authors, experts on the subject. Each of them has explained the concept of industrial relations based on his/her experiences and ideas. Let us now consider some definitions of 'Industrial Relations' as stated by the experts in order to understand its meaning and nature.

(1) **Prof. Dale Yoder** defines the term 'Industrial Relations' as, *the designation of a whole field of relationships that exist because of the necessary collaboration of men and women in the employment process of the industry.*

(2) **Prof. T. N. Kapoor** made it clear that, *industrial relations refer to a dynamic and developing concept which is not limited to the complex of relations between trade unions and management but also refers to the general web of relationship normally obtaining between employers and employees - a web much more complex than the simple concept of labour-capital conflict.*

(3) **According to Prof. V. B. Singh,** *industrial relations are an integral aspect of social relations arising out of employer-employee interaction in modern industries, which are regulated by the State, the legal system, and the workers' and employers' organisations at the industrial level, and of the pattern of industrial organisation (including management) capital structure (including technology), compensation of labour force and a study of market forces - all at the economic level.*

(4) The International Labour Organisation (ILO) has also pointed out that, *"Industrial relations indicate either the relationship between state and employers' organisation and workers' organisation or the relations between occupational organisations themselves."*

In a broad sense, 'industrial relations' is the topic of study of the personnel or human resource management and, its logical corollary, good industrial relations - one, that is, necessary for the development of a given enterprise and its employees. That apart, it is also important from the viewpoint of not only industrial peace, but also for the industrial and economic development of a given country.

1.3 Nature and Characteristics or Features of Industrial Relations

Nature of Industrial Relations

Industrial relations do not constitute a simple relationship. They are, in fact, a set of functional, inter-dependent complexities involving various variables, namely, economic, political, social, legal, etc. In other words, they are multi-dimensional in nature.

Industrial relations are the outcome of employment relationship, namely, the relations that exist between the employer and his employees while in the course of conducting work operations in a given industrial enterprise. In this regard, the trade unions, as responsible institutions can also play an important role in shaping industrial relations in many ways.

Further, the appropriate government also influences and shapes the industrial relations by way of rules, agreements, legislation, industrial relation policies, etc. Hence, industrial relations are governed by the system of legislations and regulations relating to the work, workplace and people at work.

Features / Characteristics of Industrial Relations

There are many characteristics or features of the industrial relations which make the nature of industrial relations abundantly clear. Some of them are given below:

(1) The concept of 'Industrial Relations' is a dynamic and evolving concept. It is described as that relationship which exists between employers or management of the enterprise concerned and the employees; or, amongst the employees and their organisations; or, employers, employees and their trade unions and the government. Such relationship necessarily flows out from employment relationship.

(2) Industrial relations do not constitute a simple relationship; they are, in fact, a set of functional, inter-dependent complexities involving various factors or variables, such as, economic, political, social, psychological, legal factors or variables. Further, they can be changed or affected because of the changes in the factors or variables mentioned above.

(3) Industrial relations do not exist in a vacuum. They are created out of employee-employer relationship in a given industrial activity. Without the existence of a minimum of two or more parties, industrial relationship cannot exist. They are - (a) Workers and their organisations; (b) Employers or management of the enterprise; and (c) Government.
The three aforesaid parties thus form the mainstay of industrial relations.

(4) The important objectives of industrial relations are, namely, to develop a healthy labour-management or employee-employer relations; maintenance of industrial peace; avoidance of industrial strife; and, for enabling growth of industrial democracy, etc.

(5) Industrial relations as a part of a branch of personnel management or human resources management is mainly concerns itself, among other things, with the study of the people in relation to their work, the problems arising amongst employees at work. That apart, it also applies equally *vis-à-vis* safeguarding the interests of both the employers and employees.

(6) Industrial relations may be either an individual relation or collective relations. An individual relation implies the relations between an employer and his employees in his/her enterprise; while collective relations are the relations between an employer and his employees or their trade unions at various levels. Thus, the connotation of collective relations is much wider than those of industrial relations. Collective relations also include the relations that one has with the Government, as the regulating authority.

(7) Industrial relations are the product of economic, social, and political system arising out of the employment in the industrial field.

(8) Industrial relations are determined by various factors. These factors can be classified into two groups, namely -
(a) Institutional factors, and (b) Economic factors.

Institutional factors include the labour or industrial legislation, government policy relating to labour and industry, impact and development of the trade unions, etc. In contrast, the economic factors include the ownership of the enterprises, capital structure, technology, composition of labour force, the demand and supply of labour, expectations of workers, economic conditions prevailing in the country concerned, etc.

(9) In a nutshell, the industrial relations are those relations that are affected by the conflicts as well as the co-operative attitude and aptitude of the parties concerned.

1.4 Scope of Industrial Relations

Industrial relations are an important aspect of social and economic relations arising out of the employer-employee relations and interactions in the industrial field. They are regulated by the Government in different ways. This involves the study of the legal aspects relating to labour and industries, employers' and workers' associations at different levels.

The industrial relations are part and parcel of industrial life and include various aspects, topics for their study. The important aspect or topics which are included in the study of industrial relations are as follows:

(1) It is given that in industrial relations, the relations between the parties relating to the enterprises or industries are studied and they include -
   (a) Employer-employee relations or the relations between the management and the employees working in the given enterprise.
   (b) Employee relations, i.e., relations between the employees working together.
   (c) Relations between the trade unions and the management.
   (d) The relations that exist between the industry, government and the society, at large.

(2) Business enterprises, workers or employees, trade unions do not exist in isolation. They are, in fact, a part of the larger economic, social and political systems. Hence, the study of the industrial relations also includes various environmental issues like, country's labour policy, legal system, attitudes and aptitudes of the employers, employees, trade unions, political and social environments, economic conditions, etc.

(3) The main aspects of the industrial relations are promotion of sound and healthy labour-management relations, maintenance of industrial peace, development of industrial democracy, etc. Hence, various topics relating to these aspects become the part of the study of industrial relations.

(4) The various other aspects relating to the industrial conflicts or industrial disputes too are very important topics from the viewpoint of maintaining good industrial relations. Hence, the causes of industrial disputes are analysed and, accordingly, steps are taken for their resolution. There are statutory and non-statutory measures for conflict resolution. All these aspects are studied in detail in the industrial relations.

(5) Collective bargaining and its types, process of collective bargaining and other related topics are studied in order to find out solutions to the recurrent problems of industrial conflicts or disputes.

(6) The study of certain Acts, such as, the Industrial Disputes Act, the Trade Union Act, Payment of Bonus Act, the Factories Act, etc., are necessary for improving the industrial relations. Hence, the study of the related labour laws is included in the scope of the industrial relations.

(7) Welfare measures, whether statutory or non-statutory provided by the employers, trade unions, government, etc., creates, maintains all improves the labour-management relations which substantially contribute to industrial peace. Hence, their study becomes inevitable in industrial relations.

1.5 Objectives and Importance of Industrial Relations

The following are the objectives and importance of Industrial Relations which may be outlined as below:

(1) To protect and safeguard the interests of both employer(s) and employees by creating proper understanding and goodwill amongst the concerned parties, i.e., employers, employees and their unions in the industrial field which participate in the process of production and distribution of the goods and services.

(2) To bring about industrial peace and develop harmonious relations. Such harmonious industrial relations are essential for not only increasing the overall productivity of the employees but also the production of goods and services.

(3) To enhance the economic status of the employees by increasing their wage rates and by giving other benefits. This, in turn, helps to increase the productivity by lessening the tendencies of high turnover and absenteeism.

(4) To eliminate, or remove the causes of strikes, lock-outs, *gheraos* by considering the difficulties of the employees. For this purpose, reasonable wages, improved working conditions and standard of living and fringe benefits can be provided wherever and whenever possible.

(5) To regulate the production and industrial activities by minimising industrial conflicts through state control or by any other possible means.

(6) To establish and develop the industrial democracy based on labour partnership in sharing of profits and also of managerial decisions, i.e., workers' participation in management.

(7) To avoid industrial conflicts/disputes and thereby its consequences.

(8) To encourage and develop the trade unions' working so as to improve the strength of the employees.

(9) To establish proper rapport between the management/employer and employees.

(10) To solve the problems of the employees through mutual negotiations and consultation with the employer/management.

(11) To lay down such considerations as may promote proper understanding and thereby facilitate co-operation in order to ensure better participation of the employees and thus enhance the overall industrial productivity.

1.6 Measures for the Development of Good Industrial Relations/ Factors in Industrial Relations

Good industrial relations must be developed between the management and the employees as well as their unions for the speedy economic development. I.L.O. suggested certain principles for the promotion of healthy, harmonious industrial relations.

Other authorities and experts on the subject also have suggested certain measures for the development of good, healthy, harmonious industrial relations. Some important measures to develop the employee-employer relations are mentioned as below:

(1) It is very important, in this regard to note that good, healthy and harmonious industrial relations mainly hinges on the employer's and trade unions' capacity to deal with various industrial problems freely and properly. Hence, steps must be taken to create proper understanding between the employers, employees and their unions for creating and maintaining very good, harmonious relations. If all of them understand their responsibilities and thereby learn to appreciate the advantages of healthy, harmonious relations, then, they would be able to deal with various labour-management issues properly and successfully. For this purpose, a rapport must be established between the management, employees and their unions.

(2) It is essential to lay down certain considerations for promoting proper understanding, creativity and co-operation with a view to raise industrial productivity, and ensure better participation of employees, etc. This helps to pre-empt the chances of industrial conflicts/disputes from happening.

(3) In order to maintain and develop the goal of better employer-employee relations and healthy atmosphere, the trade unions must contribute substantially by doing all it can, to not only avoid industrial conflicts but also to safeguard the interests of its members. On the other hand, the organisations must also contribute and do all it can to avoid unhealthy, unethical atmosphere in the industrial field concerned.

(4) In order to develop employee-employer relations, a proper and effective communication channel should be established between the employees and their organisations.

(5) For developing the employee-employer relations, a very good system of collective bargaining should be established and, for that purpose, necessary procedure ought to be laid down so as to successfully facilitate collective bargaining.

(6) The employers should also take necessary steps to promote various welfare schemes for their employees. The steps taken by the employer(s), in this respect, helps remove at the bud many causes of industrial conflicts/disputes.

(7) The role of the government is also very important in this regard for both maintaining and developing good industrial relations. By passing various Acts,

such as, the Industrial Act, the Trade Union Act, the Payment of Wages Act, etc., the Government has contributed a lot to create a harmonious climate for establishing good industrial relations and thereby industrial peace.

Thus, it can be said that the following, namely, willingness on the part of the employers to solve the problems of their employees, the existence of strong, responsible and democratic trade unions, collective bargaining, independent machinery for settlement of industrial disputes, a policy of no discrimination etc., are essential for the development of the healthy harmonious employee-employer relations.

1.7 Evolution of Industrial Relations in India

During the first decade of this 21st century and the last two decades of 20th century, it was discovered that industrial tensions are one of the most tangible manifestations of disagreements and conflicts of interests in India. Generally, the employers and their employees have to face various issues or problems, such as, the fair rates of wages and salaries, working conditions, the interpretation of contracts of employment, privileges, responsibilities of trade unions, etc.

Without a doubt, the aforesaid clashes are nothing new, but they, in their present day form, do reflect a major development in the society. The problems of industrial relations, as we understand it today, were not in existence in the past when the system of industrial production was very simple. With the advent of modern industries, post industrial revolution, things *vis-à-vis* production has changed dramatically.

Today, on the other hand, labour is not merely an unorganised mass of ignorant and unconscious workers as it was in the past. As a result, the employers have to deal with their employees through the medium/agency of trade unions. The trade unions have substantially increased the strength and consciousness of their members.

The trade unions now play a very important role in the field of industrial relations. In a sense, to a great extent, industrial peace depends much on the actions, reactions and interactions of the trade unions. Besides, the employers and their organisations, employees and their organisations, the other party affecting industrial relations is the Government.

It is found that the Government regulates the labour/ industrial relations in all countries of the world. In some countries, the Governments of the respective countries have laid down certain bare minimum rules for observance by the employers and their employees.

While in some other countries, the legislation covers a wide area of relationships between the employers and the employees. In India, the Government of India has enacted procedural and substantive laws to regulate the industrial relations. In order to know the development of the industrial relations in India, we have to consider basically three important factors or aspects, namely:

(1) Labour policy and labour legislation,
(2) Growth of the trade unions, and
(3) Industrial disputes and their settlement.

Labour Policy and Labour Legislation

During the pre-independence days and especially, during the early period of the colonial rule, the British rulers in India were mainly concerned with getting an ample supply of cheap labour for the production of goods for the industries mostly owned by their fellow brethren.

Naturally, the regulation of labour and their employment mainly aimed at keeping the labour costs of the industries owned by the British in India as low as possible. It is, therefore, not surprising that the British rulers did not take any pains *vis-a-vis* improving the working conditions of the Indian workers. Their conditions only started changing after 1918, i.e., after the end of the First World War.

The International Labour Organisation [ILO] was established in 1919 with a view to solve the workers' problems. The important objects of ILO are to remove injustice and hardship faced by the workers all over the world over besides improving their living conditions with a view to establish universal and lasting peace based upon social justice. The influence of the functioning of the ILO on the labour policy and labour legislation in India cannot be underestimated.

After 1920, the Government started taking certain steps to improve the working conditions of the workers employed in the factories and to provide a certain amount of security. The influence of the ILO and the pressure of public opinion in India due to the extremely unsatisfactory conditions of factory workers compelled the Government to pass certain Acts for introducing the measures to improve the same.

To name a few - The Workmen's Compensation Act, 1923, the Trade Unions Act, 1926, the Trade Disputes Act, 1929, the Payment of Gratuity Act, 1936, the Employers' Liability Act, 1938 were amongst the most significant legislative measures passed by the Government of India to protect the interests of the employees.

The Royal Commission on Labour was appointed in 1929 by Government of India. The report of the Commission brought the labour problems in India in sharp focus and also provided the comprehensive data regarding the conditions of the Indian workers. The important consequence of the report of the Royal Commission was passing of the Factories Act, 1934, and the Payment of Wages Act, 1936. Though the limited statutory provisions were made by the Government of India during the period of the British rule, there did not emerge a very comprehensive labour policy covering various aspects of industrial relations during the pre-independence period.

In the post-independence period, the Government of free India took steps necessary to develop economy in all directions. The Industrial Truce Resolution, 1947, set the tone and direction of new labour policy. The major emphasis in this was on the mutuality of interests of management and labour and the method to be adopted laid stress on mutual discussion and settlement of disputes in a proper manner. That resolution gave a proper push to the industrial relations in the expected direction.

In 1950, the Constitution of India was adopted. The Constitution has emphasised that:

(1) There should be no exploitation of the workers, weaker sections of the society,

(2) There should be fair distribution of the national income among the people,

(3) There should be provision for social security for the needy and distressed workers/employees and

(4) There should be promotion of industrial harmony for the continuous development of the industrial sector.

Thus, the Directive Principles of the State Policy as embodied in the Constitution of India lay special stress on the goal of 'Welfare State,' by directing the Government to follow certain principles which are essential to secure a social order for the promotion of welfare of the people.

In this regard, it has been clearly stated in the Constitution of India that, "The State shall endeavour to secure by suitable legislation or economic organisation, or in any other way, to all workers, agricultural, industrial or otherwise, work a living wage, conditions of work ensuring a decent standard of life and full enjoyment of leisure and social and cultural opportunities." This reflects the attitude of the constitution as regards workers and their working and living conditions.

The Indian Government decided to adopt economic planning for the development of her economy. The Five-Year Plan provides a broad framework and approach to the Government of India in so far as framing suitable labour policy - one, that is, in alignment with its overall economic development strategy.

The Second Five Year Plan (1956-1961) aimed at the goal of establishing a socialistic pattern of society and also emphasised the need of creating an industrial democracy as a prerequisite for establishing it.

The wage issue was at the heart of the problem of industrial relations and, even today, it continues to occupy an important place in the context of healthy industrial relations. Recognising the importance of the problem, the First Five Year Plan recommended the increase in wages of the workers to remove the anomalies or where the existing wage rates were abnormally low. It was decided to set up the permanent wage boards with a tripartite composition in each State and at the Centre to deal comprehensively with all aspects relating to wages of the workers employed.

It was realised that, the creation of the industrial democracy and industrial peace were necessary for the healthy development of industrial relations. Labour legislation and the enforcement machinery set up for its implementation, at best, could only provide a suitable framework wherein the employers and their employees could function.

From this point of view, under the Industrial Disputes Act, amended in 1950, a three-tier system of Labour Court, Industrial Tribunals and the National Tribunal were set up. A Code of Discipline was also evolved in 1958 in order to reduce the industrial disputes. Thus, efforts were made to strengthen the industrial relations during 1950-1960, i.e., during the first two five year plans.

In the next decade, the attention was focussed on the fixation of minimum wage rates, reduction in disparities, wage differential, etc. Special attention was given to three aspects during the Forth Five-Year Plan Period, namely:

(1) Improvement in the field of labour legislation for the protection, safety and welfare of workers,

(2) Orientation of workers and employers in order to solve the labour problems, and

(3) Execution of programmes, which had a large bearing on the welfare of workers for workers' education, provision of facilities for imparting higher skills and training to workers, social securities, etc.

The Fifth Five Year Plan envisaged better food, nutrition and health standards, higher standard of education and training, improvement in discipline and morale, more productive technology and management practices.

The Sixth Five Year Plan (1980-85) laid more stress on effective implementation of the measures in the different legislative enactments and also in extending the coverage of the Employees State Insurance Scheme, the Employees' Provident Fund and Family Pension Scheme.

Special programmes were planned by the State Governments too for the agricultural workers, artisans, handloom weavers, leather workers, fishermen and other unorganised workers in the urban as well as in the rural areas. During the Sixth Plan period, bonus payments and some social security benefits were brought under the statutory arrangements.

It was in mid-1991, that the Government of India announced the new economic policy for the seven major areas of our economy, namely, trade policy, industrial policy, fiscal policy, agricultural policy, financial policy, poverty alleviation and employment policy, human resource policy.

The New Economic Policy of 1991 has consolidated and reinforced the process of industrial restructuring. The era of privatisation, globalisation and liberalisation has begun because of the New Economic Policy. The process of industrial restructuring began in the decade of 1990 introduced the radical measures to release the Indian industries from an artificial environment of high protection and regulations. The process is still continued.

Modern industrialisation and economic growth which have taken place in the first six-seven years of the 21st century call for the increased use of legislation not merely for tackling the existing labour, social and economic problems but also for creating such industrial conditions as would seem to be very conductive for establishing a just and healthy conditions.

It is expected that the employers and their employees shall realise the importance of industrial democracy and good industrial relations for productivity and efficiency of industry. They must make all efforts to resolve their disputes through the route of joint consultation so as to fulfil the purpose of sound industrial relations. In this regard, the Government would like to help them by amending the existing acts, if necessary, and, passing suitable new acts whenever and wherever necessary.

From the brief view taken so far as regards the labour policy and the efforts of the Government to protect the interests of the workers, we come to know that the Government has tried to give proper shape to the employee-employer relations or industrial relations by passing various Acts.

A large number of labour legislations have been enacted to promote the conditions of the workers working in different sectors of the economy. The important Acts passed to protect the interests of the employees and to improve the industrial relations are mentioned as below.

1. The Factories Act, 1948.
2. The Workmen's Compensation Act, 1923.
3. The Employees' State Insurance Act, 1948.
4. The Employees' Provident Fund (and Miscellaneous Provisions) Act, 1952.
5. The Payment of Gratuity Act, 1972.
6. The Maternity Benefit Act, 1961.
7. The Payment of Wages Act, 1936.
8. The Minimum Wages Act, 1948.
9. The Industrial Disputes Act, 1947.
10. The Industrial Employment (Standing Orders) Act, 1946.
11. The Trade Unions Act, 1926.
12. The Payment of Bonus Act, 1965.
13. The Indian Mines (Amendment) Act, 1959.
14. The Coal Mines (Conservation and Safety) Act, 1952.
15. The Plantation Labour Act, 1951.
16. The Indian Railway Act, 1930.
17. The Indian Merchant Shipping Act, 1923.
18. The Indian Dock Labourers' Act, 1923.
19. The Dock Workers' (Regulation of Employment) Act, 1948.
20. The Contract Labour (Regulation and Abolition) Act, 1970.
21. The Bombay Industrial Relations Act, 1946.
22. The Maharashtra Recognition of Trade Unions and Prevention of Unfair Labour Practices Act, 1971.

23. The Bombay Shops and Establishment Act, 1948.
24. The Employment of Children Act, 1938 which was replaced by The Child Labour (Prohibition and Regulation) Act, 1986.
25. Equal Remuneration Act, 1976.
26. The Bonded Labour System (Abolition) Act, 1976.
27. The Employers' Liability Act, 1938.
28. The Employment Exchanges (Compulsory notification of Vacancies) Act, 1959.

1.8 Approaches Towards the Study of Industrial Relations

(1) Psychological Approach to Industrial Relations
- The problem of IR have their origin in the perceptions of the management, unions and the workers. The conflicts occur between labour and management because every group negatively perceives the behaviour of the other.
- The problem is further aggravated by various factors like the income, level of education, communication, values, beliefs, customs, goals of persons and groups, prestige, power, status, recognition, security, influence, perceptions, etc.
- Industrial peace is mainly a result of proper attitudes and perceptions of the two parties.

(2) Sociological Approach to Industrial Relations
- G. Margerison, an industrial sociologists, holds the view that the core of industrial relations is the nature and development of the conflict itself.
- Margerison argued that conflict is the basic concept that should form the basis of the study of industrial relations.
- According to this approach, there are two major conceptual levels of industrial relations. One is the intra-plant level where situational factors like job content, work task, and technology, and interaction factors produce three types of conflict i.e. distributive, structural, and human relations. These conflicts are being resolved through collective bargaining, structural analysis of the socio-technical systems and man-management analysis respectively.
- The second level is outside the firm and mainly concerns with the conflict resolved at the intra-organisation level. However, this approach rejects the special emphasis given to rule determination by the "System and Oxford Model". In its place, it suggests a method of inquiry, which attempts to develop sociological models of conflicts.

(3) The Gandhian Approach to Industrial Relations
- Gandhiji can be called one of the greatest labour leaders of modern India. His approach to labour problems was completely new and refreshingly human. He held definite views regarding fixation and regulation of wages, organisation and functions

of trade unions, necessity and desirability of collective bargaining, use and abuse of strikes, labour indiscipline, workers participation in management, conditions of work and living, and duties of workers.
- The Ahmedabad Textile Labour Association, a unique and successful experiment in Gandhian trade unionism, implemented many of his ideas.
- Gandhiji had immense faith in the goodness of man and he believed that many of the evils of the modern world have been brought about by wrong systems and not by wrong individuals. He insisted on recognising each individual worker as a human being. He believed in non-violent communism.
- Gandhiji laid down certain conditions for a successful strike. These are: (a) the cause of the strike must be just and there should be no strike without a grievance; (b) there should be no violence, and (c) non-stikers or-blacklegs- should never be molested.
- He was not against strikes but pleaded that they should be the last weapon in the armoury of industrial workers and hence should not be resorted to, unless all peaceful and constitutional methods of negotiations, conciliation and arbitration are exhausted.
- His concept of trusteeship is a significant contribution in the sphere of industrial relations. According to him, employers should not regard themselves as sole owners of mills and factories of which they may be the legal owners. They should regard themselves only as trustees, or co-owners. He also appealed to the workers to behave as trustees, not to regard the mill and machinery as belonging to the exploiting agents but to regard them as their own, protect them and put to the best use they can.
- In short, the theory of trusteeship is based on the view that all forms of property and human accomplishments are gifts of nature and as such, they belong not to any one individual but to society as a whole. Thus, the trusteeship system is totally different from other contemporary labour relations systems. It aimed at achieving economic equality and the material advancement of the "have-nots" in a capitalist society by non-violent means.
- Gandhiji realised that relations between labour and management can either be a powerful stimulus to economic and social progress or an important factor in economic and social stagnation. According to him, industrial peace was an essential condition not only for the growth and development of the industry itself, but also in a great measure, for the improvement in the conditions of work and wages.
- At the same time, he not only endorsed the workers' right to adopt the method of collective bargaining but also actively supported it.
- He also pleaded for perfect understanding between capital and labour, mutual respect, recognition of equality, and strong labour organisation as the essential factors for happy and constructive industrial relations. For him, means and ends are equally important.

(4) Socio-Ethical Approach to Industrial Relations
- Though not much widely accepted, but one of the often discussed approach to I. R. is the socio-ethical approach.
- This approach holds the view that industrial besides having a socio-logical base does have some ethical ramifications, as good industrial relations can only be maintained when both the labour and management realise their moral responsibility in contributing to the said task.

(5) Industrial Relations Approach
- John Dunlop put forth his theory on Industrial Labour Relations in 1950. According to Dunlop, the modern industrial relations system consists of three players:
  (a) management organisations, i.e. employers,
  (b) workers and formal/informal ways they are organised, i.e. labour unions and
  (c) government agencies.
- These players and their organisations are located within three environmental constraints: the market, distribution of power in society and technology. Within this environment, the players interact with each other, negotiate and use economic/political power in the process of determining rules that constitute the output of the industrial relations system.
- Dunlop's model identifies three key factors to be kept in mind while conducting an analysis of the management-labour relationship:
(a) Environmental or external factors are economic, technological, political, legal and social forces that impact employment relationships.
(b) Characteristics and interactions of the key players in the employment relationship. The key players are labour, management and the Government.
(c) Rules that are derived from these interactions and which govern the employment relationship.
- Effectively, industrial relations is the system which produces the rules of the workplace. Such rules are the result of interactions between the three players, i.e. the workers/unions, employers and associated organisations and the government.
- It believes that, management, labour and the government possess a shared ideology which helps to define their roles within the relationship and provide stability to the system.

(6) HR Approach to Industrial Relations
- In the words of Keith Davies, human relations are "the integration of people into a work situation that motivates them to work together productively, co-operatively and with economic, psychological and social satisfactions."
- According to him, the goals of human relations are: (a) to get people to produce, (b) to co-operate through mutuality of interest, and (c) to gain satisfaction from their relationships.

- The human relations school founded by Elton Mayo and later propagated by Roethlisberger, Whitehead, W. F. Whyte, and Romans offers a coherent view of the nature of industrial conflict and harmony.
- The human relations approach highlights certain policies and techniques to improve employee morale, efficiency and job satisfaction. It encourages the small work group to exercise considerable control over its environment and in the process helps to remove a major irritant in labour-management relations.
- But there was reaction against the excessive claims of this school of thought in the sixties. Some of its views were criticised by Marxists, pluralists, and others on the ground that it encouraged dependency and discouraged individual development, and ignored the importance of technology and culture in industry.
- Taking a balanced view, however, it must be admitted that the human relations school has thrown a lot of light on certain aspects such as communication, management development, acceptance of workplace as a social system, group dynamics, and participation in management.

1.9 Definitions and Nature of a Trade Union

The term 'Trade Union' is commonly used to refer to the organisation of workers or employees formed to protect their rights and to enhance their welfare through collective action. Many experts stated their definition of trade union keeping certain views and ideas. Following are some of the important definitions of trade union.

(1) **C. D. H. Cole:** *"A trade union means an association of workers in one or more occupation - an association carried on mainly for the purpose of protecting and advancing the members' economic interests in connection with their daily work".*

(2) **J. Gunnison:** *"A trade union is a monopolistic combination of wage-earners who stand to the employers in a relation of dependence for the sale of their labour and even for its production and that the general purpose of the association is, in view of that dependence, to strengthen their power to bargain with the employers".*

(3) **R. A. Lester:** *"A trade union is an association of employees designed primarily to maintain or improve the conditions of employment of its members".*

(4) **R. A. Lester:** *"A trade union is an association of employees designed primarily to maintain or improve the conditions of employment of its members".*

(5) **Sidney and Beatrice Webb:** *"A trade union is a continuous association of wage earners for the purpose of maintaining or improving the conditions of their working lives".*

Nature of Trade Union

From these definition of a trade union we come to know that:
1. A trade union is any combination.
2. Such combination can be formed by,
    (a) employers and employers; or
    (b) workmen and workmen; or
    (c) employers and workmen.

3. The purpose of forming such combination is to regulate the relations between such persons who forms the combination.
4. Such combination can be temporary or permanent.
5. A trade union is formed for imposing certain restrictive conditions on the conduct of any trade or business.
6. A trade union may include any federation of two or more trade unions.
7. The Trade Union Act does not affect any agreement
   (a) between partners as to their own business.
   (b) between employer and employees regarding their employment and
   (c) which is in consideration of sale of goodwill of a business or of instruction in any profession, trade or handicraft.

In ordinary parlance, trade union means an association of workmen formed to protect their own interest. But the expression 'trade union' includes both workers' and employers' organisations. The intention in covering organisations of employers under this Act is to put both the workers and employers organisations on par in matters of rights and responsibilities.

A trade union may be registered, unrecognised or recognised trade union. The important point of distinction between registration and recognition is that registration is done with the Registrar, while recognition is by the management as a collective bargaining agent. It is not obligatory to get the trade union registered. However, the members of the registered and recognised trade unions enjoy certain benefits while the members of an unregistered trade union do not. Previously, according to Section 4 of the Trade Union Act of 1926, any seven or more members of a trade union were allowed to apply to the Registrar for registering the trade union in Form - A. But the Trade Union Act of 1926 was amended in 2001 and the limit for registering a trade union has been increased to 10% or One Hundred whichever is less, subject to a minimum of seven.

Features of Trade Unions

We came to know certain features of trade unions from which the nature of trade unions become clear. Following are some of the important features of trade unions.

(1) Trade unions are voluntary organisations formed to protect and promote the interests of their members. They are formed to achieve certain objectives.
(2) The trade unions are the associations either of employers or employees or of independent workers. Thus, there are trade unions of blue-collar workers, white collar employees, employers, self-employed people, etc.
(3) Trade unions increase the bargaining capacity and strength of their members and protect them from exploitation.
(4) Trade unions help to improve the conditions of working of their members.

(5) Generally, it is found that trade unions are relatively permanent associations and are not casual.

(6) A trade union may include any federation of two or more trade unions.

(7) Trade unions can be registered under the Trade Union Act according to the provisions of the Act. However, the registration is not compulsory.

(8) Registered trade unions enjoy certain rights and privileges. The Trade Union Act of 1926 has imposed certain duties and liabilities on the registered trade union.

(9) Trade unions play an important role in creating and maintaining good and healthy industrial relations and peace. They also help to improve the material and cultural standards of their members by organising educational and cultural activities, sports and such other activities.

Though there are many definitions of trade union stated by the authorities in the field from their point of views, the legalistic definition is required to be considered for the purposes of solving industrial disputes and matters related to trade unions.

1.10 Growth of Trade Unions

Trade unionism had its origin in the factory system which made its appearance in England after the second half of the 18th century. Along with the modernisation of industries, namely, producing goods on a mass-scale with modern machines and employing thousands of workers, trade union movement has grown rapidly.

Trade unions, as the associations of wage-earners or salaried employees strive for not only maintaining the conditions of their working lives but also insofar as securing them a better and healthier status in industry and, as an extension, in society. Thus, in a way, they facilitate industrial growth and industrial relations to develop properly.

In the 18th century, there were well-developed and well-organised craftsmen guilds in the fields of textiles, blacksmithy, goldsmithy, metalware, pottery, carving, etc. These guilds used to perform certain functions, such as, regulating the working hours of craftsmen, quality and quantity of goods to be produced, prices of the goods produced, etc. But these craft guilds consisted of both workers and producers or entrepreneurs. Therefore, they cannot be compared with the trade unions of today.

Trade unions in the modern sense emerged in India only after the beginning of the factory system, i.e., in the middle of the 19th century. The factory system wakes the issues of the employment of many women and children, long and excessive hours of work and many other evils of industrialisation. To fight against such evils, some social reformers started an agitation in Mumbai in 1875 under the guidance and leadership of Mr. Sorabjee Shapurjee Bengalee. They appealed to the Government to introduce legislation for the improvement of working conditions of the workers.

As a result, the first Factory Commission was appointed in Mumbai in 1875 and the first Factories Act was passed in 1881. That Act was not adequate and its provisions were highly disappointing. Hence, there was felt the need to do more rigorous efforts to establish workers' unions on a sound basis.

In 1884, Mr. Narayan M. Lokhande organised an agitation in Bombay and later on called a meeting of workers in order to make representation before the Labour Commission. Mr. N. M. Lokhande did all the efforts and established 'Bombay Mill Hands Association' in 1890. It was the first modern-type labour organisation or association established in India.

Some important labour organisations were the Amal-Printers' Union in Calcutta (1905), the Bombay Postal Union (1907), the Kamgar Hitvardhak Sabha and the Social Service League (1910). It was just the beginning of the trade union movement in India. Though up to 1918, some labour organisations were formed, they were not in the true sense of trade unions but essentially labour welfare organisations.

After the conclusion of the First World War, the trade union movement began in the truly modern way. The credit for establishing a union on a systematic basis goes to Mr. B.P. Wadia. He did all the efforts to form a trade union and it started working in 1918. The period of some eleven years from 1924 to 1935 is considered as the period of 'Left Wing Trade Unionism.' Since 1924, the signs of militant tendencies and revolutionary trade unionism in the labour movement became apparent in India.

During 1924-1935, the communists became powerful and thus captured the labour movement in India. Discrimination against the Indian workers, the growth of Indian National Movement, the revolution in Russia were all some of the important factors responsible for giving a fillip to the Indian labour movement.

The Indian Trade Union Act, which was passed in 1926, is a landmark in the history of trade union movement in India. This Act gave the trade unions legal status and immunity to its officers and members from civil and criminal liability for concerted actions. The original Act of 1926 was amended in 1929 in order to provide for the procedure of appeal against the decision of Registrar.

In 1937, under provincial autonomy, the registered trade unions were given special representation in the provincial legislatures which further encouraged the registration of trade unions. Then, immediately after the Independence, the Trade Union Amendment Act, 1947, was passed which provided for the compulsory recognition of the trade unions by the employers under the orders of 'Labour Court.'

The Indian Trade Union (Amendment) Act, 1960, made certain changes in Sections 2, 3, 4, 14, 16 and 26 of the Act. Subsequently, by the Amendment 38 of the Act 1964, the word 'Indian' was deleted.

The Government introduced the Trade Union Bill on 13th May, 1988, to replace the earlier legislation. The Bill suggested comprehensive amendments in the Trade Union Act. Now, the Act requires a trade union to be registered within sixty days of the receipt of the application.

Thus, the registration of the trade unions has become time-bound. Besides this, it has also been provided for a statutorily recognised collective bargaining agent for a unit or for an industry and term of such an agent is fixed for three years. By passing amendments (whenever necessary) to the Act, a sincere attempt has been made to safeguard the interests of the workers and to improve the industrial relations, in tune with the changing times.

Post Independence, we are witnessing a spurt both in the number of trade unions and their members. Both at the plant level and, at the national level, the trade unions are now more closely organised and are playing a very significant role in protecting the interests of their members. At present, there are more than twelve central trade union organisations and the affiliated trade unions are about 20,000 having the membership of more than 300 lakhs.

The Indian National Trade Union Congress [INTUC], All India Trade Union Congress [AITUC], United Trade Union Congress [UTUC], Bharatiya Mazdoor Sangh [BMS], Hind Mazdoor Kisan Panchayat [HMKP], Centre of Indian Trade Unions [CITU], etc., are some of the central trade union organisations. It can also be noted that almost all major political parties in India have their own trade unions, which, often function as their 'Labour Wings.'

1.10.1 Growth of National Level Federations of Trade Unions

Two factors are relevant from the point of view of growth of trade unions in India. They relate to the trade union law and to political parties and their policies. Undoubtedly, the provisions of the Trade Unions Act has contributed to formation of many trade unions. Needless to add that there are many more unregistered trade unions.

Another factor to be noted is that the major political parties such as the Congress, Communist, Socialist, Bharatiya Janata Party etc. have helped to develop trade unions. Each of these parties has a federation at the apex i.e. national level to which unions at the plant and State level are affiliated. It is found that the organisational pattern of a trade union federation is usually three-tiered. Units exist at the plant or shop level, state and the national level. At present, there are following important National Level Federations of trade unions.

(1) All India Trade Union Congress (AITUC)

It was established in the year 1920. It is linked with the communist philosophy and it is affiliated to the Communist Party of India. It is very strong in West Bengal, Tamil Nadu, Kerala, Andhra Pradesh, Punjab, Delhi etc. It's members are drawn mostly from engineering, petroleum, building and constructions. In 1979, it had a total of 13,07,471 members which increased to 26,41,301 upto 2002. At present, its members are more than 30 lakhs.

(2) Indian National Trade Union Congress (INTUC)

The INTUC which was organised in 1947 is the labour wing of the Congress Party with the active support and encouragement of the Congress leaders. Its main aim, besides other objectives, is to bring about a peaceful and non-violent solution to industrial disputes and to maintain smooth industrial relations. It has strong roots in West Bengal, Assam, Bihar, Gujarat and Maharashtra. It had 23,88,451 members in 1979 which increased to 30,70,795 in

2002. Today, number of its members is more than 33 lakhs. The largest number of its members are drawn from the textile industry, the tea plantations in Assam and West Bengal, the jute industry in West Bengal, the transport and mining-cum-metallic industries etc. It is the largest national federation of trade unions.

(3) Hind Mazdoor Sabha (HMS)

HMS national federation came into existence into 1948. The INTUC is the first, AITUC is the second, while HMS is the third largest federation of trade unions having the membership of more than 15 lakh workers. The methods employed by this federation are peaceful and democratic. It has adopted the socialist philosophy and has linkages with socialist parties. It's members are mostly drawn from the railways, cotton textiles, coal mining, engineering etc. The Hind Mazdoor Panchayat (HMP) is an off-shoot of the Socialist Party which is another national level trade unions' federation with socialist tendency and philosophy.

(4) Centre of Indian Trade Unions [CITU]

The Centre of Indian Trade Unions came into existence on 30th May, 1970. Two important points of its existence have been the unity and struggle. The CITU was organised as a result of split in the AITU which was a sequel to the split in the CPI.

The CITU's main aims and objectives are to fight against all encroachments on economic and social rights of workers and for the enlargement of their rights and liberties, to fight against hazards of unemployment, to have progressive improvement in wage rates and to improve the living standards of workers. It had 8,17,805 members in 1979. The membership increased upto 11, 12,328 with 2231 affiliated trade unions in 2002. Today, there are more than 13 lakhs members of the CITU.

Besides the above mentioned federations of trade unions, there are others like the United Trade Union Congress, the National Labour Organisation, the All India Bank Employees' Association, the Indian Federation of Working Journalists, the National Federation of Indian Railway men etc.

No doubt that the trade union movement is flourishing in India. It is because of the changing political and socio-economic atmosphere in our country, spreading of ideas about democracy, awareness spread amongst the workers of their rights, spread of education, etc. These factors alone cannot be accounted for expansion of trade union movement. But some other important factors are the establishment of more central organisations, the growth of the political parties at the national as well as the regional levels and rapid economic development. As a result, number of registered trade unions and members of trade unions submitting returns are continuously increasing.

From 1999 to 2008, number of registered trade unions has increased by about 31%, that is, to 84,642 registered unions. Out of the registered trade unions, only 9709 unions (11.47%) have submitted returns during 2008 while out of total registered trade unions 18602, only 2937 unions (i.e. 15.8%) submitted their returns for the year 2010. The average membership per union was 1735 in 2010. Following table gives us an idea at a glance about the growth of the registered trade unions and membership of trade unions submitting returns.

Growth of Registered Trade Unions and their Membership 1996 to 2010

Year	Number of Registered Trade Unions	Number of Unions Submitting Returns	Membership of Unions Submitting Returns				Total Membership ('000)	Average Membership Per Union
			Men		Women			
			Number ('000)	Percentage	Number ('000)	Percentage		
1	2	3	4	5	6	7	8	9
1996	58,988	7,242 / 12.3	4,250	75.9	1,351	24.1	4,601	77
1997	60,660	8,872 / 14.6	6,504	87.8	905	12.2	7,409	83
1998	61,992	7,403 / 11.9	6,104	84.2	1,145	15.8	7,249	97
1999	64,817	8,152 / 12.6	5,190	81.0	1,218	19.0	6,408	78
2000	66,056	7,253 / 11.0	4,510	83.2	910	16.8	5,420	74
2001	66,624	6,531 / 9.8	4,392	74.8	1,481	25.2	5,873	89
2002	68,544	7,812 / 11.4	5,102	73.2	1,871	26.8	6,973	89
2003	74,649	7,258 / 9.7	4,854	77.3	1,423	22.7	6,277	86
2004	74,403	5,252 / 7.1	2,954	87.0	443	13.90	3,397	64
2005	78,465	8,317 / 10.6	6,334	72.6	2,385	27.4	8,719	104
2006	88,440	8,471 / 9.6	7,754	86.5	1,206	13.5	8,960	106
2007	95,783	7,408 / 7.7	5,751	73.0	2,126	27.0	7,877	106
2008	84,642	9,709 / 11.5	7,420	77.5	2,154	22.5	9.574	98
2009	22,284*	3,861 / 17.3	4,388	67.7	2,092	32.3	6,480	167
2010	18,602*	2,937 / 15.8	3,185	62.5	1,912	37.5	5,097	173

1.11 Objectives and Functions of Trade Unions

Objectives of Trade Unions

The basic objectives of trade unions are to unite the workers or employees to increase their strength and power to bargain with any class or group on equal footing and to protect and promote the interests of the workers and the conditions of their employment. The interest of the workers lies in getting reasonable wages, improved working conditions, job

security. The trade unions must do all efforts to stop exploitation of labour and improve their standard of living, terms and conditions of their employment. For achieving these objectives, trade unions perform various functions. Following are some of the important functions performed by trade unions.
(1) To do all efforts to unite the workers and to increase their strength and bargaining power and also to make the supply side of labour to gain monopolistic position.
(2) To protect the interests of the members through continuous efforts on better wages, improving the terms and conditions of employment and standard of living.
(3) To generate self-confidence among the workers.
(4) To take up welfare measure for improving the morale of the workers.
(5) To conduct various training and development programmes for increasing the efficiency and productivity of workers.
(6) To minimise the helplessness of workers by making them stand-up unitedly and creating and/or increasing their resistance power through collective bargaining.
(7) To protect the members and workers against victimisation and injustice by their employers.
(8) To do all efforts to encourage sincerity, honesty and discipline among the workers.
(9) To give a better status to workers.
(10) To educate the workers to become more responsible and responsive to the needs of their organisations.
(11) To act as a bridge between the management and workers.
(12) To do the whole hearted efforts to create and improve cordial labour management-industrial relations by avoiding industrial disputes.
(13) To do efforts for workers' participation in management. Workers' participation gives to workers a sense of importance, pride and accomplishment. It also provides them an opportunity for self-expression; a feeling of belonging to their places of work and a sense of workmanship and creativeness. It helps to provide for the integration of their interests with their management and makes them the joint partners in their enterprises.

Functions of Trade Union
The National Commission on Labour (NCL) has stated certain basic functions of trade unions which are mentioned below.
(1) To secure fair wages for workers.
(2) To promote identity of interests of workers with their industry.
(3) To safeguard the security of tenure and also to improve conditions of service.
(4) To enlarge opportunities for promotion and training.
(5) To promote working and living conditions.
(6) To provide for educational, cultural and recreational facilities to enrich their lives.
(7) To do all efforts to promote individual and collective welfare of workers.
(8) To facilitate technological advancement by broadening the understanding the views of workers in the issues involved in their jobs.
(9) To offer responsive co-operation in improving levels of production the productivity, discipline and high standards of quality.

The NCL also enjoined following important responsibilities upon the trade unions.
(a) To do all efforts for promoting national integration.
(b) Properly instilling a sense of responsibilities towards industry and society in their members.

From the functions considered above it can be concluded that the trade unions must not only function for protecting and improving wages and conditions of labour; but they should do all efforts related to matters by which workers are likely to be affected. Moreover, they should change their views or outlook, activities, functions and practices to suit the prevailing economic, political, social and cultural conditions to be more useful and effective.

Questions for Discussion

1. State and explain the meaning of 'Industrial Relations.'
2. Explain the features of 'Industrial Relations.'
3. Describe the scope of Industrial Relations.
4. Discuss the objectives and importance of Industrial Relations.
5. Explain the measures which can be introduced to develop the industrial relations.
6. Explain the development of industrial relations in the post-independence period.
7. Explain the concept of trade unions.
8. Explain the objectives and functions of trade unions.
9. Describe the trade union movement in India.
10. Write short notes:
    (a) Nature of industrial relations
    (b) Nature of Trade Union
    (c) Approaches for the Study of industrial relations
    (d) Industrial relations and Labour Legislation in India
    (e) Features of trade unions

Questions from Previous Pune University BBA Examinations

1. Define the term Trade Union. Explain the Growth of Trade Unions. **October 2012**

Ans.: Refer to Article 1.9 and Article 1.10 of this Chapter.

2. Define the term Industrial Relation. Explain the Scope and Importance of Industrial Relation. **April 2014**

Ans.: Refer to Articles 1.2, 1.4 and 1.5 of this Chapter.

5. Write Short Notes:

   (A) Importance of Industrial Relations. **October 2010, 2011**

Ans.: Refer to Article 1.5 of this Chapter.

   (B) Growth of Trade Union. **October 2010**

Ans.: Refer to Article 1.10 of this Chapter.

✱✱✱

Chapter 2...

Industrial Disputes, Collective Bargaining and Workers Participation in Management

Contents ...

2.1 Meaning, Definition and Causes of Industrial Disputes

2.2 Model Grievance Procedure

2.3 Types of Conflict Resolution: Negotiation, Investigation, Mediation, Conciliation, Arbitration and Adjudication, Works Committee, Conciliation Officer, Board of Conciliation, Court of Enquiry, Labour Court, Industrial Tribunal and National Tribunal

2.4 Collective Bargaining: Meaning, Characteristics, Importance, Process, Pre-requisites and Types

2.5 Employee Engagement: Concept, Importance and Employee Engagement in India

2.6 Workers Participation in Management (WPM): Meaning, Pre-requisites, Advantages and Disadvantages, Levels and Types

- Questions for Discussion
- Questions from Previous Pune University BBA Examinations

2.1 Meaning, Definition and Causes of Industrial Disputes

(1) Meaning and Definition of Industrial Disputes

The dictionary meaning of 'conflict' is a struggle, a fight or a strong disagreement; while by 'dispute' is meant quarrelling. In the literature on industrial relations, the word 'conflict' and 'dispute' are used more or less as synonymously. A conflict is an expression of disagreement. Industrial conflict is rather a general concept. When it acquires a specific dimension, it becomes an industrial dispute. Industrial disputes are open manifestations of the feeling of dissatisfaction of employees/workers, in question.

The definition of the term 'Industrial Dispute' is given in the Industrial Disputes Act, 1947. According to Section 2(k), *'Industrial Dispute' means any dispute or difference between employers and employers or between employers and workmen, or between workmen and workmen, which is connected with the employment or non-employment or the terms of employment or with the conditions of labour, or of any person.*

(2) Causes of Industrial Disputes

The employer and his employees jointly form the integral parts of one and the same organisation. But, many a times, the strategies of each party are guided by their own vested interests. As a result, it is inevitable that the attitudes and interests of one party come in direct conflict with that of the other party. To overcome such a scenario, each of the parties need to adopt a holistic view, namely, that there are certain areas wherein in the interests of both the parties, i.e., the employers and employees are the same; whereas, in some other areas, there could be disagreements - one that has the potential to trigger conflicts.

There are various factors which give rise to industrial conflicts or disputes. It is, therefore, very difficult to identify a single factor, as a cause of industrial conflicts or disputes as multifarious causes blended together result in industrial conflicts or disputes. However, various factors or causes of industrial conflicts can be broadly grouped in the following important categories:

- (a) Economic factors or causes;
- (b) Industrial factors;
- (c) Management attitudes towards its employees;
- (d) Factors relating to the implementation of labour laws;
- (e) Psychological factors;
- (f) Other causes or factors.

(a) Economic Factors or Causes:

The workers demand increase in wage rates, overtime payments and other allowances. The management opposition is always there in that respect. Bonus is the other important issue. Despite the Payment of Bonus Act, in place, conflicts over the rate of bonus have been common. Bonus was the cause of more than 7 per cent of total number of industrial conflicts or disputes in India.

Sometimes, industrial conflicts crop up following the demand of labour for economic security. The most important security for the workers is their jobs. It is but natural that the workers always try to protect their jobs. It is the feeling of insecurity that leads the workers to go on strikes against retrenchments and dismissals.

(b) Industrial Factors:

Industrial factors are mainly related to working conditions and welfare of the workers. Working conditions include the length of working hours, physical work environment, safety measures, terms and conditions of employment pertaining to dismissal, functions and duties of the workers, etc. While welfare of workers refers to such services, facilities and amenities, such as, rest and recreation rooms, canteen facilities, transportation facilities, etc. They contribute to the improvements in the conditions under which the workers are employed. If the management remains reluctant in respect of these aspects, then, these conflicts, in due course of time, could lead to industrial unrest. That apart, poor personnel administration could also be the cause of industrial conflicts.

(c) Management Approach Towards its Employees/Workers:

If the approach of the management towards the problems, difficulties etc., of its employees are not positive, conflicts definitely arise. The following few points make this amply clear. They are:

(i) When management does not take any initiative to find out the solutions for solving industrial disputes even when the trade unions want the management to do so, it ends up angering the workers.

(ii) Many a times, the management concerned refuses to recognise a particular trade union or unions which have the full support of workers. The workers naturally resist such an attitude, thereby leading to industrial conflict or dispute.

(iii) When the management takes all the decisions relating to recruitment, transfers, promotions, etc., without consulting the employees; the employees, in turn, become non-cooperative and, at times, resort to strikes, as a mark of protest.

(iv) Inter-role conflicts may develop when the role of the supervisors is ambiguous.

(v) When the management expects its supervisors to assist in integrating the new employees, while the experienced and senior employees expect the supervisors to protect their interest, rights and treat everyone consistently, certain conflicts may develop. Such conflicts are known as 'Inter-sender conflicts.'

(vi) The employees expect its management to provide certain services and benefits for promoting harmonious employee-employee relations. But when their management does not take necessary steps to provide those benefits and services, conflicts invariably develop.

(d) Factors Relating to the Implementation of Labour Laws:

Although many Acts have been passed for promoting the harmonious relations and labour welfare; their provisions are seldom properly implemented by the employers concerned, leading invariably to avoidable industrial conflicts.

(e) Psychological Factors:

There are some psychological causes of industrial conflicts. The satisfaction of the workers with their jobs is not only based merely on their wages, hours of work, working conditions, but also so on the extent to which they enjoy their work and feel that it is worthwhile. When they do not get mental or psychological satisfaction and the management denies the opportunities for the workers to satisfy their urge for self-expression, personal achievement, etc., then, this fuels unrest and thereby to industrial conflicts.

(f) Other Causes or Factors:

We have already noted that there are certain external factors which give rise to industrial conflicts. These external factors are those causes or factors which are not directly connected with the given enterprise, as for example, in a case, wherein the workers of a given enterprise go on strike to express solidarity with the workers of some other enterprise, who are on strike. The other important external factor is the political factor, wherein the workers go on strikes to protest against certain legislative measures or government policies, etc. As a result, the working activity of their organisation is disturbed.

Essentials of Industrial Dispute:

For any dispute to be called as an industrial dispute, it should satisfy the following essentials:

(a) There must be a difference or dispute (i) between employers and employers, (ii) between workmen and workmen, or (iii) between workmen and employers.

(b) A workman concerned with the dispute should not be employed in any administrative or managerial capacity.

(c) Industrial dispute must pertain to an industrial matter, or

(d) It may be connected with the employment or non-employment or the terms of employment.

(e) Industrial dispute may be concerned with the condition of labour of any person.

(f) Industrial dispute implies a real and substantial difference having some element of persistency and continuity till resolved and, if not adjusted, it is likely to endanger the industrial peace of the undertaking.

(3) Forms and Types of Industrial Disputes:

The industrial disputes can take the form of strikes, *gheraos*, *bandhs*, lock-outs, etc. A strike is nothing but a stoppage of work initiated or supported by a trade union or trade unions. The workers/employees go on strike with a view to bring pressure upon their employer to resolve the dispute, grievance or constrain him to accept certain terms and conditions. The strikes can be of different types, i.e., primary strikes and secondary strikes. Stay away strikes, sit-down or, tool down, or open down strikes, go-slow tactics, token strikes, etc., are some of the examples of primary strikes. Sympathetic strikes, i.e., supporting or showing solidarity to workers unions of other industry in support of their cause or demands, fall under secondary strikes.

On the other hand, when an employer closes down the factory or place of work or refuses to continue the employment of his employees in order to force them to agree to his terms and conditions during the pendency of an industrial dispute, the resulting situation is a lock-out.

The main types of the industrial disputes can be classified in the following manner:

(a) Industrial disputes which arise out of deadlocks in the negotiations for a collective agreement. Such disputes are known as 'Interest Disputes'.

(b) Industrial disputes which take place or arise from day-to-day grievances or complaints of the employees. Such disputes are known as 'Grievance Disputes.'

(c) Some industrial disputes arise from the acts of interference through the exercise of the rights to act or to organise leading to unfair labour practices. They are the ones which relate to unfair labour practices.

(d) Some industrial disputes relate to the right of a trade union to represent a particular class or category of employees for certain purposes, such as, collective bargaining. They can be called as 'Recognition Disputes.'

2.2 Model Grievance Procedure

Meaning of 'Grievance'

It is very difficult to define the concept of 'Grievance' precisely. But it is defined in several ways by the experts in the field of management considering various points relating to grievance. Some important definitions stated by the experts are stated below:

(a) **Dale S. Beach**, *"Any dissatisfaction or feeling of injustice in connection with one's employment situation that is brought to the attention or notice of management".*

(b) **E. B. Flippo,** *"The grievance is a type of discontent which must be expressed. It is usually more formal in character than a complaint. It can be valid or ridiculous, and must grow out of something connected with company operations or policy. It must involve an interpretation or application of the provisions of the labour contract".*

(c) **Prof. Arun Monappa and Prof. Mirza Sayadain,** *"Grievances are manifestations of workers' dissensions against working conditions, terms of service, leave and holidays and management decision.*

(d) **Keith Davis,** *"Grievance is any real or imagined feeling of personal injustice which an employee has concerning his employment relationship".*

(e) **Jucicus, Michael J.**, *"A grievance is any discontent or dissatisfaction, whether expressed or not, whether valid or not, arising out of anything connected with the company which an employee thinks, believes or even feels to be unfair, unjust or inequitable".*

(f) **The International Labour Organisation** defines a grievance as a complaint of one or more workers with respect to their wages, allowances, conditions of work and interpretation of service conditions or stipulations covering such arrears as overtime, leave, transfer, promotions, seniority, job assignment and termination of service.

(g) **According to the National Commission on Labour,** *"Complaints affecting one or more individual workers in respect of wage payments, overtime, leave, transfer, promotion, seniority, work assignment and discharges would constitute grievances".*

From the above mentioned definitions, we can definitely say that a grievance is sign of an employee's discontent or dissatisfaction with his job or work and its nature. When an employee has certain expectations, aspirations which he wants to be fulfilled by the management where he is working and if his management neglects or fails to satisfy that employee's needs, expectations, there develops the feeling of dissatisfaction or discontent and as a result, a grievance may take place. It is thus clear that a grievance is employee expectation and management practice of not paying proper attention to that. The cause of grievances are many. If proper care is not taken in time, there is discontent or dissatisfaction among the employees which generally results in a turmoil affecting the working or functioning of the organisation adversely. Hence, the grievances must be redressed at the earliest possible moment considering the cause of dissatisfaction of the employees concerned.

Features of Grievance:

If we study and analyse the above stated definitions, we shall come to know the following important features of grievance.

(a) Grievance is a concept which implies dissatisfaction or dissensions of the employees when at work.

(b) It can be verbal or written, valid and legitimate, untrue or false, imaginary or ridiculous.

(c) It arises out of something connected with the job, working conditions, amenities, promotions, increments or such other matter.

(d) A grievance may be that of an individual employee or of a group of employees.

(e) Grievances generally give rise to unhappiness, frustration, discontent, indifference to work, poor morale, etc., and disturb the employees concerned.

(f) Grievances ultimately lead to inefficiency of workers and low productivity.

(g) The effects or the results of grievance are harmful on the employees as well as on the organisation in which the employees work.

(2) Causes of Grievances

There are certain real causes of grievances while there can be imaginary or apparent causes of grievance. It is found that sometimes, an employee feels that the physical conditions and circumstances under which he has to work are unsafe and unpleasant or irritating. This leads to his discontent. But on close observation, an impartial observer may find that the main cause of the discontent or the grievance of that employee is not the physical irritating conditions, but the employee does not like his supervisor for one or other reason. It is also found that many employees are habituated to find faults, to lodge complaints for petty reasons and they have always grievances against their officers. Hence, they are known as 'chronic grievers' or 'habituated grievers'. Many times, doubts and fears give rise to grievances. Management policy and particular attitudes towards the employees are also responsible for grievances. Thus, there can be many reasons or causes of grievance. Some important causes are enumerated below:

[A] Grievances of Employees

(a) Undesirable, unsatisfactory working conditions.
(b) Complaints about dampness, fumes, noise, unsafe conditions.
(c) Inadequate welfare facilities, amenities.
(d) Demands for individual wage adjustments, bonus.
(e) Continuity in service and service conditions.
(f) Complaints about the incentive system.
(g) Complaints about a particular supervisor, foreman, officer.
(h) Complaints about the job classifications.
(i) Objections regarding the general method or manner of supervision.
(j) Complaints or dissatisfaction about compensation.
(k) Interpretation of seniority rules, promotions, increments, etc.
(l) Disciplinary action or disciplinary discharge, lay-off.
(m) Improper manner of imposition of fines, penalties.
(n) Duty leave, sick leave and other types of leaves.
(o) Transfers.
(p) Changing of shifts.
(q) Recovery of dues.
(r) Suspension.
(s) Super-annuation, retirement.
(t) Victimisation, favouritism, feeling of neglect.
(u) Violation of contracts relating to collective bargaining.
(v) Non-availability of inputs in time.

[B] Causes of Grievances of Management against its Employees

(a) Disobedience on the part of employees.

(b) Going on leave without prior permission, absenteeism, etc.

(c) Indiscipline.

(d) Illegal strikes.

(e) Illusion or wrong conclusions.

(f) Go slow tactics.

(g) Improper methods adopted by the trade unions in dealing with management.

(h) Arrogant behaviours of the employees.

(i) Reckless charges by the employees, trade unions leaders against the supervisors, management.

Whatever may be a cause or causes of grievances, efforts must be taken to find out the best possible solutions or methods of settling them and for that purpose, there should be an effective grievance redressal procedure.

(3) Grievance Procedure

The main purpose of grievance procedure is to eliminate dissatisfaction by settling the grievances and to ensure fair and equitable treatment for the employees so that environment, constructive work producing healthy industrial relations, can be maintained for the benefit of all.

A grievance procedure is the formal mechanism for dealing with employees' grievances. It has several steps which an aggrieved employee can take in sequence for the redressal of his grievance or grievances.

A grievance may be that of an individual employee or a group of employees. A grievance procedure is laid down only for individual-level grievances, whereas the collective bargaining is used for redressing the group grievances.

It may be noted here that a grievance procedure can be of two types: (1) An Open-door type, or (2) A Step-ladder type.

In an open-door policy, management allows an employee who has a grievance to go directly to it for redressal of his grievance, or even to meet the highest authority of an enterprise. Of course, this policy is useful in the case of small enterprises. For large organisations, a ladder-step policy is suitable. In ladder step policy, there can be three-step, four step or five step grievance procedure depending upon the need and size of the organisation.

In practice, it is found that a grievance procedure differs from an enterprise to enterprise. Some enterprises accept two or three step procedure. Generally, such enterprises are small, while the large unionised companies may have six or even more than six-step grievance procedures. You will get an idea about the grievance handling procedure from the following diagrams.

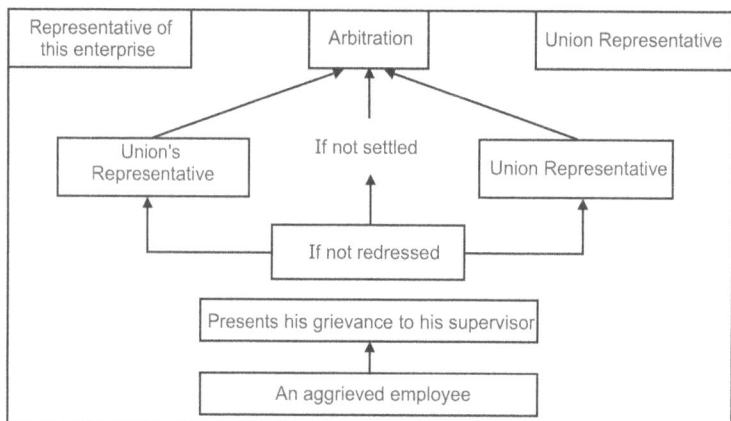

Fig. 2.1: A Grievance Handling Procedure in a Small Enterprise

If a grievance is settled at an early stage, it is obvious that there is no need to approach the other superior officers or persons for grievance redressal.

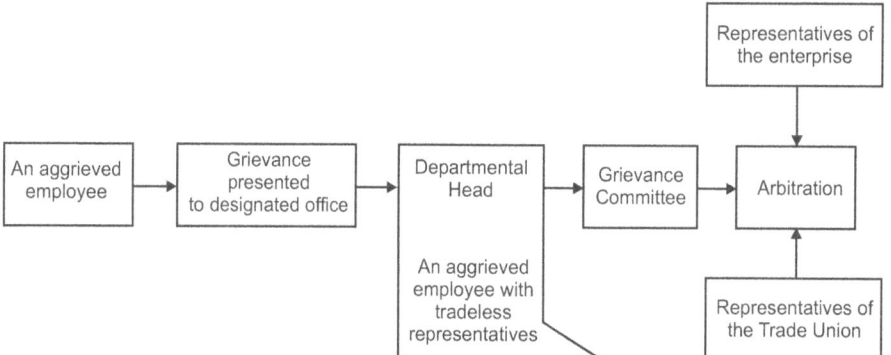

Fig. 2.2: A Grievance Handling Procedure in a Large Unionalised Enterprise

The National Commission on Labour has suggested the Model Grievance Procedure in which there are certain steps for the redressal or settling of a grievance. The summary of these steps is as follows:

(a) When there is any grievance, the aggrieved employee, at the outset, has to approach his immediate superior or supervisor and to inform him regarding his grievance.

(b) If that aggrieved employee is not satisfied or his superior has not given any reply or response, the employee should make an appeal to the departmental head either in person or accompanied by his departmental representative.

(c) If the departmental head does not pay attention to the grievance or solution or decision given by him is not acceptable to the aggrieved employee, then the aggrieved employee can resort to the Bipartite Grievance Committee constituted by the representative of the management and the employees, trade unions.

(d) In the Committee, if there are unanimous decisions on the grievance, communicates the same to the management for the implementation. If the committee could not take the decision unanimously, it places all the relevant records concerning the grievance before the management and the management thereupon takes the decision.

(e) If the aggrieved employee is not satisfied with the decision of the management, he has the right to appeal against the decision of the management.

(f) When no agreement is reached at this stage, the grievance is referred to arbitration.

The steps mentioned above in the grievance redressal procedure are not statutory. There is voluntariness in so far as the implementation of the Model Grievance Procedure is concerned.

A grievance becomes a dispute when there is no redressal of a grievance through a grievance handling machinery or procedure or the management's decision is not acceptable to the aggrieved employee.

(4) Legislative Aspects of the Grievance Redressal Procedure in India

In India, at present, we find that some industries have formulated the grievance procedures formulated by themselves, while in some enterprises, the Model Grievance Procedure has been adopted. But there are three important Acts which deal with provisions of the Acts applicable. These three Acts are:

(a) The Industrial Employment (Standing Orders) Act of 1946.
(b) The Factories Act of 1948.
(c) The Industrial Disputes Act of 1947.

Before Independence, the settlement of the day-to-day grievances of the employees did not receive much legislative attention. However, the Industrial Employment (Standing Orders) Act of 1946 has provided for the framing of standing orders for every establishment employing one hundred or more workers and it is also made clear in the Act that these orders should contain, among other things, provisions for redressal of grievances of workers against unfair treatment and wrongful exploitation by the employer or his agents. The Act has a limited applicability and it does not provide for bipartite discussions or any powerful measure for a prompt redressal of the grievances.

The Factories Act of 1948 provides for the appointment of a welfare officer in every factory ordinarily employing five hundred or more workers [Section 49 (1)]. These officers, thus appointed, look after the complaints and grievances of the workers employed in the factories to which the Factory Act of 1948 is applied. According to the provisions of the Factories Act, the State Government have framed rules which enjoin upon Labour Welfare Officers to ensure the settlement of grievances.

In the Industrial Disputes Act of 1947, we find certain provisions relating individual industrial disputes relating to discharge, dismissal, retrenchment, etc. Provisions have been made in the Industrial Disputes Act of 1947 for the investigation and settlement of industrial disputes by appointing authorities. The Industrial Disputes Act, 1947 has been amended in

2010 and the provisions have been made for setting up "Grievance Redressal Machinery" in Section 9-C. The provisions of Section 9-C are as under:

Grievance Redressal Machinery [Section 9-C]
1. Every industrial establishment employing twenty or more workmen shall have one or more Grievance Redressal Committee for the resolution of disputes arising out of individual grievances.
2. The Grievance Redressal Committee shall consist of equal number of members from the employer and the workmen.
3. The Chairperson of the Grievance Redressal Committee shall be selected from the employer and from among the workmen alternatively on rotation basis every year.
4. The total number of members of the Grievance Redressal Committee shall not be more than six:
   Provided that there shall be, as far as practicable, one woman member if the Grievance Redressal Committee has two members and in case the number of members are more than two, the number of women members may be increased proportionately.
5. Notwithstanding anything contained in this section, the setting up of Grievance Redressal Committee shall not affect the right of the workman to raise industrial dispute on the same matter under the provisions of this Act.
6. The Grievance Redressal Committee may complete its proceedings within thirty days on receipt of a written application by or on behalf of the aggrieved party.
7. The workman who is aggrieved of the decision of the Grievance Redressal Committee may prefer an appeal to the employer against the decision of Grievance Redressal Committee and the employer shall, within one month from the date of receipt of such appeal, dispose of the same and send a copy of his decision to the workman concerned.
8. Nothing contained in this section shall apply to the workmen for whom there is an established Grievance Redressal Mechanism in the establishment concerned.

2.3 Types of Conflict Resolution: Negotiation, Investigation, Mediation, Conciliation, Arbitration and Adjudication, Works Committee, Conciliation Officer, Board of Conciliation, Court of Enquiry, Labour Court, Industrial Tribunal and National Tribunal

Conflict Resolution

Conflict demands attention because when the sources of tension are left unattended, they tend to smoulder or rankle long after the explosions have taken place. Often, the accumulation of minor conflicts over a period of time, if not addressed timely, leads to major explosions in various situations. Therefore, for proper resolution of conflicts, top priority must be accorded to any programme concerning itself with harmonising industrial relations and maintaining industrial peace in the country.

Conflicts can be resolved by any one or a combination of measures put together, having due regard to the nature of conflict or conflicts. Generally, the thumb rule followed in conflict resolution is "to try to move conflict from a 'lose-lose' or 'win-lose' emphasis to a 'win-win' emphasis." If creative solutions are found out, both parties to the conflicts stand to benefit.

For proper resolution of industrial conflicts, there should be clear identification of the underlying causes and sources of conflicts, redirection of tensions towards productive accomplishments, integration of the ideas of the parties concerned of the conflict in question so as to achieve proper solutions in the overall best interests of both the employees and their organisation, in a spirit of mutual co-operation and, one guided by proper attitudes and aptitudes, etc.

In a scenario wherein there are conflicts of interest, then, adequate efforts in an accommodative spirit, i.e., of give and take needs to be made for rendering collective bargaining successful. Conflicts of interest are compromisable and hence, 'give and take' policy can be adopted to resolve such conflicts.

Conflicts that arise due to day-to-day grievances can also be resolved by making collective agreement, employment contract, work rules, etc. There are different ways of handling the industrial conflicts considering the nature of the conflicts. In this regard, it should be remembered that prevention is always better than cure. Hence, no effort should be spared to prevent the occurrence of the conflicts. Preventive measures can be taken both at the organisational and macro levels.

At the enterprise level, good personnel management backed by cordial and healthy employer-employee relationship definitely goes to contribute to industrial peace, which, in turn, helps to nip in the bud any industrial conflicts from happening. The participation of labour in management, a good employer-employee communication system, a proper understanding of the situation by the employees as well as the employer, i.e., by both the parties, mutual respect for each others' rights, a proper discharge of responsibilities by both the parties etc., are very important if industrial conflicts are to be avoided. Besides this, there should be in place proper procedures for finding out solutions to the conflicts, as and when they arise.

Types of Conflict Resolution
(1) Negotiation
- Negotiation is one of the principal means of settling labour disputes. However, due to lack of trust between the employers and workmen or their trade unions or because of inter-rivalry of the trade unions where the employers get the upper hand and are in a commanding position, negotiations often fail.
- Through an Amendment in the Act by Act 46 of 1982 Chapter II B, certain individual disputes can be sent to Grievance Settlement Authority. Under this

Chapter, Section 9 C has made it obligatory for the employers to make provisions for Grievance Settlement Authority, for settlement of industrial disputes connected with an individual workman employed in an establishment in which fifty or more workmen are employed or have been employed on any day in the preceding twelve months. This amendment however, despite being made thirty two years back, has not yet seen the light of the day.

(2) Investigation

Investigation is conducted by a board or court appointed by the Appropriate Government. It can be either compulsory or voluntary. When the investigation is conducted on an application made by either or both the parties to the conflict/dispute, it is a voluntary investigation. But when the Government appoints a court of inquiry, on its own motion, to investigate into the matters concerning the conflict/dispute in question without the consent of the parties concerned, such investigation is compulsory. The method of investigation helps to analyse the facts and reasons of disputes/ conflicts in order to reach some amicable solution or solutions. During the pendency of investigation, neither are strikes and lock-outs allowed nor can the conditions of employment be changed.

(3) Mediation

Mediation can be defined as "a process by which a third party brings together the parties or groups having conflicts amongst them not only to iron out the differences existing between them but also to find out a better solution or a specific proposal for putting an end to the conflict or dispute in question through negotiations."

Mediation takes place with the consent of both the parties. The mediator is rightly described as 'confidential advisor' and 'Industrial Diplomat'. He performs a messenger's service or job for the parties concerned without bringing his pressure to bear upon them.

The main aim of mediation is always to find out a solution to the existing conflict/dispute by bringing about a voluntary agreement. Mediation intends a positive and affirmative action by some third party to bring about a settlement of industrial disputes. It encourages the parties concerned to arrive at a decision without any force or orders from the mediator. His job is to bring the parties to the conflicts/ disputes together in his presence and by formulating suitable and substantive proposals for ironing out the differences of the parties, i.e., employers, employees or trade unions with a view to resolve them.

In fact, there are three kinds of mediators as suggested by Prof. Pigou. These mediators are –

    (a)   The eminent outsider,

    (b)   The non-governmental board, and

    (c)   The board connected with some part of the Government system of the country.

(4) Conciliation

Conciliation is one of the important methods of the settlement of industrial conflicts/disputes. It is an attempt to bring about a reconciliation *vis-à-vis* the differing views of the parties to the disputes/conflicts so as to bring about an agreement. Conciliation is considered as the friendly intervention by a neutral person to help the parties concerned to settle their differences peacefully.

Conciliation can be defined as "a process by which the parties to the conflicts/disputes are brought together by the conciliation machinery with a view to persuading them to arrive at a mutually acceptable agreement for settling the conflicts. It is really a process of rational and orderly discussions of conflicts or disputes between the parties under the able guidance of a conciliator. Conciliating machinery consists of a conciliation officer and the board of conciliation. The main task of conciliation is to offer advice and make necessary suggestions to the parties concerned on the controversial issues. Conciliation can be either voluntary or compulsory.

As a matter of fact, conciliation and mediation are considered as equivalent terms involving third party intervention for resolving the conflicts or for promoting voluntary settlement of disputes. Prof. H. W. Davey, the author of *Contemporary Collective Bargaining* point out that, the distinction between 'mediation' and 'conciliation' is almost hair-splitting. In practice, conciliation shades off into mediation. The difference between them is essentially one of degree rather than kind.

It seems that 'mediation' is a wider term than conciliation. Conciliation is limited to encouraging the parties concerned to discuss the differences between them. This, it does, by helping the parties concerned to develop their own proposed solutions. While, mediation implies a stronger form of intervention and a mediator can suggest certain proposals to the parties to settle the conflicts.

(5) Arbitration

Arbitration is yet another method available for bringing about settlement of conflicts. It is a means of securing an award on a conflict issue by reference to a third party.

Arbitration is a process in which a dispute/conflict is submitted to an outsider who impartially makes a decision which is generally binding on both the parties to the conflict.

Voluntary arbitration implies that the two parties to the conflict/dispute are unable to sort out their differences by themselves or with the help of mediator or conciliator, and therefore, they agree to submit their conflict to some impartial authority, whose decision they are ready to accept. In voluntary arbitration, parties to the conflict voluntarily refer their conflict to arbitration before it is referred for adjudication. The important aspects of voluntary arbitration are as under:

- (a) There is voluntary submission of dispute/conflict to an arbitrator in the voluntary arbitration.
- (b) Thereafter, necessary investigations are done.
- (c) Voluntary arbitration may be specifically required for conflicts arising under agreements.
- (d) The enforcement of an award is not necessary and binding on the parties concerned. There is no compulsion in that respect as the arbitration is voluntary.

(6) Adjudication

Adjudication is the ultimate legal remedy for the settlement of unresolved industrial conflicts/disputes. Adjudication or compulsory arbitration as the method of settlement of conflicts is generally utilised when the parties concerned fail to arrive at a settlement through the other voluntary methods.

Adjudication involves the intervention in the conflict/dispute by a third party appointed by the Appropriate Government for the purpose of deciding the nature of final settlement. When the reference of adjudication is made by the aforesaid Government without the consent of either or both the parties to the dispute/conflict, it is known as compulsory adjudication. The Industrial Disputes Act, 1947, provides for a three-tier system of adjudication consisting of - (a) Labour Courts; (b) Industrial Tribunals; and (c) National Tribunals. These adjudication bodies decide the industrial disputes/conflicts referred to them by the Appropriate Government and pass their awards.

(7) Works Committee

Refer to Article 3.4.1 (Point 1) of Chapter 3.

(8) Conciliation Officer

Refer to Article 3.4.1 (Point 2) of Chapter 3.

(9) Board of Conciliation

Refer to Article 3.4.1 (Point 3) of Chapter 3.

(10) Court of Enquiry

Refer to Article 3.4.1 (Point 4) of Chapter 3.

(11) Labour Court

Refer to Article 3.4.2 (Point 1) of Chapter 3.

(12) Industrial Tribunal

Refer to Article 3.4.2 (Point 2) of Chapter 3.

(13) National Tribunal

Refer to Article 3.4.2 (Point 3) of Chapter 3.

2.4 Collective Bargaining: Meaning, Characteristics, Importance, Process, Pre-requisites and Types

(1) Meaning and Definitions of Collective Bargaining

The term 'Collective Bargaining' is composed of two words. (a) Collective, and (b) Bargaining. The word 'collective' is opposite to the word 'individual' as it implies 'group'; while 'bargaining' pertains to 'negotiation' or 'haggling'. In other words, by 'collective bargaining' refers to negotiation by a group. It is obvious that collective bargaining or negotiations require joint sessions of the representatives of workers/employers and management/employers.

Thus, collective bargaining is opposite to that of individual bargaining and it takes place between organised groups of employees with either a single employer or multiple employers. It is so-called because employees, as a group, select their representatives to meet and discuss in joint sessions their differences with the management or employer and the collective bargaining helps in ironing out many differences between employees and their management.

The term 'collective bargaining' was coined by Sydney and Beatrice Webb of Great Britain, which is considered the 'home of Collective Bargaining.' This is based on the belief that the bargaining capacity of an individual worker is weak *vis-à-vis* his employer, who is often powerful. To overcome such an inequitable situation, the workers concerned opt for the mechanism of 'collective bargaining' wherein through their collective efforts, they stand a better chance of taking up their cause from a position of strength *vis-à-vis* their employer or employers, as the case may be.

It is this idea (collective bargaining) that gave birth to the establishment of modern day trade unions, which, in turn, helped the workers to stay organised and thereby gain bargaining advantage, which would have otherwise been not possible but for the mechanism of collective bargaining. This plays an important role in the context of wage determination besides many other things.

Many experts in the field of management and economics have defined the term 'Collective Bargaining'. Let us consider some of the important definitions in order to understand their nature and characteristics.

Definitions of Collective Bargaining:

(a) In the **Encyclopedia of Social Sciences**, "Collective Bargaining' is defined as, *a process of discussion and negotiation between two parties, one or both of whom is a group of persons acting in concert. The resulting bargain is an understanding as to the terms and conditions under which a continuing service is to be performed. More specifically, collective bargaining is a procedure by which employees and a group of employees agree upon the conditions of work*".

This implies that they both, by understanding each other's problems and viewpoints, develop some framework of good industrial relations by way of collective bargaining and both may carry their daily association by seeking co-operation for their mutual benefits.

(b) **R.F. Hoxie**, *Collective bargaining is the mode of fixing the term of employment by means of bargaining between an organised body of employees and an employer or an association of employers usually acting through organised agents. The essence of collective bargaining is a bargain between interested parties and not a degree from outside parties.*

(c) **Dale Yoder**, "*Collective bargaining is essentially a process in which employees act as a group in seeking to shape conditions and relationships in their employment*".

(d) **Reynolds L.G**, "*Trade unions try to advance the interests of their members mainly by negotiating agreements usually termed, 'Union contracts' or 'Collective Agreements' – with employers. The process by which these agreements are negotiated, administered and enforced are included in the term Collective Bargaining*".

(e) **Archibald Cox**, "*Collective Bargaining is the resolution of industrial problems between the representatives of employers and the freely designated representatives of employees acting collectively with a minimum of government dictation*".

(f) **J. H. Richardson**, "*Collective bargaining takes place when a number of work people enter into a negotiation as a bargaining unit with an employer or group of employers with the object of reaching an agreement on the conditions of the employment of the work people*".

(2) Characteristic Features of Collective Bargaining

The following are the important salient features or characteristics of collecting bargaining:

(a) Collective bargaining is opposite to individual bargaining. In collective bargaining, organised group or groups of employees and either a single employer or multiple employers takes part. It is called collective bargaining because the employees through their representatives negotiate with their management about working conditions, terms of employment etc.

(b) It is a two-party process. Obviously, these two parties are the representatives of workers and the employer or employers or people managing the enterprise.

(c) The above mentioned two parties get an opportunity for clear and face-to-face negotiations.

(d) Collective bargaining is a mutual give and take process and not a take it or leave it method of arriving at settlement of any dispute. Collective bargaining can become successful only when the workers through their representatives and management want to make it successful. There must be some bargaining; the attitude of both the parties must be positive. There should not be any animosity or reprisal.

(e) Collective bargaining is a continuous process. When we use the word 'process' it implies time lag. It does not end with merely negotiation. It begins and ends with a contract. Changes, if required, can be made in the contract, according to one's needs. Contracts once entered into cannot be permanent.

(f) Collective bargaining is a dynamic and flexible process. When we say that collective bargaining is a continuous process, it implies that certain or some changes can be brought about. It has fluidity and ample scope for a compromise. If it is not dynamic, flexible, collective bargaining can not became successful.

(g) The ultimate objective of collective bargaining is to solve the problems or disputes and establish regular stable and sound industrial relations between the employees and their employers.

(h) Collective bargaining is the practical way of industrial democracy wherein workers and their employers participate to achieve certain objectives. It is really a process or method of a joint formulation of the policies of the enterprise concerned on various matters which affects the workers directly at the workplace. It is a good form of inter-disciplinary system that helps promote industrial jurisprudence.

(i) Collective bargaining is a process which includes all the efforts from preliminary preparations to the presentation of conflicting viewpoints, collection of related necessary facts of correct decisions in order to solve the problems or disputes of the needs and objectives of employees and employers who work together in the given organisation.

(j) Collective bargaining is not a competitive process but is essentially a complementary process. This implies that each party needs something that the other party has. A worker can do all that he can as far as productive efforts insofar as enhancing efficient production go - one, that is expected of him from the employer concerned; while the employers have the capacity to pay for those efforts in return. Collective bargaining is a special type of transaction involving a complex process. It is not a simple transaction based on 'take–it–or–leave-it' method. In collective bargaining, the workers and management are highly dependent upon each other. Both parties by acting in a spirit of co-operation stand to gain from the agreement reached through its instrumentality.

(k) Collective bargaining is a voluntary process wherein workers and management participate on their own motion in the process of negotiation for discussing the issues concerned thoroughly and, thereafter, arrive at a solution for the well-being and growth of their enterprise, as a whole.

(l) Collective bargaining covers the negotiations of contracts, grievance procedure and settlement of disputes as well as economic sanctions. In the process of collective bargaining, the participation of workers through their trade unions and their management is essential. The end objective of collective bargaining is to help secure labour-management agreement or contract without any assistance from a third party.

(3) Importance of Collective Bargaining

We have already studied the various important aspects such as characteristic features, principles, types of collective bargaining, bargaining process and contents of collective bargaining, contracts, etc. Now you can understand properly the functions and importance of collective bargaining. Let us first consider some important functions of collective bargaining, which are as follows:

Prof. Arthur D. Butler, the author of the book, *Labour Economics and Institutions*, has classified the important features under the following three heads. They are:

(a) Collective bargaining as a process of social change;

(b) Collective bargaining as a peace treaty between two parties in continual conflicts or disputes;

(c) Collective bargaining as a system of industrial jurisprudence.

(i) The function of collective bargaining as a process of social change includes various aspects relating to the establishment of adjustment and balance of power between two conflicting groups. It is a technique of bringing about the rearrangements in the power hierarchy of competing groups. It is not merely confined to the economic relations between the employers and their employees. It helps the wage-earners to enhance their social as well as economic position.

(ii) It is also an important function of collective bargaining to bring about truce, i.e., stoppage of fighting or disputes by agreement, compromise for establishing peace and cordial relations between the two parties in a state of continual conflict.

(iii) The function of collective bargaining as a system of industrial jurisprudence is also very important. In a real sense, collective bargaining is a method of introducing civil rights into industry. In other words, it is a democratic method of bargaining. It requires the management to follow rules, terms and conditions while managing its organisation. In this sense, it is a rule-making process. It is a judicial process because in every collective bargaining agreement, there are provisions regarding the interpretation of the agreement entered into. In a nutshell, collective bargaining is a system which establishes, revises and administers many of the rules which govern the workplace and its conditions.

Following discussion would make the importance of collective bargaining, clearer.

Collective bargaining is very important for solving the problems of workers arising at the plant or industry level. The solutions to the common problems can be found directly through negotiations between the parties concerned from the standpoint of employees, trade unions and management, and, therefore, is very beneficial. If it works well, it develops a sense of responsibility and self-respect amongst the workers concerned and contributes significantly to workers' morale and productivity.

Moreover, it also helps to restrict management's freedom of action which is beneficial from the view point of workers. Further, the inclusion of provision for seniority and promotions in the collective bargaining agreement promotes a sense of job security among the workers. It helps to reduce the cost of labour turnover to the management.

At the macro level, i.e., from the view of economic and industrial development of the whole economy, successful collective bargaining results in the establishment of peaceful industrial climate which, in turn, increases the pace of the efforts towards economic and social development by eliminating obstacles coming in the way of development which are related to industrial unrest.

It can be said that as vehicle for industrial peace, collective bargaining has no equal. It encompasses the entire spectrum of democratic principles - right from the political field to the industrial field. It facilitates to help build a system of industrial jurisprudence by introducing civil rights in industry. Thanks to collective bargaining, the affairs relating to workers' job, his working conditions, promotions, transfers, wages and overtime payments, and leaves, etc., is conducted by the management through the mechanism of rules rather than arbitrary decisions.

Collective bargaining helps:
(a) to solve the industrial disputes,
(b) to prevent the industrial disputes,
(c) to create industrial peace in a democratic way,
(d) to secure a prompt and fair redressal of grievances,
(e) to avoid interruptions in work which may follow strikes, go-slow tactics, etc.
(f) to achieve efficient operations of the plants,
(g) to improve economic conditions of the employees,
(h) to provide a flexible means for the adjustment of wages and employment terms and conditions to economic changes and technological changes in the industry.
(i) to provide a solution to the problem of sickness in industry, of old age pension benefits and other fringe benefits.
(j) to create healthy and co-operative atmosphere and sound industrial relations in the enterprise concerned.
(k) to promote the stability and prosperity of the given enterprise as well as of the industrial sector.

(4) Process of Collective Bargaining

Collective bargaining is a continuous, flexible, dynamic and mobile process which covers the negotiations of contracts, the grievance procedures and the settlement of disputes as well as economic sanctions. In this process, the participation of workers through their trade unions and their management is essential. The end process of collective bargaining is the labour-management agreement or contract without the assistance of any third party. It is both, at the same time, a device and a procedure used by workers to safeguard their interests. It is really a technique by which the needs and objectives of workers and their employers are met, and hence, it is an integral part of the industrial society. The essence of collective bargaining lies in the readiness of the two parties to a dispute to reach an agreed and mutually satisfying settlement. Hence, there are two important stages in collective bargaining. These stages are:

[a] The Negotiation stage, and
[b] The stage of Contract Administration.

(a) The Negotiation Stage

For collective bargaining, there must exist for negotiation purposes, certain issues, problems, and demands. In this regard, certain proposals are put forward for consideration of the parties concerned and, thus, begin the process of collective bargaining. The negotiation stage itself involves four important steps, which are as follows:

(i) Identification of Problem or Issue

If the problem or problems or issues are not identified, how can the collective bargaining process begin? There must be some base to begin collective bargaining. In fact, the nature of problem or issue influences to a great extent the whole process of collective bargaining. If the problem is serious, it is accorded high priority and thereby discussed immediately. The nature of the problems, or issues or demands influences the selection of representatives, their number, periods of negotiation and agreement that is reached ultimately. Hence, it is very important from the point of view of both the parties to be very clear about the problems or issues before entering into negotiations.

(ii) Preparation for Negotiations

Negotiations may commence at the instance of workers or of management. When it is decided to solve the problem, to find the solution for the issue through collective bargaining process, both the parties start preparing themselves for negotiations. It is obvious that the preparation starts with the negotiations and the selection of representatives. The selected representatives collect all the necessary information relating to the problem and study various aspects in order to present their views effectively. Their authority and powers during negotiations are also clearly spelt out. Preparation for negotiations also entails fixing up of time for negotiations, period of negotiations etc. The period of negotiation may vary depending upon the circumstances.

(iii) Negotiation Procedure or Technique

For the purpose of negotiations, a negotiation committee comprising three to six members is formed, according to one's needs. It is considered that as far as possible, such committee should be small. If such committees are large, they tend to become unwieldy - one, that is, not only difficult to assemble but also prone to be disorderly. The management committee works as a team. A chief spokesman from the management side leads the committee. A chief spokesman is also called as a chief negotiator or principal negotiator.

The committee plans the negotiations and the chief negotiator covers a strategy of action, directs and presides over the process. He presents the nature and contents of problem, its intensity and the views to both the parties. Thereafter, the representatives of both the parties are allowed to present their views. There can be arguments and counter arguments, proposals and counter proposals. For making it successful, the representatives of both the parties must keep a positive attitude and do all that they reasonably can to reach an amicable solution. Finally, when a solution is reached, it is put on the paper after considering all the legal and other aspects. If no amicable solution could be reached, both the parties may opt for arbitration.

(iv) Follow-up Action Stage

The contents of the agreement should be circulated among all the employees so that they come to know exactly what has been agreed upon between their representatives and management. This is very important so as to make clear all the factual points to the employees for whom, the collective bargaining is done. For this purpose, meetings of the people concerned should be held so that they can implement the agreement properly and effectively.

(b) Contract Administration Stage

When the process of negotiation is completed, the contract is signed. But the implementation of the contract is as important as making a contract. Prof. Williamson and Prof. Harris remarked in the context that, "If anything is more important to industrial relations than the contract itself, it is the administration of the contract. The progress in collective bargaining is not measured by the mere signing of an agreement. Rather, it is measured by the fundamental human relationships agreement." The trade unions and the management concerned are required to honour the contract in both letter and spirit.

(5) Pre-requisites of Collective Bargaining

Insofar as the pre-requisites for collective bargaining are concerned, the apt proverb to quote in this context would be - "where there is a will, there is a way." The same should be remembered and followed. By keeping a positive attitude, both the parties, i.e., the employers and the trade unions must with sufficient determination come together to make the collective bargaining exercise successful for solving the problems at hand.

There are certain essential conditions or pre-requisites which have been suggested by the experts in the field. These conditions must exist so as to make the exercise of collective bargaining meaningful and effective. The basic conditions are stated as below:

(a) The primary condition or pre-requisite for successful collective bargaining is the existence of well-organised and fully recognised trade unions. The trade unions must be unanimously supported by their members. The trade unions too must have well-defined policies in place.

(b) There must be positive attitude all around. The management, the trade unions concerned and their members must understand that collective bargaining does not imply litigation as it does under adjudication. All the parties to the collective bargaining must determine to resolve their differences on their respective claims in a peaceful and co-operative manner.

(c) Collective bargaining can prove to be an effective technique of settling industrial disputes, problems of employees etc., provided there is a spirit of give and take between the parties concerned. The word 'bargaining' implies 'give and take' and not 'take it or leave it' attitude. The former attitude needs to be followed for making collective bargaining successful.

(d) Collective bargaining is best conducted at plant level. If it is done, various problems can be given proper attention, according to the enormity or importance of the problems. As far as possible, there should be one trade union in a plant. If there is more than one trade union, one trade union, that has, more followers should be recognised as the sole bargaining agent of all the workers in the given organisation.

(e) There is no legal sanction behind the terms and conditions voluntarily agreed upon. Hence, all the parties concerned must do all the things and acts in good faith on the basis of mutual agreement. There must be unanimity between the parties on the implementation of collective bargaining contract.

(f) Employees as well as employers through their representatives should negotiate on the points of differences or on demands with a view to reaching an agreement. Trade unions should not put forward unreasonable demands and their management must consider their reasonable demands. There must be proper dialogue between the two parties. In this regard, it must be noted that rigid attitudes prove detrimental to successful collective bargaining and, therefore, must be avoided at all costs.

(g) The success of collective bargaining would depend much upon the moral fibre of trade union leaders as well as the management. Hence, there must be a complete and true understanding and appreciation of each others' viewpoints.

(h) There must be face-to-face meetings between the parties to the collective bargaining and they make all efforts to keep traditional prejudices at bay.

(i) Negotiations must be based on facts and figures.

(j) Unfair labour practices must be avoided for ensuring the collective bargaining functions properly.

(k) There should not be any uncertainty about the fields or areas in which the parties concerned are legally required to bargain collectively.

(l) When negotiations result in an agreement, its terms, conditions etc., should be put down in writing and embodied in a document in order to avoid any ambiguity. If no agreement is reached, the parties in question should be open to the routes of conciliation, mediation or arbitration for resolving the issue at hand.

(m) The agreement once entered into must be honoured and implemented properly.

(n) It is very essential to incorporate a provision of arbitration. There may be disagreement on the interpretation of the terms and conditions of the agreement.

If the disputes arise in respect of terms and conditions of the agreement, the same can be referred to a third party for bringing about a amicable solution - one, that is, final and binding - to the problem in question. This is very important pre-requisite for successful collective bargaining.

(6) Types of Collective Bargaining

Collective bargaining can be broadly classified under the following three heads. They are, namely:

(a) A single employer or a single plant bargaining.

(b) A multiple plant bargaining.

(c) A multi-employer bargaining.

(a) A Single Employer or a Single Plant Bargaining:

In this form or type, collective bargaining takes place between the management and a single trade union. We find this type of collective bargaining in India. There can also be the bargaining between the management and more than one trade unions in the enterprise.

(b) A Multiple-plant Bargaining:

This type of bargaining usually takes place between a single factory or establishment having many plants and the workers employed in all those plants.

(c) A Multi-employer Bargaining:

It is the type of collective bargaining between all the trade unions in the same industry through their federal organisations and the federations of employers. This type of bargaining is possible both at the local as well as regional level.

It is found that a trade union starts negotiating with a single employer and while still in its course, it so happens that its jurisdiction enlarges to cover the entire region or industry groups. The actual jurisdiction, however, depends upon the strength of the trade unions.

Bargaining on the basis of a single plant is mostly conducted through the local trade unions. But when there are different problems related to an industry or a group of industries, there is national level bargaining.

It is found that there are national federations in India. They have greater control and they exercise their powers in the bargaining process effectively, and hence, there is an increasing tendency toward multi-employers bargaining.

2.5 Employee Engagement: Concept, Importance and Employee Engagement in India

(1) Employee Engagement (Concept)

(a) Employee engagement is an emergent property of the relationship between an organisation and its employees.

(b) An "engaged employee" is one who is fully absorbed by and enthusiastic about his work and so takes positive action to enhance the organisations reputation and interests.

(c) Employee engagement is not the same as employee satisfaction.

(d) Employee engagement is a workplace approach designed to ensure that the employees are committed to their organisational goals and values, motivated to contribute to organisational success, and are able at the same time enhance own sense of well-being.

(2) Importance of Employee Engagement

(a) **Increased Productivity:** When employee feel more engaged, they are likely to become more productive. They work with more zeal and energy. They implement the necessary improvement with little or no direction.

(b) **Reduced Labour Turnover:** Engaged employees are more likely to stay with a company on a long-term basis, saving the business, the large costs involved with hiring and training replacement staff.

(c) **Improved Customer Service:** Improved customer service is one of the most widely recognised sign of employee engagement. Happy people are not only obvious but they are contagious so when a business engages their employees, the positive impact on their customers is not only immediate but can be significant.

(d) **Employee Satisfaction:** Employee engagement increases the job satisfaction level of the employees. Employees that are engaged and satisfied are essential for the success of the business as they have a high level of commitment and loyalty.

(e) **Innovation:** There is a close relationship between innovation and employee engagement. Engaged employees perform at a higher level and bring passion and interest to their job, which often leads to innovation in the workplace.

(f) **Profitability:** Companies with more engaged employees tend to have a higher profitability rates. When employees are engaged, they become more productive and efficient, positively affecting the company's bottom line.

(3) Employee Engagement in India

(a) After globalisation, many Indian companies offer various employee engagement programmes to its employees.

(b) These engagement programmes aims to achieve the following objectives:

(i) Change in thinking of employees.

(ii) Sharpen their skills.

(iii) Change how they behave.

(iv) Create sustained motivation and momentum.

(v) Cultivate a workplace that works.

(c) Normally, majority of Indian Companies introduces the following employee engagement programmes:
  (i) Monetary and non-monetary incentives to provide motivation to employees.
  (ii) Safety programmes to prevent costly mishaps.
  (iii) Wellness programmes to lower the health-care costs.
  (iv) Service anniversary programmes to support retention.
(d) Companies like HUL, Bajaj Auto Ltd., TCS, Infosys, Wipro, Tata Steel Ltd., Cipla offers various engagement programmes to its employees.
(e) Nowadays, even the small and medium scale companies in India started implementing employee engagement programmes to strengthen their employees.

2.6 Workers Participation in Management (WPM): Meaning, Pre-requisites, Advantages and Disadvantages, Levels and Types

(1) Meaning of Workers Participation in Management

The concept of workers' participation in management has been a vague and debatable issue in the field of industrial relations and hence, it has acquired different meanings for different people. It is difficult to define the concept of workers' participation very clearly because it is associated with varying practices in different countries, its content and form being in accordance with the socio-economic objectives of a country. However, it seems that the concept of workers' participation in management has its roots in the human relations movement in the domain of industrial organisations. The humanitarian approach to labour has brought about a new set of values for labour and management.

Definitions of Workers Participation in Management

(a) **Keith Davis:** *"Workers' participation in management is a mental and emotional involvement of a person in a group which encourages him to contribute to the goals and share responsibilities in them".*

(b) **C. B. Memoria:** *"Workers' participation in management is a system of communication and consultation either in formal or informal way by which employees of organisation are kept informal about the affairs of the undertaking and through which they express their opinion and contribute to management decisions".*

(c) **International Labour Organisation [I.L.O.]:** *"Workers' participation may, broadly, be taken to cover all terms of association of workers and their representatives with the decision-making process, ranging from exchanging of information, consultations, decisions and negotiations to more institutionalised forms such as the presence of workers' member on management or supervisory boards or even management by workers themselves as practised in Yugoslavia".*

(d) **McGregor Douglas:** *"The term workers' participation implies a formal method of providing an opportunity for every member of the organisation to contribute his brain and ingenuity as well as his physical efforts to the improvement of organisational effectiveness".*

(2) Pre-requisites of Workers Participation in Management

It is needless to say that workers' participation in management, besiders other things, provides a better status to workers and helps to create industrial democracy. It also makes workers more responsible and responsive to the needs of their organisation. Moreover, it creates a feeling of involvement among workers and it acts as a bridge between the management and workers. Hence, it is very essential to create suitable atmosphere for making the workers' participation in management successful. Following are some of the important pre-requisites or conditions for the successful functioning of workers' participation schemes in management.

(a) The attitude of an organisation/management should be constructive and progressive. It must sincerely and whole heartedly accept the concept of workers' participation and must be prepared to give a fair trial to the schemes of workers' participation.

(b) Both parties should have genuine faith, mutual trust in the system and in each other. Moreover, they must be willing to work together.

(c) There should be progressive management and it should recognise its obligations, responsibilities etc. towards their unions.

(d) Trade union must be strong and democratic with a genuine and prudent leadership. The union leaders should have genuine desire to participate in the management. The attitude of union leaders should be positive, co-operative and not aggressive.

(e) There should be closely and mutually formulated objectives for successful participation by management as well as trade unions.

(f) There should be effective two-way communication for making the workers' participation successful. For that purpose, frequent meetings of representatives of workers and their employers/management should be held to discuss various issues relating to workers' participation schemes and to conduct negotiations for the solution of pending problems. Both the parties should do all the efforts to develop a favourable attitude towards the schemes of participative management.

(g) Workers should be given proper education and training as regards the schemes of workers participation. Along with workers, supervisory staff should also be associated with the management.

(h) The follow-up actions on the decisions of the participating forums should be ensured.

(i) There should be full recognition of the rights and claims of both the parties. Workers should be no doubt conscious of their rights, but at the same time, emphasis must also be laid on their responsibilities.

(j) Workers' participation in the management cannot be effective unless the state of labour-management relations in the organisation is healthy. Besides this, workers' participation in management cannot be effective unless there is an adequate machinery for collective bargaining.

(3) Objectives of Workers Participation in Management

Workers' participation in management is considered as a means of self-realisation in work. Further, it helps to meet the psychological needs of workers at work by eliminating to a large extent the feeling of futility, isolation and consequent frustration that they face in normal industrial setting. The objectives of workers' participation in management may vary from country to country because socio-economic development, political philosophy, industrial relations scene, attitudes of working class and of trade unions are different. However, the objectives of workers' participation in management which are considered as very important are mentioned below.

(a) To develop good industrial relations.

(b) To create and increase better understanding among the workers about their role and place in the process of attainment of organisational goals and objectives.

(c) To stimulate workers for higher productivity for the benefits of themselves for the advantage of their organisations and society at large.

(d) To satisfy the workers' social and esteem needs.

(e) To create among the workers the feeling of dignity and self-respect.

(f) To strengthen labour-management co-operation for maintaining industrial peace and harmony.

(g) To establish industrial democracy.

(h) To avoid external interference.

(i) To build the dynamic human resource systematically.

(j) To share financial and other information about the organisation for the purpose of collective bargaining.

(4) Advantages of Workers Participation in Management

The basic idea or principle behind the workers' participation in management is to increase the workers' influence in the management of an enterprise or an organisation to which they belong in order to solve their problems relating to their work. Following points make clear the benefits or advantages of workers' participation in management.

(a) It helps to promote good and healthy industrial relations for creating and maintaining industrial peace.

(b) It creates a better understanding in workers about their role, responsibilities and place in the process of attainment of organisational goals. It, in turn, leads to workers' commitment to their work and towards their organisation.

(c) It helps to improve the quality of decision making as workers/ employees can offer useful suggestions and recommendations regarding the working and for solving their problems.

(d) It eliminates the differences of opinion between workers and their management and facilitates team work.

(e) When workers' participation is effective, it increases a sense of confidence and trust in the minds of workers towards the management. As a result, workers give full co-operation and accept the change without much resistance. This also helps to avoid strikes and lockouts.

(f) When workers co-operate fully and whole heartedly, it leads to higher productivity and efficiency.

(g) Workers' participation in management satisfies the social and esteem needs of the workers.

(5) Disadvantages of Workers Participation in Management

Workers' participation in management has to overcome a lot of limitations to succeed. Some of these limitations are:

(a) Today technology and organisations are extremely complex and hence specialised work-roles are necessary. Due to this employees can not participate effectively in matters beyond their particular environment.

(b) Everybody need not necessarily want participation.

(c) Trade unions are not pro participative management and hence do not promote it.

(d) Employers are unwilling to share power with the workers' representatives.

(e) Managers consider participative management a fraud.

(6) Levels of Workers Participation in Management

Workers' participation in management is important for maintaining the smooth and healthy industrial relations. It helps the workers to protect their interests. Management and workers are benefited thereby. The workers' participation is possible at all levels of management. Much depends upon the nature of functions, the strength of the workers, the attitudes of the trade unions and also that of management. The areas and degrees of the workers' participation can differ considerably at different levels depending upon the circumstances, needs etc.

Broadly speaking, there can be four stages of participation. At the initial stage, participation may be informative and associative participation. In such type of participation, the members are entitled to receive information, to give and discuss suggestions on the general economic condition of their organisation, the state of market, production, sales programmes, organisation, long-term plans of growth and development etc. At the consultative participation level, the workers are consulted on various matters such as welfare facilities, adoption of new technology and the problems emanting from it, safety measures etc. These aspects are directly related to the workers. In administrative participation, there is a greater degree of sharing of authority and responsibility of management functions. In such participation, the members are given a little more autonomy in exercising administrative and supervisory powers in respect of certain matters like welfare and safety measures, operation of training and development programmes, preparation of schedules of working hours, breaks, holidays etc. Decision-making participation is the highest form of participation. However, the management always likes to maintain its decision-making authority intact.

The workers' participation in management involves participation through representative of workers. Hence, its level can be considered in this context also. Generally, there can be following three levels at which workers' participation in management can take place.

- **(a) Shop-floor level:** At shop-floor, shop-floor councils or committees are constituted. In such committees, the representatives of management and workers are included. They consider and discuss various matters, problems relating to a particular shop.
- **(b) Plant level:** There are many plants of an organisation or company which are located in different geographical areas. When this is the situation, plant level participation of workers in management proves to be useful and advantageous for maintaining good industrial relations. Where a company or an enterprise has a single plant, plant level participation is not needed. Various matters, problems are dealt at the plant level which have relevance for all shop-floors and they cannot be solved at shop-floor level.
- **(c) Enterprise level:** At enterprise level, workers' participation for constructive co-operation is much needed. Such participation can be in the forms of management committees, co-partnership representation of workers at the level of Board of Directors.

(7) Types of Workers Participation in Management

The forms or methods in which workers can participate in management vary, depending upon the pattern of management, levels of management, size of the factory, authority delegated to subordinates, areas in which participation is sought etc. Certain methods are specified by the legal framework while certain methods are evolved in the process. In India some methods have been prescribed by law while many other methods have been suggested through guidelines formulated by the Government.

When workers participate in management either through formal mechanism or through informal procedures, it is considered as an instance of participative management. For this effective functioning, both the parties i.e. labour and management, must be keenly interested. It is obvious that management interest basically lies in reducing cost and in improving the productivity. On the other hand, workers are interested to increase their earnings and to get various facilities. When earnings increase through sharing gains in productivity, a harmony of interests can be promoted. Hence, if participation is to be made effective and successful as a process or device, it should be integrated properly with a scheme of improving productivity as well as gain sharing.

Participation can be ascending participation or descending participation. In ascending participation, workers are given an opportunity to influence managerial decisions at higher levels through their elected representatives. While in descending participation, workers may be given more powers to plan and make decisions about their work.

Following are the important forms or methods of workers' participation in management.

(a) Works Committee

A works committee is a forum provided under the Industrial Disputes Act of 1947 for explaining the difficulties of the parties concerned with the disputes. It endeavours to maintain cordial relationship even though there are disputes or differences between the parties to the disputes. The success of work committees mainly depends on the efforts and co-operation of both the parties to the disputes.

Section 3 (1) of this Act provides for a Works Committee. According to this section, in the case of any industrial establishment in which one hundred or more workmen are employed or have been employed on any day in the preceding twelve months, the appropriate Government may by general or special order require the employer to constitute in the prescribed manner a Works Committee consisting of representatives of employers and workmen engaged in the establishment. However, the number of representatives of workmen on the committee shall not be less than the number of representatives of the employer. The representatives of the workmen shall be chosen in the prescribed manner from among the workmen engaged in the establishment and in consultation with their trade union, if any, registered under the Indian Trade Unions Act, 1926. Section 3 (2) further provides that it shall be the duty of the Works Committee to promote measures for securing and preserving amity and good relations between the employer and workmen and, to that end to comment upon matters of their common interest or concern and endeavour to compose any material difference of opinion in respect of such matters.

Industrial Disputes Act, 1947 promotes the settlement of industrial disputes firstly by voluntary negotiations. The Works Committees are the prominent efforts towards that goal. Works Committees are joint committees having equal number of the representatives of employers and workmen. The constitution of Works Committee is must in an industrial establishment wherein one hundred or more workmen are employed on any day in preceding twelve months. Works Committee is an internal media for settlement of Industrial Disputes Act within the industry.

Duties or Functions of Works Committee

Sub-Section 2 of Section 3 of this Act enumerates the duties or functions of a Works Committee which are as follows:

(i) To remove the disparities between employers and workmen;

(ii) To promote measures for securing and preserving amity, and friendly and good relations between the employers and workmen;

(iii) To that end, to comment upon all matters of their common interest or concern;

(iv) To make efforts to compose any material difference of opinion in respect of various matters. These matters include so many aspects such as welfare of workers, provision and supervision of various recreational facilities, training of workmen and their wages, bonus, gratuity, working conditions including discipline, promotions, transfers etc. Thus, it seems that there is no subject concerning the relation between the employers and workmen which the Works Committee is precluded from considering. However, following points must be remembered in this connection.

1. Findings of the Works Committee are advisory or recommendatory and not mandatory. It cannot decide and pass final judgement. Its duty is only to comment because it is mainly a negotiating organ. It is the function of the Works Committee to promote measures for harmonious, and friendly and good relations between the employers and workmen.

2. Works Committees are not intended to supersede or supplement the trade unions for the purpose of collective bargaining. They are not authorised to consider real changes or substantial changes in the service conditions. They are not a substitute of trade unions.

The success of a works committee mainly depends upon (a) the responsible and positive attitude on the part of management and (b) the wholehearted implementation of its recommendations. Being a legal provision, works committees have been constituted in most of the organisations.

(b) Joint Management Councils

A Joint Management Council (JMC) consists of representatives of management and workers. The J. M. Council performs advisory role on various matters specified. The J. M. Council is expected to be consulted on matters relating to the administration of standing orders, welfare measures, rationalisation, retrenchment etc. The important functions performed by a J. M. Council are as follows:

(i) A.J.M.C. is to be consulted by the management on the matters like standing orders, rationalisation, retrenchment, closure, reduction of operations.

(ii) To receive information, to discuss and offer suggestions on general economic situations, market position, production and marketing programmes, methods of production, long-term capital budgeting decisions, modernisation, development and growth etc.

(iii) To shoulder administrative responsibilities like maintaining welfare measures, safety measures, training schemes and progammes, payment of rewards, scheduling of working hours, problems of indiscipline, absenteeism etc. A J. M. Council takes up and suggests the measures in respect of the matters mentioned above.

It should be noted that J.M. Council merely performs the advisory role on the matter specified and its recommendations are not accepted as a mandatory requirement. Further, various matters which are likely to be sorted out through collective bargaining such as wages, bonus etc. are kept out of its purview. Similarly, it does not deal with the personal problems of an individual worker.

In India, a large number of J. M. Councils are established. However, the real contribution of the councils is limited.

Following are the important reasons of the limited success of the J. M. Councils:

(i) Trade unions generally oppose to such councils as the trade unions feel that their importance may be reduced in course of time. Hence, their attitude towards the J. M. Council becomes negative.

(ii) The attitude of employers or managements of the organisations is not progressive and favourable for the effective working of the J. M. Councils.

(c) Workers' Participation on the Board of Directors:

Appointments of employees' or workers' representatives on the Board of Directors is an important form or method of workers' participation in management. The basic idea behind this method is that the workers' representation of the Board of Directors' Level may help to establish industrial democracy and to create and maintain better employer- employee relations. As workers' representatives are appointed on the Board of Directors, it is expected that they would do all the efforts to protect the interests of their workers.

Under this method, the representatives are either elected or nominated, may be two or three, by the workers who attend the meeting of the Board and participate in their deliberations. The representatives of workers on the Board of Directors do all the efforts to bring to the notice of other directors the views, problems etc. of the workers and give suggestions. Thus, they participate in the process of problem solving and decision-making at the top level. However, this method is not much effective in bridging the gap between workers and their management because of the following important reasons:

(i) As the workers' representatives are in minority they cannot bring any pressure on the other Directors. As a result, suggestion of the representatives of workers are not given proper or due attention and the gap between the two parties continue.

(ii) The Board meetings are held mainly to discuss managerial problems and not the problems of workers. Naturally, the workers' representatives get limited opportunities to discuss views, problems etc. of the workers.

(iii) Decision-making process at the board level is rather complex, complicated which require specific skills than alternative form of participation for which workers' representatives neither possess skills nor they have mental set.

(iv) There are rival trade unions. Naturally, workers' representatives appointed on the Board cannot put forward the views, problems, suggestions which are acceptable to all the workers. Moreover, participation at the board level weakens the bargaining power of trade unions as they have to accept the decisions of the Board having their own representatives.

(d) Suggestion Scheme

Under this scheme, workers are associated with the management through their suggestions on various matters relating to their working. A suggestion committee or suggestion screening committee is constituted with equal representation from management and workers. Workers are encouraged to give their suggestions to the management. The committee constituted for that purpose screens and evaluates the suggestions received from workers. The suggestions are accepted if they are found suitable and useful. Rewards are also given to those workers who give constructive suggestions for the benefit of all. Suggestion boxes are kept at convenient places in some organisations. The suggestions also can be given to a joint committee of workers and management or to the departmental heads.

(e) Shop Councils

A shop council is a method or a form of workers' participation in management wherein for each department or a shop in an unit, a shop council is constituted. Each shop council is consisted of an equal number of representatives of employers and workers. The employers' representatives are nominated by the management. All such representatives are nominated from within the unit concerned.

The workers' representatives are obviously from among the workers of their department or shop concerned. The number of members of each shop council is determined by the employers in consultation with the recognised trade union. Generally, the total number of a shop council does not exceed twelve. Various decisions of a shop council are arrived at on the basis of consensus and not by the process of voting. A shop council works for a minimum period of two years. In other words, the tenure of a shop council is for a period of two years. This method of workers' participation was launched in India in 1975.

Functions of Shop Councils

Following are the important functions of the shop councils:

(i) To assist the management in achieving production targets.

(ii) To take necessary steps to improve productivity, efficiency and to increase production to the optimum.

(iii) To eliminate wastage and to do all efforts to utilise effectively manpower and machine capacity.

(iv) To recommend various steps to reduce absenteeism in the shop or department considering the causes of absenteeism.

(v) To make suggestions for providing safety measures.

(vi) To assist to maintain general discipline in the shop or department.

(vii) To provide various welfare measures for efficient running of the shop or department.

(viii) To do all efforts to provide various physical facilities such as lighting, ventilation, dust control, noise control etc.

(ix) To ensure proper flow of adequate two-way communication between the management and workers for efficient working of the shop or department.

(f) Joint Councils

There is a participation of management and of workers in the Joint Councils. These councils work for the whole unit and their membership remains confined to those who are actually engaged in the organisation. The tenure of the Joint Councils is for two years.

The Chief Executive of the unit works as the chairman and workers' members of the council nominate the Vice-Chairman. The Secretary is appointed by the Joint Council.

The Joint Councils meet once in four months, but the periodicity of the meeting varies from unit to unit, it may be once in a month, quarter etc.

The decisions are taken in the Joint Council meeting by the process of consensus and the management implements the discussions within one month.

Under the 20-Point Economic Programme, factories employing five hundred or more workers constituted Joint Councils.

A Joint Council performs certain functions.

Functions of Joint Councils

Following are important functions performed by Joint Councils from which their nature becomes clear.

(i) To increase the output by fixation of standards.

(ii) To consider various matters which could not be solved by shop councils.

(iii) To do all efforts to develop the skills of workers by providing them necessary and adequate training facilities.

(iv) To encourage the employees for research and to give awards to workers involving creative work.

(v) To prepare a schedule of working laws.

(vi) To ensure full and proper utilisation of finished goods.

(vii) To provide general health, welfare and safety measures for the unit of the plant.

(g) Unit Councils

The scheme of workers' participation was launched in 1977 in commercial and service organisations in the public sector. The scheme envisaged setting up of unit councils in those units which employ at least One hundred workers. The organisations where unit councils are set up include hotels, restaurants, hospitals, transport undertakings, (railway air, sea, road transport services), educational institutions, ports and docks, provident fund and pension organisations, banks, insurance companies, municipalities, warehousing corporations etc.

The scheme provides for unit level councils. These councils are basically set up to eliminate factors which hinder progress and hamper operations. Efforts are made to improve methods of operations.

Under this scheme of unit councils, each unit council consists of an equal number of representatives of management and workers. The actual number of the representatives is determined by the management in consultation with the recognised trade union, registered trade unions or the workers as per the needs. However, total number of the representatives does not exceed twelve. The management's representatives are nominated by the management who are from the unit concerned.

The decisions of a unit council are taken on the basis of consensus and not by the process of voting. The unsettled matters are referred to the joint council for consideration. Every decision of a unit council is implemented by the concerned parties within a period of a month, unless otherwise stated in the decision itself. The management makes necessary arrangements for the recording of minutes of the meetings and designate one of its representatives as a secretary for this purpose. The secretary is entrusted the responsibility to report on the action taken on the decisions at the subsequent meetings of the council.

A unit once formed, functions for a period of two years. The council can meet as frequently as is necessary but at least once in a month. The Chairman of the council is a nominee of the management while worker members of the council elect a vice-chairman from amongst themselves. The functions of the unit councils are more or less similar to those of joint councils. However, the main functions of a unit council are to create necessary conditions for attaining higher productivity and efficiency and to provide better customer services.

Functions of Unit Council

Other functions performed by the unit councils are mentioned below.

(i) To create conditions for healthy employer-employee relations.
(ii) To create and improve conditions for reducing absenteeism and recommend measure for the purpose.
(iii) To identify areas of inadequate or inferior services and to take necessary constructive and corrective steps to eliminate the contributing factors and to evolve improved methods of operations.
(iv) To institute a proper and suitable system of rewards for eliminating pilferage and all types of corruption.
(v) To ensure effective flow of adequate two-way communication between the management and workers for making the working of unit councils successful.
(vi) To suggest the measures for improving the physical conditions of working such as lighting, ventilation, internal lay-out, setting up of customers' service points etc.
(vii) To make recommendations for improving health, safety and welfare measures for an efficient working of the unit.

(h) Co-partnership

Under co-partnership, workers/employees are made equal partners i.e. owners of the organisation in which they work as employees. In co-partnership, workers or employees participate in the equity capital of their organisation. The shares are allotted to them either on cash payment basis or in-lieu of various incentives payable in cash. Thus, they become the shareholders of their organisation and can exercise control over it as other shareholder do. The workers by becoming co-partners, can participate in both i.e. sharing of profits and participating in management as shareholders. In this way, workers are given a higher status and they are connected with their organisation in a dual capacity. They, thus, can elect their representatives as directors and protect their interests. This helps to create better understanding between the management and employees which is essential for good industrial relations. It also helps in integrating the employees with their organisation and become the part-owner of the organisation to the extent of their shareholding. However, the workers do not get real control over the management and they cannot participate in management because of their negligible shareholding. The scope of workers' participation in management through co-partnership is quite limited.

(i) Auto-management

Under Auto-management scheme, workers are given wider powers in management. The industrial unit is established by the State but the day-to-day management is entrusted in the hands of workers working in the unit. Various targets e.g. production, sales etc. are decided at the government level, but other activities, functions are managed by the workers collectively. It is obvious that this method of workers' participation in management is suitable in socialist or communist countries. It exists in Yugoslavia. But it is not suitable to the Indian Economic System.

Questions for Discussion

1. Define Industrial Disputes. Explain the causes of Industrial Disputes.
2. Describe the Model Grievance Procedure.
3. Describe the Various Types of Conflict Resolution.
4. What is Collective Bargaining? State its characteristics.
5. Explain the Importance of Collective Bargaining.
6. State the Types of Collective Bargaining.
7. State the Importance of Employee Engagement.
8. What is Worker's Participation in Management? State its pre-requisites.
9. State the advantages and disadvantages of Workers Participation in Management.
10. Explain the various types of Workers Participation in Management.
11. Write Short Notes:
    (a) Conflict Resolution (b) Causes of Grievances
    (c) Works Committee (d) Court of Enquiry
    (e) Process of Collective Bargaining (f) Employee Engagement
    (g) Levels of Workers Participation in Management

Questions from Previous Pune University Examinations

1. Define Workers Participation in Management. Discuss few important types of WPM. **October 2010**

   Ans.: Refer to Article 2.6 of this Chapter.

2. Explain Collective Bargaining with its Process. **October 2010** OR

   Define Collective Bargaining and Explain its Process. **April 2011**

   Ans.: Refer to Article 2.4 of this Chapter.

3. Explain Collective Bargaining with its Need and Detailed Process. **October 2011**

   Ans.: Refer to Article 2.4 of this chapter.

4. Write a detailed Note: Grievance Redressal Machinery. **October 2011** OR

   Ans.: Refer to Article 2.2 of this chapter.

   Explain Procedure for Grievance Redressal Machinery. **April 2014**

   Ans.: Refer to Article 2.2 of this Chapter.

5. Write a detailed note on Causes and Types of Industrial Conflicts. **April 2012**

   Ans.: Refer to Article 2.1 of this Chapter.

6. What do you mean by Collective Bargaining ? State the Characteristics and pre-requisites of Collective Bargaining. **October 2012**

   Ans.: Refer to Article 2.4 of this Chapter.

7. What is Workers Participation in Management ? Discuss various Forms of Workers Participation in Management. **October 2012**

   Ans.: Refer to Article 2.6 of this Chapter.

8. What do you mean by Collective Bargaining ? State the Characteristics and Importance of Collective Bargaining. **April 2014**

   Ans.: Refer to Article 2.4 of this Chapter.

9. Write Short Notes:

   (A) Causes of ID. **April 2011** OR

   Causes of Industrial Dispute. **October 2011**

   Ans.: Refer to Article 2.1 of this Chapter.

   (B) Concept of Workers Participation in Management. **April 2012**

   Ans.: Refer to Article 2.6 of this Chapter.

10. What do you mean by WPM ? Explain the Statutory Types of Conflict Resolution. **April 2014**

    Ans.: Refer to Article 2.6 of this Chapter.

***

Chapter 3...

The Industrial Disputes Act, 1946 and the Factories Act 1948

Contents ...

The Industrial Disputes Act, 1946

- 3.1 Introduction
- 3.2 Objects of the Act
- 3.3 Definitions
- 3.4 Machinery for Settlement of Industrial Disputes
    - 3.4.1 Conciliation Machinery
    - 3.4.2 Adjudication Machinery
- 3.5 Procedure and Powers of the Authorities [Section 11]
- 3.6 Strikes and Lock-outs
    - 3.6.1 Strikes
    - 3.6.2 Lock-outs
    - 3.6.3 Prohibition of Strikes and Lock-outs in Public Utility Services [Section 22]
    - 3.6.4 General Prohibition of Strikes and Lock-outs [Section 23]
    - 3.6.5 Illegal Strikes and Lock-outs [Section 24]
    - 3.6.6 Distinction between Strike and Lock-out
- 3.7 Lay-off and Retrenchment
    - 3.7.1 Lay-off
    - 3.7.2 Retrenchment
    - 3.7.3 Rights of Workman Laid-off for Compensation [Section 25-C]
    - 3.7.4 Conditions Precedent to Retrenchment of Workmen [Section 25-F]
    - 3.7.5 Procedure for Retrenchment
    - 3.7.6 Re-employment of Retrenched Workman [Section 25-H]
    - 3.7.7 Difference between Lock-out and Lay-off
    - 3.7.8 Difference between Retrenchment and Lock-out
    - 3.7.9 Distinction between Retrenchment and Lay-off

3.8 Closure of an Industrial Undertaking [Section 25 FFA]

    3.8.1 Compensation to be Paid to Workmen in Case of Closing Down of Undertaking [Section 25FFF]

    3.8.2 Procedure of Closing Down an Undertaking [Section 25-O]

3.9 Penalties

The Factories Act, 1948

3.10 Introduction

3.11 Objects and Scope of the Act

3.12 Definitions

3.13 Authorities

3.14 Provisions Relating to Worker's Health

3.15 Provisions Relating to Safety of Workers

3.16 Provisions Relating to Welfare of Workers

3.17 Provisions of Chapter VIII relating to Annual Leave with Wages

3.18 Penalties

- Questions for Discussion
- Questions from Previous Pune University Examinations

The Industrial Disputes Act, 1946

3.1 Introduction

The First World War which broke out in 1914 lasted for about four years. At the close of the war, there was a great outbreak of industrial unrest which led to the passing of the first Industrial Trade Disputes Act. This Act was known as the Trade Disputes Act, 1929. Chapter III and Chapter IV of this Act were related to the establishment of tribunals for investigation and settlement of Trade Disputes.

During the Second World War, several emergency measures were introduced by the Central Government. In 1942, Rule 81-A was added with a view to restrain strikes and lock-outs. This Rule 81-A gave powers to the Central Government to make orders prohibiting strikes, lock-outs etc., with regard to any trade disputes unless reasonable notice was given. At the close of the year 1942, the Government promulgated an order under Rule 81-A, whereby the party proposing to go on strike or lock-outs was required to issue an advance fourteen days' notice for doing so.

Shortly, thereafter, the Industrial Disputes Act, 1947, was passed which embodies the important provisions of the Trade Disputes Act, 1929, as well as the important principles of

Rule 81-A. The Industrial Disputes Act, 1947, too was amended several times. The Industrial Disputes (Amendment) Act, 1982, provided for extensive changes. It had recast many terms used in the main Act, such as, Workman, Industry, Industrial Establishments, etc. The rules regarding closure, lay-off, reinstatement, retrenchment, etc., too were altered. Moreover, certain new concepts as well as rules had been introduced, namely, a time limit for adjudication of disputes, a model grievances redressal procedure etc. The latest amendment was carried out in August, 1996. This Act, i.e., The Industrial Disputes (Amendment) Act, 1996, received the assent of the President of India on 16th August, 1996.

3.2 Objects of the Act

The Industrial Disputes Act, 1947, can be described as a milestone in the history of Industrial Laws in India. It is one of the self-contained Acts. It provides one with the necessary machinery and procedure for the investigation and settlement of industrial disputes. The Act is mainly passed:

(1) To secure and maintain industrial peace by preventing and settling industrial disputes between the employers and workmen, or employers and employees.

(2) To promote those measures that is necessary for securing amity and good relations between employers and workmen through the mechanism of internal works committees.

(3) To promote good relations through an external machinery of conciliation, Courts of Inquiry, Labour Courts, Industrial Tribunals and National Tribunals.

(4) To ameliorate the condition of workmen by redressal of grievances of workmen through a statutory machinery.

(5) To provide for job security to the workmen employed in industries.

(6) To prevent illegal strikes and lock-outs.

(7) To encourage collective bargaining.

3.3 Definitions

(1) Appropriate Government [Section 2(a)]

'Appropriate Government' means –

(a) In relation to any industrial dispute concerning any industry carried on by or under the authority of the Central Government or by a railway company or concerning any such industry as may be specified in this behalf by the Central Government or in relation to an industrial dispute concerning a Dock Labour Board established under Section 5-A of the Dock Workers (Regulation of Employment) Act, 1948 (9 of 1948), or the Industrial Finance Corporation of India established under Section 3 of the Industrial Finance Corporation Act, 1948, or the Employees State Insurance Corporation established under Section 3 of the Employee's State Insurance Act, 1948, or the Board of Trustees constituted under

Section 3-A of the Coal Mines Provident Fund and Miscellaneous Provisions Act, 1948, or the Central Board of Trustees and the State Boards of Trustees constituted under Section 5-A and Section 5-B, respectively, of the Employees Provident Fund and Miscellaneous Provisions Act, 1952, or the Indian Airlines and Air India Corporations established under Section 3 of the Air India Corporations Act, 1953, or the Life Insurance Corporation of India established under Section 3 of the Life Insurance Corporation Act, 1956, or the Oil and Natural Gas Commission established under Section 3 of the Oil and Natural Gas Commission Act, 1959, or the Deposit Insurance and Credit Guarantee Corporation established under Section 3 of the Deposit Insurance and Credit Guarantee Corporation Act, 1961 (47 of 1961), or the Central Warehousing Corporations Act, 1962 (58 of 1962), or the Unit Trust of India established under Section 3 of the Unit Trust of India Act, 1963 (52 or 1963), or the Food Corporation of India established under Section 3, or a Board of Management established for two or more contiguous States under Section 16, of the Food Corporations Act 1964 (37 of 1964), or the International Airports Authority of India constituted under Section 3 of the International Airports Authority of India Act, 1971 (43 of 1971), or a Regional Rural Bank established under Section 8 of the Regional Rural Banks Act, 1976 (21 of 1976), or the Export Credit and Guarantee Corporation Limited or the Industrial Reconstruction Corporation of India Limited; Rural Bank established under Section 3 of the Regional Rural Banks Act, 1976 (21 of 1976), or [the Banking Service Commission established under Section 3 of the Banking Service Commission Act, 1975 (42 of 1975), a banking or an Insurance Company, a mine, an oilfield, a Cantonment Board or a major port, the Central Government; and

(b) In relation to any other industrial dispute, the State Government.

(2) Arbitrator [Section 2(aa)]

In the Industrial Disputes Act, 1947, the definition of 'Arbitrator' is given in Section 2 wherein it is only stated that **'Arbitrator'** includes an umpire.

(3) Average Pay [Section 2(aaa)]

'Average pay' means the average of the wages payable to a workman;

(a) in the case of monthly paid workman, in the three complete calendar months;

(b) in the case of weekly paid workman, in the four complete weeks;

(c) in the case of daily paid workman, the twelve full working days, preceding the date on which the average pay becomes payable if the workman had worked for three complete calendar months or four complete weeks or twelve full working days, as the case may be, and where such calculation cannot be made, the average pay shall be calculated at the average of the wages payable to a workman during the period he actually worked.

From the above definition, it becomes clear that Section 2(aaa) lays down the basis as to how the average pay of a workman is to be calculated.

When the average pay cannot be calculated on the above mentioned basis, the average is to be calculated as the average of wages payable to a workman during the period he actually worked. While calculating the average wages to a daily paid workman, weekly or other holidays should be excluded.

(4) Muster Roll

Muster roll simply means official list. Section 25-D of the Industrial Disputes Act, 1947, provides that notwithstanding that workmen in any industrial establishment have been laid off, it is the duty of every employer to maintain for the purposes of Sections 25-A to 25-J, a muster roll and also to provide for the making of entries properly therein by workmen who may present themselves for work at the establishment at the appointed time during normal working hours. Thus, muster roll proves to be very useful for calculating an average pay.

(5) Award [Section 2(b)]

'Award' means an interim or a final determination of any industrial dispute or of any question relating thereto by any Labour Court, Industrial Tribunal or National Industrial Tribunal and includes an arbitration award made under Section 10-A.

From the above mentioned definition of 'award,' it becomes clear that award is of the following two kinds or types.

(a) Interim or a final determination of industrial dispute or of any other question relating thereto by any Labour Court, Industrial Tribunal or National Tribunal, and

(b) An arbitration award made under Section 10-A. The important provisions relating to award have been made in Section 16, 17, 17-A.

(6) Board [Section 2(c)]

'Board' means a Board of conciliation constituted under this Act.

Section 5 of the Industrial Disputes Act, 1947, provides for the constitution of a Board of Conciliation.

The appropriate Government may as occasion arises, by notification in the Official Gazette, constitute a Board of Conciliation for promoting the settlement of any industrial dispute. Thus, the settlement of an industrial dispute is the main purpose behind the constitution of a Board of Conciliation. A Board of Conciliation consists of a chairman and two or four members as the appropriate Government thinks it fit. The chairman of a Board of Conciliation shall be an independent person. The other members of a Board of Conciliation are appointed in equal numbers to represent the two parties to the dispute. Each party is to recommend the names of their representatives. But, if they do not recommend the names of their representatives, the appropriate Government selects such members.

Provisions relating to the constitution, duties of Board of Conciliation have been made in Sections 5 and 13 of this Act, which we shall consider at an appropriate place.

(7) Closure [Section 2(c)]

'Closure' means the permanent closing down of the place of employment or part thereof.

The definition of the term 'closure' is given in the State Acts of Maharashtra and Madhya Pradesh, which is as follows:

"'Closure' means the closing of any place or a part of a place of employment or the total or partial suspension of work by an employer or the total partial refusal by an employer to continue to employ persons employed by him whether such closing, suspension or refusal is or is not in consequence of an industrial dispute."

By closure of an undertaking is meant the closing of industrial activity and, as a result, workmen employed in such undertaking are rendered jobless. When an undertaking is closed, compensation is required to be paid to the workmen working in such undertaking. Provisions have been made in Section 25-FFF of the Industrial Disputes Act, 1947, regarding the compensation to be paid to workmen in case of closing down of undertaking.

(8) Conciliation Officer [Section 2(d)]

'Conciliation Officer' means Conciliation Officer appointed under this Act.

The Appropriate Government appoints such number of persons as it thinks fit to be conciliation officers by notification in the Official Gazette. A conciliation officer can be appointed for a specified area or specified industries in a specified area or for one or more specified industries and either permanently or for a limited period. Such conciliation officers are charged with the duty of mediating in and promoting the settlement of industrial disputes.

The conciliation officers thus appointed are the public servants within the meaning of Section 21 of the Indian Penal Code, 1960. The provisions relating to the appointment and duties of the conciliation officers have been made in Sections 4 and 12, respectively.

(9) Conciliation Proceeding [Section 2(e)]

'Conciliation proceeding' means any proceeding held by a conciliation officer of Board under this Act.

(10) Controlled Industry [Section 2(ee)]

'Controlled Industry' means any industry the control of which by the Union has been declared by the Central Act to be expedient in the public interest.

Here, it must be remembered that only when the declaration is made by the Central Act that the control of industry by the Union is necessary or suitable in the public interest. then and only then, an industry is called a controlled industry.

(11) Court [Section 2(f)]

'Court' means a court of enquiry constituted under this Act.

Section 6 of this Act empowers the Appropriate Government to appoint a Court of Inquiry for enquiring into any matter appearing to be connected with or is relevant to an industrial dispute. A court may consist of one independent person or of such number of independent persons, as the Appropriate Government may think it fit and where a court of inquiry consists of two or more members, one of them is appointed as the chairman. All members of the Court of Inquiry are deemed to be public servants within the meaning of Section 21 of the Indian Penal Code.

(12) Employer [Section 2 (g)]

'Employer' means

(a) In relation to an industry carried on by or under the authority of any department of the Central Government or a State Government, the authority prescribed in this behalf, or where no authority is prescribed, the head of the department;

(b) In relation to an industry carried on by or on behalf of a local authority, the chief executive officer of that authority.

This definition of an 'employer' is not exhaustive. But, it must also be noted that, it does not limit its sphere merely to businesses run by the Government or local authority. This Act applies to all industries carried on either by an individual or an association.

(13) Executive [Section 2(gg)]

'Executive' in relation to a trade union, means the body by whatever name called, to which the management of the affairs of the trade union is entrusted.

(14) Industry [Section 2(J)]

'Industry' means any systematic activity carried on by co-operation between an employer and his workmen (whether such workmen are employed by such employer directly or by or through any agency, including a contractor) for the production, supply or distribution of goods or services with a view to satisfy human wants to wishes (not being wants or wishes which are merely spiritual or religious in nature), whether or not –

(i) Any capital has been invested for the purpose of carrying on such activity; or

(ii) Such activity is carried on with a motive to make any gain or profit and includes –

  (a) Any activity of the Dock Labour Board established under Section 5-A of the Dock Workers (Regulation of Employment) Act, 1948.

  (b) Any activity relating to the promotion of sales or business or both carried on by an establishment.

(15) Industrial Dispute (Section 2(k)

'Industrial dispute' means any dispute or difference between employers and employers or between employers and workmen, or between workmen and workmen, which is connected with the employment or non-employment or the terms of employment or with the conditions of labour, of any person.

For any dispute to be considered an industrial dispute, it should satisfy the following essentials:

(a) There must be a difference or dispute (i) between employers and employers (ii) between workmen and workmen or (iii) between workmen and employers.

(b) A workman concerned with the dispute should not be employed in any administrative or managerial capacity.

(c) Industrial dispute must pertain to an industrial matter or

(d) It may be connected with the employment or non-employment or the terms of employment.

(e) Industrial dispute may be concerned with the condition of labour of any person.

Industrial dispute implies a real and substantial difference having some element of persistency and continuity till resolved and, if not adjusted timely, it is likely to endanger the industrial peace of the given undertaking.

(16) Industrial Establishment or Undertaking [Section 2(ka)]

'Industrial establishment or undertaking' means an establishment or undertaking in which any industry is carried on;

Provided that where several activities are carried on in an establishment or undertaking or undertakings and only one or some of such activities is or are an industry or industries, then –

(a) if any unit of such establishment or undertaking carrying on any activity, being an industry, is severable from the other unit or units of such establishment or undertaking such unit shall be deemed to be a separate industrial establishment or undertaking;

(b) If the predominant activity or each of the predominant activities carried on in such establishment or undertaking or any unit thereof is an industry and the other activity or each of the other activities carried on in such establishment or undertaking or unit thereof is not severable from and is, for the purpose of carrying on, or aiding the carrying on of, such predominant activity or activities, the entire establishment or undertaking or, as the case may be, unit thereof shall be deemed to be an industrial establishment or undertaking.

(17) Insurance Company [Section 2(kk)]

'Insurance Company' means an insurance company as defined in Section 2 of the Insurance Act, 1938, having branches or other establishments in more than one state.

(18) Labour Court [Section 2(kkb)]:

'Labour Court' means a Labour Court constituted under Section 7.

According to Section 7 of this Act, the Appropriate Government may constitute one or more Labour Courts for the adjudication of industrial disputes relating to any matter specified in the Second Schedule. The Appropriate Government may also entrust certain other functions to Labour Courts. A Labour Court consists of one person only who is appointed by the Appropriate Government [Section 7(2)].

The provisions relating to jurisdiction, duties, qualifications, disqualifications etc., have been made in Section 7 of the Industrial Disputes Act, 1947.

(19) Major Port [Section 2(1a)]

'Major port' means a major-port as defined in clause (8) of Section 3 of the Indian Ports Act, 1908.

(20) Mine [Section 2(1b)]

'Mine' means a mine as defined in clause J of Section 2(1) of the Mines Act, 1952.

(21) National Tribunal [Section 2(11)]

'National Tribunal' means a National Industrial Tribunal Constituted under Section 7-B.

The Central Government is authorised under this Act to constitute one or more National Industrial Tribunals for the adjudication of industrial disputes, which involve questions of national importance or such disputes in which the industrial establishments situated in more than one state are interested or affected by such disputes. A National Tribunal consists of one person only and such person is appointed by the Central Government. Certain functions or duties are entrusted to National Tribunal, as the Central Government deems fit.

(22) Office-bearer [Section 2(111)]

'Office-bearer' in relation to a trade union includes any member of the executive thereof, but does not include an auditor.

(23) Prescribed [Section 2(m)]

'Prescribed' means prescribed by rules made under this Act.

(24) Public Utility Service [Section 2(n)]

'Public utility service' means:

(a) Any railway service or any transport service for the carriage of passengers or goods by air;

    (i) Any service in, or in connection with the working of, any major port of dock;

(b) Any section of an industrial establishment on the working of which the safety of the establishment or the workmen employed therein depends;

(c) Any postal, telegraph or telephone service;

(d) Any industry which supplies power, light or water to the public;

(e) Any system of public conservancy or sanitation;

(f) Any industry specified in the First Schedule which the Appropriate Government may, if satisfied that public emergency or public interest so requires, by notification in the Official Gazette, declare to be public utility service for the purposes of this Act, for such period as may be specified in the notification.

Provided that the period so specified shall not, in the first instance, exceed six months but may by a like notification, be extended from time to time, by any period not exceeding six months, at any one time, if in the opinion of the Appropriate Government, public emergency or public interest requires such extension;

(25) Railway Company [Section 2(o)]

'Railway Company' means any railway company as defined in Section 3 of the Indian Railways Act, 1890.

(26) Settlement [Section 2(p)]

'Settlement' means a settlement arrived at in the course of conciliation proceeding and includes a written agreement between the employer and workmen arrived at otherwise than in the course of conciliation proceeding where such agreement has been signed by the parties thereto in such manner as may be prescribed and a copy thereof has been sent to an officer authorised in this behalf by the Appropriate Government and Conciliation Officer.

(27) Trade Union [Section 2(gg)]

'Trade Union' means a trade union registered under the Trade Union Act, 1926,

According to Section 2(h) of the Trade Union Act, 1926, a trade union means any combination formed primarily for the purpose of regulating the relations between workmen and employers or between workmen and workmen or between employers and employers for imposing restrictive conditions on the conduct of any trade or business and includes any federation of two or more trade unions.

(28) Tribunal [Section 2(r)]

'Tribunal' means an Industrial Tribunal constituted under Section 7-A and includes an Industrial Tribunal constituted before the 10th March 1975, under this Act.

Industrial Disputes Act, 1947, provides for the constitution of one or more Industrial Tribunals. The Appropriate Government may constitute one or more Industrial Tribunals for the adjudication of industrial disputes relating to any matter specified in the Second Schedule or the Third Schedule appended to this Act.

(29) Village Industries [Section 2(rb)]

'Village Industries' has the same meaning assigned to it in clause (h) of Section 2 of the Khadi and Village Industries Commission Act, 1956.

(30) Wages [Section 2(rr)]

'Wages' means all remuneration capable of being expressed in terms of money, which would, if the terms of employment, express or implied, were fulfilled, be payable to a workman, in respect of his employment or of work done in such employment, and includes –

- (a) Such allowances (including dearness allowance) as the workman is for the time being entitled to;
- (b) Such value of any house accommodation, or of supply of light, water, medical attendance or other amenity of any service or of any concessional supply of food grains of other articles;
- (c) Any travelling concession; but does not include –
  - (i) Any bonus;
  - (ii) Any contribution paid or payable by the employer to any pension fund or provident fund or for the benefit of the workman under any law for the time being in force;
  - (iii) Any gratuity payable on the termination of his service;
- (d) Any commission payable on the promotion sales or business or, both.

In the above mentioned definition of 'wages', the two terms, namely, bonus and gratuity are used. Let us make clear the meaning of these two terms.

(31) Bonus

Bonus is an extra payment made to workmen by their employer in addition to their wages, allowances and usual fringe benefits. The Payment of Bonus Act, 1965, has made various provisions so far as payment of bonus is concerned. The payment of bonus to the workmen to whom the Payment of Bonus Act is applicable does not depend on the profit of their employers or their will. According to its provisions, the bonus is required to be paid to the employers.

(32) Workman [Section 2(s)]

'Workman' means any person (including an apprentice) employed in any industry to do any manual, unskilled, skilled, technical, operations, clerical or supervisory work for hire or reward, whether the terms of employment, be express or implied, and for the purposes of any proceeding under this Act in relation to an industrial dispute, includes any such person who has been dismissed, discharged or retrenched in connection with, or as a consequence of, that dispute, or whose dismissal, discharge, or retrenchment has led to that dispute, but does not include any such person –

(a) Who is subject to the Air Force Act, 1950 or the Army Act, 1950 or the Navy Act, 1957; or

(b) Who is employed in the Police Service or as an officer or other employee of a prison; or

(c) Who is employed mainly in a managerial or administrative capacity; or

(d) Who, being employed in a supervisory capacity, draws wages exceeding one thousand and six hundred rupees per month or exercises, either by the nature of the duties attached to the office or by reason of the powers vested in him, functions mainly of a managerial nature.

3.4 Machinery for Settlement of Industrial Disputes

In the preamble of the Industrial Disputes Act, 1947, it is stated that, "An Act to make provisions for the investigation and settlement of industrial disputes and for certain other purposes." Thus, this Act intends the prevention and settlement of industrial disputes by making necessary provisions and, for that purpose, various authorities with sufficient powers are constituted under it to bring about settlement between the parties concerned. These authorities are both internal as well as external.

The three modes, namely, voluntary settlement and conciliation, adjudication and arbitration have been provided for settlement of disputes under the Industrial Disputes Act, 1947. Works Committees, Conciliation Officers, Boards of Conciliation and Courts of Inquiry are the authorities under this Act which make use of conciliation as a method of settlement of industrial disputes. These authorities are meant to facilitate settlement of industrial disputes or, if needed, inquire into them, but in no case, can they make any awards, i.e., one, that would be binding on the parties concerned.

The adjudication authorities, in this regard, are - labour courts, Industrial Tribunals and National Tribunal.

The provisions relating to voluntary reference of dispute to arbitration have been made in Section 10-A, have already been studied by us while considering the definition of arbitrator.

3.4.1 Conciliation Machinery

(1) Works Committees [Section 3]

A 'works committee' is a forum provided for under this Act for expressing the difficulties of the parties concerned as regards their disputes. It endeavours to maintain cordial relationship even though there are disputes or differences between the parties to the disputes. The success of work committees mainly depends on the efforts and co-operation of both the parties to the disputes.

Section 3(1) of this Act provides for a Works Committee. According to this section, in the case of any industrial establishment in which one hundred or more workmen are employed or have been employed on any day in the preceding twelve months, the Appropriate Government may, by general or special order, require the employer to constitute in the prescribed manner, a Works Committee consisting of representatives of both employers and workmen engaged in the establishment.

However the number of representatives of workmen on the committee shall not be less than the number of representatives of the employer. The representatives of the workmen shall be chosen in the prescribed manner from among the workmen engaged in the establishment and in consultation with their trade union, if any, registered under the Indian Trade Unions Act, 1926. Section 3(2) further provides that it shall be the duty of the Works Committee to promote measures for securing and preserving amity and good relations between the employer and workmen and, to that end, to comment upon matters of their common interest or concern and endeavour to compose any material difference of opinion in respect of such matters.

The Industrial Disputes Act, 1947, prescribes the use of voluntary negotiations as the first option for settling industrial disputes. In this regard, Works Committees play a prominent role. 'Works Committee' comprise joint committees having an equal number of representatives from both the employers and workmen. The constitution of Works Committee is a must in an industrial establishment wherein one hundred or more workmen are employed on any day in preceding twelve months. In a nutshell, a Works Committee is an internal or in-house media meant for facilitating the settlement of industrial disputes within a given industry.

Functions of a Works Committee

Sub-section 2 of Section 3 of this Act enumerates the duties or functions of a Works Committee as follows –

(a) To remove the disparities between employers and workmen;

(b) To promote measures for securing and preserving amity and friendly and good relations between the employers and workmen;

(c) To that end, to comment upon all matters of their common interest or concern;

(d) To make efforts to compose any material difference of opinion in respect of various matters. These matters include so many aspects, such as, welfare of workers, provision and supervision of various recreational facilities, training of workmen and their wages, bonus, gratuity, working conditions including discipline, promotions, transfers, etc. Thus, it seems that there is no subject concerning the relation between the employers and workmen which the Works Committee is precluded from considering. However, the following points must be remembered in this connection.

1. The findings of the Works Committee are advisory or recommendatory and not mandatory, in nature. It cannot decide and pass final judgement. Its duty is only to

comment since it is mainly a negotiating organ. It is the function of the Works Committee to promote measures for harmonious and friendly and good relations between the employers and workmen.

2. Works Committees are not intended to supersede or supplement the trade unions for the purpose of collective bargaining. They are not authorised to consider real changes or substantial changes in the service conditions. They are not a substitute for trade unions.

(2) Conciliation Officers [Section 4]

Section 4 of the Industrial Disputes Act, 1947, provides for conciliation officer. According to Section 4(1), the Appropriate Government, by notification in the Official Gazette, may appoint such number of persons as it thinks fit, to be conciliation officers, charged with the duty of mediating in and promoting the settlement of industrial disputes. Section 4(2) further states that a Conciliation Officer may be appointed for a specified area or for specified industries in a specified area or for one or more specified industries either permanently or for a limited period. Thus, Section 4 makes it clear that a conciliation officer may be appointed by the Appropriate Government –

(a) Either permanently or for a limited period;

(b) For a specified area or for a specified industry in a specified area; or

(c) For one or more specified industries.

The Appropriate Government appoints such number of Conciliation Officers as it thinks fit.

The Conciliation Officers thus appointed are the public servants within the meaning of Section 21 of Indian Penal Code, 1960 [Section 11(6) of Industrial Disputes Act, 1947].

Duties of the Conciliation Officers [Section 12]:

The main duties of the conciliation officers consist of mediating in and promoting the settlement of industrial disputes.

According to Section 12 of this Act, the duties of the Conciliation Officers are as follows –

(a) To Hold Conciliation Proceedings

Where any industrial dispute exists or is apprehended, the Conciliation Officer may, or where the dispute relates to a public utility service and a notice of strike or lock-out under Section 22 of this Act has been given, shall hold conciliation proceedings in the prescribed manner [Section 12(1)]

Thus, it is obligatory on the part of Conciliation Officers to hold conciliation proceedings in public utility services where –

(i) An industrial dispute exists, or

(ii) An industrial dispute is apprehended; or

(iii) Where notice of a strike or a lock-out is given under Section 22 of this Act.

(b) Investigation of an Industrial Dispute:

For the purpose of bringing about a settlement of the dispute without delay, the Conciliation Officer shall investigate the dispute and all matters affecting the merits and the right settlement of the dispute, and may do all such things as he thinks fit for the purpose of inducing the parties to come to a fair and amicable settlement of the dispute [Section12(2) Thus, it is expected that the Conciliation Officers should take necessary steps to conduct conciliation proceedings expeditiously and, for doing so, certain discretionary powers are vested with the Conciliation Officers for conducting the proceedings in such a manner as they think proper.

(c) Memorandum of Settlement:

If the settlement of the dispute or of any matter in dispute arrived at in the course of the conciliation proceedings, the Conciliation Officer shall send a report thereof to the Appropriate Government or an officer authorised in this behalf by it together with a memorandum of the settlement signed by the parties to the dispute [Section 12(3)].

(d) Submission of Report with Facts to the appropriate Government:

If no settlement is arrived at, the conciliation officer, as soon as practicable after the close of the investigation, shall send to the Appropriate Government a full report setting forth the steps taken by him for ascertaining the facts and circumstances relating to the dispute and, for bringing about a settlement thereof, together with a full statement of such facts and circumstances, and the reason on account of which in his opinion a settlement could not be arrived at [Section 12(4)].

(e) Reference to a Board, Labour Court, Tribunal or National Tribunal:

On a consideration of the report referred to in sub-section 4 of Section 12, if the Appropriate Government is satisfied that there is a case for reference to a Board, Labour Court; Tribunal or National Tribunal, it may make such reference. Where the appropriate Government does not make such reference, it shall record and communicate to the parties' concerned its reasons therefor [Section 12(5)].

(f) Submission of Report within Fourteen Days

A report under this section shall be submitted within fourteen days of the commencement of the conciliation proceedings or within such shorter period as may be fixed by the Appropriate Government [Section 12(6)]. Provided that subject to the approval of the Conciliation Officer the time for the submission of the report may be extended by such period as may be agreed upon in writing by all the parties to the dispute [Proviso to Section 12(6)].

Commencement and Conclusion of Conciliation Proceedings

According to Section 20(1), a conciliation proceeding shall be deemed to have commenced on the date on which a notice of strike or lock-out under Section 22 is received by the Conciliation Officer. It is deemed to have concluded –

(a) Where a settlement is arrived at, when a memorandum of settlement is signed by the parties to the dispute, or

(b) Where no settlement is arrived at, when the report of the conciliation office by the Appropriate Government [Section 20(2)].

(3) Board of Conciliation [Section 5]:

Section 5 of the Industrial Disputes Act, 1947, provides for the constitution of a Board of Conciliation, Section 5 is reproduced as below –

The Appropriate Government may as occasion arises, by notification in the Official Gazette, constitute a Board of Conciliation for promoting the settlement of any industrial dispute [Section 5(1)].

A Board shall consist of a chairman and two or four other members as the Appropriate Government thinks fit [Section 5(2)].

The chairman shall be an independent person and the other members shall be persons appointed in equal numbers to represent the parties to the dispute and any person appointed to represent a party shall be appointed on the recommendation of the party [Section 5(3)]. Provided that if any party fails to make a recommendations as aforesaid within the prescribed time, the Appropriate Government shall appoint such person as it thinks fit to represent that party [Proviso to Section 5(3)].

Validity of Sitting of a Board of Conciliation

A Board having the prescribed quorum may act, notwithstanding the absence of the Chairman or any of its members or any vacancy in its number [Section 5(4)]. Provided that if the Appropriate Government notifies the Board that the services of the Chairman or of any other member have ceased to be available, the Board shall not act until a new chairman or member, as the case may be, has been appointed [Proviso to Section 5(4)]

Quorum of the Board of Conciliation

The quorum necessary to constitute a sitting of a Board of Conciliation is as follows –

(a) Where the number of members is three Quarum - two members; and

(b) Where the number of members is five Quarum - three members.

Reference of Disputes to a Board of Conciliation

Where the Appropriate Government is of the opinion that any industrial dispute exists or is apprehended, it may at any time, by order in writing, refer the dispute to a Board of Conciliation for promoting a settlement thereof [Section 10(1)].

Where the parties to an Industrial Disputes Act apply in the prescribed manner, whether jointly or separately, for a reference of the dispute to a Board of Conciliation, the Appropriate Government, if satisfied that the persons applying represents the majority of such party, shall make reference, accordingly [Section 10(2)].

Duties of a Board of Conciliation

Thus, a Board of Conciliation is a body of persons appointed by the Appropriate Government by notification in the Official Gazette for the purpose of promoting the settlement of an industrial dispute. Section 13 of this Act provides for the following duties of the Board of Conciliation. They are, namely -

(a) **Efforts to Bring About a Settlement :** Where a dispute has been referred to a Board of conciliation under this Act, it shall be the duty of the Board to bring about a settlement of the same and, for this purpose, the Board shall in such manner as it thinks fit and without delay, investigate the dispute and all matters affecting the merits and the right settlement thereof and may do all such things as it thinks fit for the purpose of inducing the parties to come to a fair and amicable settlement of the dispute [Section 13(1)].

(b) **Submission of the Memorandum of Settlement:** If a settlement of the dispute or any of the matters in dispute is arrived at in the course of conciliation proceedings, the Board shall send a report thereof to the Appropriate Government together with a memorandum of the settlement signed by the parties to the dispute [Section 13(2)].

(c) **Submission of Report with Facts, Circumstances etc.:** If no settlement is arrived at, the Board shall, as soon as practicable after the close of the investigation, send to the Appropriate Government, a full report setting forth proceedings and steps taken by the Board for ascertaining the facts and circumstances relating to the disputes and for bringing about a settlement thereof, together with full statement of such facts and circumstances, its findings thereon, the reasons on account of which, in its opinion, a settlement could not be arrived at and its recommendations for determination of the dispute [Section 13(3)].

(d) **Communication to the Parties:** If on the receipt of a report under sub-section 13(3) in respect of a dispute relating to public utility service, the Appropriate Government does not make a reference to a Labour Court, Tribunal or National Tribunal under Section 10, it shall record and communicate to the parties concerned its reasons therefor [Section 13(4)].

(e) **Submission of Reports within Two Months:** The Board of conciliation shall submit its report under this section within two months from the date on which the dispute was referred to it or within such shorter period as may be fixed by the Appropriate Government [Section 13(5)].

Provided that the Appropriate Government may, from time to time extend the time for the submission of the report by such further periods not exceeding two months in the aggregate. It is further provided that the time for submission of the report may be extended by such period as may be agreed to in writing by all parties to dispute.

Form of Report and Publication of Report

The report of a Board of Conciliation must be in writing and is required to be signed by all members of the Board. However, any member can submit a dissenting report. Every report together with the minute of dissent is required to be published by the Appropriate Government within thirty days from its receipt [Sections 16(1) and 17(1)].

All Members of a Board of Conciliation are Public Servants

It is made amply clear in the provisions of Section 11(6) that all members of a Board of Conciliation are deemed to be public servants within the meaning of Section 21 of the Indian Penal Code, 1860.

Procedure to be Followed by a Board of Conciliation

Subject to any rules that may be made in this behalf, a Board of Conciliation shall follow such procedure as it may think fit [Section 11(1)].

Commencement and Conclusion of Proceeding

A conciliation proceeding is deemed to commence from the date of order referring the dispute to the Board of Conciliation [Section 20(1)] and it is deemed to have concluded (a) when a memorandum of the settlement is signed by the parties to the dispute or (b) when the report of the Board of Conciliation is published [Section 20(2)].

Finality of the Governments Order

It is made clear in Section 9(1) that no order of the Appropriate Government or of the Central Government appointing any person as the Chairman or any other member of a Board of Conciliation shall be called into question in any manner, and no act or proceeding before any Board of Conciliation shall be called into question in any manner on the ground merely of the existence of any vacancy in, or defect in the constitution of such Board of condition.

(4) Courts of Inquiry [Section 6]

Where conciliation officers do not become successful, a Board of Conciliation takes over. The functions of such Board of Conciliation are the same as those of conciliation officers. The purpose of constituting the Boards of Conciliation is to bring about the settlement of industrial disputes. The next step in the process of settlement of industrial disputes under this Act is adjudication, for which various provisions are made in it in Sections 6, 7, 7-A and 7-B. Now, let us study one important aspect of adjudication first, i.e., Courts of Inquiry.

Composition and Appointment of Members of a Court of Inquiry

The provisions relating to composition and appointment of members of a Court of Inquiry have been made in Section 6 of this Act, which are as follows –

The Appropriate Government may as occasion arises, by notification in the Official Gazette, constitute a Court of Inquiry for enquiring into any matter appearing to be concerned with or relevant to an industrial dispute [Section 6(1)].

A court may consist of one independent person or of such number of independent persons as the Appropriate Government may think fit and where a Court consists of two or more members, one of them shall be appointed as the Chairman [Section 6(2)].

Quorum of a Court of Inquiry

According to the Rule 14 of the Industrial Disputes (Central) Rules, 1957, the quorum necessary to constitute a sitting of a Court of Inquiry shall be as follows –

(a) Where the number of members is not more than two, the quorum required is one.
(b) Where the number of members is more than two but less than five, the required quorum is two.
(c) Where the number of members is five or more, the same would be three.

Validity of sitting of a Court of Inquiry

A Court having the prescribed quorum, may act, notwithstanding the absence of the Chairman or any of its members of any vacancy in its number [Section 6(3)].

Provided that, if the Appropriate Government notifies the Court that the services of the Chairman have ceased to be available, the court shall not act until a new chairman has been appointed [Proviso to Section 6(3)].

Duties of a Court of Inquiry

The powers, duties etc. of various authorities concerned with investigation and settlement of industrial disputes are narrated in Sections 11, 14 and also in Sections 16 to 21 of Chapter IV of the Industrial Disputes Act, 1947.

The relevant portion of these sections is reproduced as below:

(a) **Appointment of Assessor or Assessors:** A Court of Inquiry may, if it so thinks fit, appoint one or more persons having special knowledge of the matter under consideration as assessor or assessors, to advise it in the proceedings before it [Section 11(5)].

(b) **Holding of an Enquiry and Submission of Report:** A court shall inquire into the matters referred to it and report thereon to the Appropriate Government ordinarily within a period of six months from the commencement of its inquiry [Section 14].

(c) **Report in Writing:** The report of a Court of Inquiry shall be in writing and shall be signed by all the members of the Board or Court as the case may be [Section 16(1)]. Provided that nothing in this section shall be deemed to prevent any member of the Court from recording any minute of dissent from a report or from any recommendation made therein [Proviso to Section 16(1)].

Publication of a report of a Court of Inquiry

Every report of a Court of Inquiry together with any minute of dissent recorded therewith shall, within a period of thirty days from the date of its receipt by the Appropriate Government, be published in such a manner as the Appropriate Government thinks fit [Section 17(1)].

Procedure to be followed by a Court of Inquiry

Subject to any rules that may be made in this behalf, a Court of Inquiry shall follow such procedure as it may think fit [Section 11(1)].

Reference of an Industrial Dispute to a Court of Inquiry

Where the Appropriate Government is of the opinion that any industrial dispute exists or is apprehended, it may at any time, by order in writing, refer any matter appearing to be connected with or relevant to the dispute to a Court of Inquiry for Inquiry [Section 10(1)]. In Section 10(2), it is further stated that where the parties to an industrial dispute apply in the prescribed manner, whether jointly or separately, for a reference of the dispute to a Court of Inquiry, the Appropriate Government if satisfied that the persons applying represent the majority of each party, shall make the reference, accordingly.

All Members of a Court of Inquiry are Public Servants

All members of a Court of Inquiry are deemed to be public servants within the meaning of section 21 of the Indian Penal Code, 1860 [Section 11(6)].

Finality of orders constituting a Court of Inquiry

No order for the Appropriate Government or of the Central Governmont, as the case may be, appointing any person as the Chairman or any other member of a Court of Inquiry shall be called into question in any manner, and no act or proceeding before any Court of Inquiry shall be called into question in any manner on the ground merely of the existence of any vacancy in, or defect in the constitution of such Court of Inquiry [Section 9(1)].

3.4.2 Adjudication Machinery

Labour courts, Industrial Tribunals and National Tribunals are adjudication authorities constituted under the Industrial Disputes Act, 1947, for the settlement of industrial disputes and bring about industrial peace. Let us now consider the provisions of this Act relating to appointments, constitution, qualifications, duties and powers etc., of these authorities.

(1) Labour Courts [Section 7]

The ultimate legal remedy for settling an unresolved industrial dispute is its reference to adjudication by the Appropriate Government. The Industrial Disputes Act, 1947, empowers the Appropriate Government to Constitute a Labour Court, Industrial Tribunals or National Tribunal to adjudicate Industrial Disputes [Section 7, 7-A, 7-B].

According to Section 7 of the Industrial Disputes Act, 1947, the Appropriate Government may, by notification in the Official Gazette, constitute one or more Labour Courts for the adjudication of industrial disputes relating to any matter specified in the Second Schedule (which is given below) and for performing such other functions as may be assigned to them under this Act [Section 7(l)]. A Labour Court shall consist of one person only to be appointed by the Appropriate Government [Section 7(2)].

Jurisdication of Labour Courts

The Second Schedule to the Industrial Disputes Act, 1947, specifies various matters within the jurisdiction of Labour Court.

Second Schedule

The matters within the Jurisdication of the Labour Courts are as follows:

(a) The propriety or legality of an order passed by an employer under the standing orders;

(b) The application and interpretation of standing orders;

(c) Discharge or dismissal of workmen including reinstatement of, or grant of relief to, workmen wrongfully dismissed;

(d) Withdrawal of any customary concession or privilege;

(e) Illegality or otherwise of strike or lock-out, and

(f) All matters other than those specified in the Third Schedule.

Qualifications and Disqualifications of a Person to be Appointed as a Presiding Officer of a Labour Court

Section 7(3) of this Act prescribes the qualifications of persons to be appointed as the presiding officers. According to Section 7(3), a person shall not be qualified for appointment as the Presiding Officer of a Labour Court, unless –

(a) he is or has been a Judge of a High Court; or

(b) he has been a District Judge or an Additional District Judge for a period of not less than three years; or

(c) he has held any judicial office in India for not less than seven years; or

(d) he has been the Presiding Officer of a Labour Court constituted under any Provincial Act or State Act for not less than five years.

Disqualifications to become Presiding Officer of a Labour Court

Section 7-C provides that no person shall be appointed to, or constitute in, the office of the presiding officer of a Labour Court; Tribunal or National Tribunal, if –

(a) He is not an independent person; or

(b) He has attained the age of sixty-five years.

Duties of a Labour Court

The duties of a Labour Court are as follows:

(a) **To Adjudicate:** It is the duty of a Labour Court to adjudicate upon the industrial disputes relating to any matter specified in the Second Schedule which is already given above and to perform all such other functions as may be assigned to it under this Act [Section 7(1)].

(b) **To hold Proceedings and Submission of Awards:** Where an industrial dispute has been referred to a Labour Court for adjudication, it shall hold its proceedings expeditiously and shall, within the period specified in the order referring such industrial dispute or the further period extended under the second proviso to sub-section 2-A of Section 10, submit its award to the Appropriate Government [Section 15].

Powers of a Labour Court

The important powers of a Labour Court are as follows:

(a) **Power to Enter the Premises:** The Presiding Officer of a Labour Court may for the purpose of inquiry into any existing or apprehended industrial dispute enter the premises occupied by any establishment to which the dispute relate, after giving a reasonable notice [Section 11(2)]

(b) **Powers of the Civil Court:** According to Section 11(3), every Labour Court shall have the same powers as are vested in a Civil Court under the Code of Civil Procedure, 1908, when trying a suit, in respect of the following matters, namely –
 (i) Enforcing the attendance of any person and examining him on oath.
 (ii) Compelling the production of documents and material objects.
 (iii) Issuing commissions for the examination of witness(es).
 (iv) In respect of such matters as may be prescribed.

(c) **Powers in respect of Judicial Proceedings:** Every inquiry or investigation by a Labour Court shall be deemed to be a judicial proceeding within the meaning of Sections 193 and 228 of the Indian Penal Code, 1860 [Section (3)(d)]

(d) **Power of Appointing an Assessor or Assessors:** A Labour Court, if it so thinks fit, may appoint one or more persons having special knowledge of the matter under consideration as an assessor or assessors to advice it in the proceeding before it [Section 11(5)].

(e) **Some Powers of a Civil Court and Status of Civil Court :** Every Labour Court is deemed to be a Civil Court for the purposes of Sections 345, 346, and 348 of the Code of Criminal Procedure, 1973 (2 of 1974) [Section 11(8)].

(f) **Power to Set Aside the Order of Discharge, Dismissal of Workman and to Direct Reinstatement :** Where an industrial dispute relating to the discharge or dismissal of a workman has been referred to a Labour Court for adjudication and, in the course of adjudication proceedings, the Labour Court is satisfied that the order of discharge or dismissal, as the case may be, was not justified, it may by its award, set aside such order of discharge or dismissal and direct the re-instatement of the workman on such terms and conditions, if any, as it thinks fit, or give such other relief to the workman including the award of any lesser punishment in lieu of discharge or dismissal as the circumstances of the case may require [Section 11-A]. It is also provided that in any proceeding under Section 11-A, the Labour Court shall rely only on the materials on record and shall not take any fresh evidence in relation to the matter [Proviso to Section 11-A].

(g) Powers of a Labour Court to allow Costs: It is stated in Section 11(7) that, "Subject to any rules made under this Act, the costs of, and incidental to, any proceeding before a Labour Court, the Labour Court shall have full powers to determine by and to whom and to what extent and subject to what conditions, if any, such costs are to be paid, and to give all necessary directions for the purposes aforesaid and such costs may, on an application made to the Appropriate Government by the person entitled, to be recovered by that Government in the same manner as an arrear of land revenue."

Thus, Section 11(7) empowers a Labour court to determine the costs of any proceedings before it and also to determine by whom and to what extent and subject to what conditions, if any, such costs are to be paid. A Labour Court is also empowered to give all necessary directions for the purposes aforesaid.

The Presiding of a Labour Court is a Public Servant:

It is made clear in the provisions of Section 11(6), that the Presiding Officer of a Labour Court is deemed to be a public servant within the meaning of Section 21 of the Indian Penal Code, 1860.

Procedure to be followed by a Labour Court:

Subject to any rules that may be made in this behalf, a labour court shall follow such procedure as it may think fit [Section 11(1)]

Finality of the Orders of the Government Constituting a Labour Court

No order of the Appropriate Government appointing any person as the presiding officer of a Labour Court shall be called into question in any manner, and no act or proceeding before any Labour Court shall be called into question in any manner on the ground merely of the existence of any vacancy in, or defect in the constitution of such Labour Court [Section 9(1)].

Filling of a Vacancy in the Office of Presiding Officer of a Labour Court

If, for any reason, a vacancy (other than a temporary vacancy) occurs in the office of the Presiding Officer of a Labour Court, the Appropriate Government shall appoint another person in accordance with the provisions of this Act to fill the vacancy, and the proceeding may be continued before the Labour Court from the stage at which the vacancy is filled [Section 8].

Reference of disputes to a Labour Court:

(a) Where the Appropriate Government is of the opinion that any industrial dispute exists or is apprehended, it may at any time, by order in writing, refer the dispute or any matter to be connected with, or relevant to the dispute, if it relates to the matter specified in the Second Schedule, to a Labour Court for adjudication [Section 10(1)(c)].

(b) Where the dispute relates to any matter specified in the Third Schedule and is not likely to affect more than one hundred workmen, the Appropriate Government may, if it so thinks fit, make the reference to a Labour Court under Section 10(1)(c) which is reproduced above [Proviso to Section 10(1)].

(c) Where the dispute in relation to which the Central Government is the Appropriate Government, it shall be competent for that Government to refer the dispute to a Labour Court constituted by the State Government [Proviso to Section 10(1)].

(d) Where the parties to an industrial dispute apply in the prescribed manner, whether jointly or separately, for a reference of the dispute to a Labour Court, the Appropriate Government, if satisfied that the persons applying represent the majority of each party, shall make the reference, accordingly [Section 10(2)].

Points of Reference and Jurisdiction

Where in an order referring an industrial dispute to a Labour Court or in a subsequent order, the Appropriate Government has specified the points of dispute for adjudication, the Labour Court shall continue its adjudication (jurisdiction) to those points and matters incidental thereto [Section 10(4)]

Prohibition of any Strike or Lock-out

Section 10(3) states that, "Where an industrial dispute has been referred to a Labour Court under this section, the Appropriate Government may, by order, prohibit the continuance of any strike or lock-out in connection with such dispute which may be in existence on the date of reference.

Forms of Award

The award of a Labour Court must be in writing and it must be signed by its Presiding Officer [Section 16(2)].

Publication of Award

According to the provisions of Section 17(1), every award of a Labour Court must be published within a period of thirty days from the date of its receipt by the Appropriate Government and it must be published in such a manner as it thinks fit.

It is stated in Section 17(2) that, "Subject to the Provisions of Section 17-A, the award published under Section 17(1) shall be final and shall not be called into question by any Court in any manner whatsoever."

Period for Submitting of an Award

An order referring an industrial dispute to a Labour Court under Section 10 shall specify the period within which such Labour Court shall submit its award on such dispute to the Appropriate Government [Section 10(2-A)].

Where such industrial dispute is connected with an individual workman, no such period shall exceed three months [Proviso to Section 10(2-A)]. But where the parties to an industrial dispute apply in the prescribed manner, whether jointly or separately, to the Labour Court for extension of such period or for any other reason, and the Presiding Officer of such Labour court considers it necessary or expedient to extend such period, he may for reasons to be recorded in writing, extend such period by such further period, as he may think fit [Proviso to Section 10(2-A)].

In computing any period specified in this section, the period, if any, for which the proceedings before the Labour Court had been stayed by any injunction or order of a Civil Court shall be excluded [Proviso to Section 10(2-A)].

It is also further provided in the Section 10(2-A) that no proceedings before the Labour Court shall lapse merely on the ground that any period specified under this sub-section had expired without such proceeding being completed.

On the Death of Parties, Proceedings do not Lapse

The provisions made in Section 10(8) of this Act relates to the proceedings pending on the death of the parties to the dispute. Section 10(8) lays down that, "No proceedings pending before a Labour Court in relation to an industrial dispute shall lapse merely by reason on the death of any of the parties to the dispute being a workman, and such labour court shall complete such proceedings and submit its award to the Appropriate Government."

(2) Industrial Tribunals [Section 7-A]

Constitution and Jurisdiction: Section 7-A of the Industrial Disputes Act, 1947, provides for the constitution of one or more Industrial Tribunals. According to Section 7-A(1), the Appropriate Government, by notification in the Official Gazette, may constitute one or more Industrial Tribunals for the adjudication of industrial disputes relating to any matter whether specified in the Second Schedule (which is already given elsewhere) or the Third Schedule and for performing such other functions as may be assigned to them under this Act. The Third Schedule appended to this Act is reproduced as below:

The Third Schedule

The matters within the jurisdiction of Industrial Tribunals are as follows:

(a) Wages including the period and mode of payment;

(b) Compensatory and other allowances;

(c) Hours of Work and rest intervals;

(d) Leave with wages and holidays;
(e) Bonus, profit-sharing, provident fund and gratuity;
(f) Shift working otherwise than in accordance with standing orders;
(g) Classification of discipline;
(h) Rules of discipline;
(i) Rationalisation;
(j) Retrenchment of workmen and closure of establishment; and
(k) Any other matter that may be prescribed.

A Tribunal shall consist of one person only to be appointed by the Appropriate Government [Section 7-A(2)].

Qualifications and Disqualifications of Presiding Officer of a Tribunal

A person shall not be qualified for appointment as the Presiding Officer of a Tribunal unless –
(a) He is or has been, a Judge of a High Court; or
(b) He has been a District Judge or an Additional District Judge for a period of not less than three years [Section 7-A(3)].

Disqualification of Presiding Officer of a Tribunal

No person shall be appointed to, or continue in the office of the presiding officer of a Tribunal, if
(a) He is not an independent person; or
(b) He has attained the age of sixty-five years [Section 7-C].

Appointment of Assessors

The Appropriate Government may, if it thinks fit, appoint two persons as assessors, to advise the Tribunal in the proceedings before it [Section 7-A(4)].

Duties of Industrial Tribunals

Section 15 of this Act describes the duties of Tribunals and, accordingly, "Where an industrial dispute has been referred to a Tribunal for adjudication, it shall hold its proceedings expeditiously and shall within the period specified in the order referring such industrial dispute or the further period extended under the second proviso to sub-section 2(A) of Section 10, submit its award to the Appropriate Government.

Powers of an Industrial Tribunal:

The powers of an Industrial Tribunal are given in Section 11 (Chapter IV) of the Industrial Disputes Act, 1947. These powers are enumerated as below:

(a) The Presiding Officer of a Tribunal may for the purpose of inquiry into any existing or apprehended industrial dispute, after giving a reasonable notice, enter the premises occupied by any establishment to which the dispute relates [Section 11(2)].

(b) Every Tribunal shall have the same powers as are vested in a Civil Court under the Code of Civil Procedure, 1908, when trying a suit, in respect of the following matters, namely -

- (i) Enforcing the attendance of any person and examining him on oath;
- (ii) Compelling the production of documents and material objects;
- (iii) Issuing commissions for the examination of witness(es);
- (iv) In respect of such other matters, as may be prescribed.

Every inquiry or investigation by a Tribunal is deemed to be a judical proceeding within the meaning of Sections 193 and 228 of the Indian Penal Code, 1860. Every court of inquiry is deemed to be Civil Court for the purposes of Sections 345, 346 and 348 of the Code of criminal Procedure, 1973.

(c) Power of Appointing an Assessor or Assessors: A Tribunal, if it so thinks fit, may appoint one or more persons having special knowledge of the matter under consideration as an assessor or assessors to advice it in the proceeding before it [Section 11(5)].

(d) Some Powers of a Civil Court and Status of Civil Court: Every Tribunal is deemed to be Civil Court for the purposes of Sections 345, 346 and 348 of the Code of Criminal Procedure, 1973 (2 of 1974) [Section 11(8)].

(e) Power to give Relief in case Discharge, Dismissal of Workman and to Direct Reinstatement: Where an industrial dispute relating to the discharge or dismissal of a workman has been referred to a Tribunal for adjudication and, in the course of adjudication proceedings, the Tribunal is satisfied that the order of discharge or dismissal, as the case may be, was not justified, it may by its award set aside such order of discharge or dismissal and direct re-instatement of the workman on such terms and conditions, if any, as it thinks fit, or give such other relief to the workman including the award of any lesser punishment in lieu of discharge or dismissal as the circumstances of the case may require [Section 11-A]. It is also provided that in any proceeding under Section 11-A, the Tribunal shall rely only on the materials on record and shall not take any fresh evidences in relation to the matter [Proviso to Section 11-A].

(f) Power of an Industrial Tribunal to Allow Costs: It is stated in Section 11(7) that, "Subject to any rules made under this act, the costs of, and incidental to, any proceeding before an Industrial Tribunal shall have full powers to determine by and to whom and to what extent and, subject to what conditions, if any, such costs are to be paid, and to give all necessary directions for the purposes aforesaid and such costs may, on an application made to the Appropriate Government by the person entitled, to be recovered by that Government in the same manner as an arrear of land revenue.

Thus, Section 11(7) empowers an Industrial Tribunal to determine the costs of any proceedings before it and also to determine by whom and to what extent and the subject to what conditions if any, such costs are to be paid. An Industrial Tribunal is also empowered to give all necessary directions for the purposes aforesaid.

The Presiding Officer of Tribunals is a Public Servant:

It is made clear in the provisions of Section 11(6) that the presiding officer of a Tribunal is deemed to be a public servant within the meaning of Section 21 of the Indian Penal Code, 1860.

Procedure to be followed by a Tribunal

Subject to any rules that may be made in this behalf, a Tribunal shall follow such procedure as it may think fit [Section 11(1)].

Finality of the Orders of the Government

No order of the Appropriate Government appointing any person as the Presiding Officer of a Tribunal shall be called into question in any manner and no act or proceeding before any Tribunal shall be called into question in any manner on the ground merely of the existence of any vacancy in or defect in the constitution of such Tribunal [Section 9(1)].

Filling of a Vacancy in the Office of Presiding Officer of a Tribunal

If, for any reason, a vacancy (other than a temporary vacancy) occurs in the office of the Presiding Officer of a Tribunal, the Appropriate Government shall appoint another person in accordance with the provisions of this Act to fill the vacancy; and the proceeding may be continued before the Tribunal from the stage at which the vacancy is filled [Section 8].

Reference of disputes to a Tribunal

(a) Where the Appropriate Government is of the opinion that any industrial dispute exists or is apprehended, it may at any time, by order in writing, refer the dispute or any matter to be connected with, or relevant to the dispute, if it relates to the matter specified in the Second Schedule or the Third Schedule to a Tribunal for adjudication [Section 10(1)(c)]. The Third Schedule is already reproduced elsewhere.

(b) Where the dispute in relation to which the Central Government is the Appropriate Government, it shall be competent for that Government to refer the dispute to an Industrial Tribunal constituted by the State Government [Proviso to Section 10(1)].

(c) Where the parties to an industrial dispute apply in the prescribed manner, whether jointly or separately for a reference of the dispute to a Tribunal, the Appropriate Government, if satisfied that the persons applying represent the majority of each party, shall make the reference, accordingly [Section 10(2)].

Points of Reference and Jurisdiction

Where in an order referring an industrial dispute to a Tribunal or in a subsequent order, the Appropriate Government has specified the points of dispute for adjudication the Tribunal shall continue its adjudication (jurisdiction) to those points and matters incidental thereto [Section 10(4)].

Prohibition of any Strike or Lock-out

Section 10(3) states that, "where an industrial dispute has been referred to a Tribunal under this section, the Appropriate Government may by order, prohibit the continuance of any strike or lock-out in connection with such dispute which may be in existence on the date of reference."

Order of Inclusion of either an Industrial Establishment or a Group or Class of Establishments

Where a dispute concerning any establishment or establishments has been or is to be referred to an Industrial Tribunal under Section 10 and the Appropriate Government is of the opinion, whether on an application made to it in this behalf or otherwise, that the dispute is of such nature that any other establishment, group or class of establishments of a similar nature is likely to be interested in, or affected by, such dispute, the Appropriate Government may, at any time of making the reference or at any time thereafter but before the submission of award, include in that reference such establishment, group or class of establishments, whether or not at the time of such inclusion any dispute exists or is apprehended in that establishment group or class of establishments [Section 10(5)]

Form of Award

The award of a Tribunal must be in writing and it must be signed by its Presiding Officer [Section 16(2)].

Publication of Award

According to the provisions of Section 17(1), every award of a Tribunal must be published within a period of thirty days from the date of its receipt by the Appropriate Government and it must be published in such manner as it thinks fit.

It is stated in Section 17(2) that, "Subject to the provisions of Section 17-A, the award published under Section 17(1) shall be final and shall not be called into question by any court in any manner whatsoever."

Period for Submitting of an Award

An order referring an industrial dispute to an Industrial Tribunal under Section 10 shall specify the period within which such Tribunal shall submit its award on such dispute to the Appropriate Government [Section 10(2-A)].

Where such industrial dispute is connected with an individual workman, no such period shall exceed three months [Proviso to Section 10(2-A)]. But where the parties to an industrial dispute apply in the prescribed manner, whether jointly or separately, to the Industrial Tribunal for extension of such period or for any other reason, and the Presiding Officer of such Tribunal considers it necessary or expedient to extend such period, he may for reasons to be recorded in writing, extend such period by such further period as he may think fit [Proviso to Section 10(2-A)].

(3) National Industrial Tribunal [Section 7-B]

Constitution of National Tribunal, its composition and appointment of presiding officer

The Central Government, by notification in the Official Gazette, may constitute one or more National Industrial Tribunals for the adjudication of industrial disputes which, in the opinion of the Central Government, involve questions of national importance or are of such a nature that industrial establishments situated in more than one state are likely to be interested in, or affected by, such disputes [Section 7-B(1)].

A National Tribunal shall consist of one person only to be appointed by the Central Government [Section 7-B(2)].

Qualifications and disqualifications of a presiding officer of National Industrial Tribunal [Section 7-B (3) and 7-C]:

Qualifications and disqualifications: A person shall not be qualified for the appointment as the presiding officer of National Tribunal unless he is or has been a Judge of a High Court [Section 7-B(3)].

No person shall be appointed to, or continue in, the office of the presiding officer of a National Tribunal if –
(a) He is not an independent person; or
(b) He has attained the age of sixty-five years [Section 7-C].

Appointment of Assessors [Section 7-B(4)]

Assessors: The Central Government may, if it thinks fit, appoint two persons as assessors to advise the National Industrial Tribunal in the proceedings before it [Section 7-B(4)].

Duties of a National Tribunal

(a) **Proceedings and Award:** Where an industrial dispute has been referred to a National Tribunal for adjudication, it shall hold its proceedings expeditiously and shall within the period specified in the order referring such industrial dispute or the further period extended under the second proviso to sub-section 2(A) of Section 10, submit its award to the Appropriate Government [Section 15].

(b) **Disputes of National Importance:** The National Tribunals are to adjudicate industrial disputes which, in the opinion of the Central Government –
   (i) involve various questions of national importance; or/and
   (ii) are of such a nature that industrial establishments situated in more than one state is likely to be interested in, or affected by, such industrial disputes.

Powers of a National Tribunal

The powers of a National Tribunal are given in Section 11 (Chapter IV) of the Industrial Disputes Act, 1947. These powers are enumerated as below:

(a) The presiding officer of a National Tribunal may for the purpose of inquiry into any existing or a apprehended industrial dispute, after giving a reasonable notice, enter the premises occupied by any establishment to which the dispute relates [Section 11(2)].

(b) According to Section 11(3), every National Tribunal shall have the same powers as are vested in a civil court under the Ccode of Civil Procedure, 1908, when trying a suit, in respect of the following matters, namely –
  (i) Enforcing the attendance of any person and examining him on oath;
  (ii) Completing the production of documents and material objects;
  (iii) Issuing commissions for the examination of witness(es);
  (iv) In respect of such other matters as may be prescribed.

Every inquiry or investigation by a National Tribunal is deemed to be a judicial proceeding within the meaning of Sections 193 and 228 of the Indian Penal Code, 1860. Every National Tribunal is deemed to be Civil Court for the purposes of Sections 345(1), 346 and 348 of the Code of Criminal Procedure, 1973.

(c) Power of Appointing an Assessor or Assessors: A National Tribunal, if it so thinks fit, may appoint one or more persons having special knowledge of the matter under consideration as an assessor or assessors to advise it in the proceeding before it [Section 11(5)].

(d) Some Powers of a Civil Court and Status of Civil Court: Every National Tribunal is deemed to be a Civil Court for the purposes of Sections 345(1), 346 and 348 of the Code of Criminal Procedure, 1973 (2 of 1974) [Section 11(8)]

(e) Power to Set Aside the Order of Discharge, Dismissal of Workman and to Direct Reinstatement: Where an industrial dispute relating to the discharge or dismissal of a workman has been referred a National Tribunal for adjudication and in the course of adjudication proceeding, the National Tribunal is satisfied that the order of discharge or dismissal, as the case may be, was not justified, it may by its award set aside the order of such discharge or dismissal and direct the re-instatement of the workman on such terms and conditions, if any, as it thinks fit, or give such other relief to the workman including the award of any lesser punishment in lieu of discharge or dismissal as the circumstances of the case may require [Section 11-A]. It is also provided that in any proceeding under Section 11-A, the National Tribunal shall rely only on the materials on record and shall not take any fresh evidence in relation to the matter [Proviso to Section 11-A].

(f) Powers of a National Tribunal to allow costs: It is stated in Section 11(7) that, "Subject to any rules made under this Act, the costs of, and incidental to, any proceeding before a National Tribunal, the National Tribunal shall have full powers to determine by and to when and to what extent and subject to what conditions, if any, such costs are to be paid, and to give all necessary directions for the purposes aforesaid and such costs may, on an application made to the Appropriate Government by the person entitled, to be recovered by that Government in the same manner as an arrear of land revenue."

Thus, Section 11(7) empowers a National Tribunal to determine the costs of any proceedings before it and also to determine by whom and to what extent and subject to what conditions, if any, such costs are to be paid. A National Tribunal is also empowered to give all necessary directions for the purposes aforesaid.

The Presiding Officer of a National Tribunal is a Public Servant

It is made clear in the provisions of Section 11(6) that the presiding officer of a National Tribunal is deemed to be a public servant within the meaning of Section 21 of the Indian Penal Code, 1860.

Procedure to be followed by a National Tribunal

Subject to any rules that may be made in this behalf, a National Tribunal shall follow such procedure as it may think fit [Section 11(1)].

Finality of the Order of the Government

No order of the Appropriate Government appointing any person as the Presiding Officer of a National Tribunal shall be called into question in any manner and no act or proceeding before any National Tribunal shall be called into question in any manner on the ground merely of the existence of any vacancy in, or defect in the constitution of such Labour Court [Section 9(1)].

Fitting of a Vacancy in the Office of Presiding Officer of a National Tribunal

If, for any reason, a vacancy (other than a temporary vacancy) occurs in the office of the presiding officer of a National Tribunal, the Appropriate Government shall appoint another person in accordance with the provisions of this Act to fill up the vacancy and the proceeding may be continued before the National Tribunal from the stage at which the vacancy is filled [Section 8].

Reference of Disputes to National Tribunal

(a) Where the Central Government is of the opinion that any industrial dispute exists or is apprehended, and -

 (i) the dispute involves any question of national importance or;

 (ii) that is of such a nature that industrial establishments situated in more than one state are likely to be interested in, or affected by such dispute, and

 (iii) that the dispute should be adjudicated by a National Tribunal, then –

The Central Government may, whether or not it is the Appropriate Government in relation to that dispute, at any time, by order in writing, refer the dispute or any matter appearing to be connected with, or relevant to the dispute whether it relates to any matter specified in the Second Schedule or the Third Schedule [these schedules are already reproduced elsewhere], to a National Tribunal for adjudication [Section 10(1-A)].

(b) Where the parties to an industrial dispute apply in the prescribed manner, whether jointly or separately, for a reference of the dispute to a National Tribunal, the Appropriate Government, if satisfied that the persons applying represent the majority of each party, shall make the reference, accordingly [Section 10(2)]

Points of Reference and Jurisdiction:

Where in an order referring an industrial dispute to a National Tribunal or in a subsequent order, the Appropriate Government has specified the points of dispute for adjudication, the National Tribunal shall continue its adjudication (jurisdiction) to those points and matters incidental thereto [Section 10(4)].

Prohibition of any Strike or Lock-out:

Section 10(3) states that, "Where an industrial dispute has been referred to a National Tribunal under this section, the Appropriate Government may by order, prohibit the continuance of any strike or lock-out in connection with such dispute which may be in existence on the date of reference.

Order of Inclusion of either an Industrial Establishment or a Group or Class of Establishments

Where a dispute concerning any establishment or establishments has been, or is to be referred to a National Tribunal under Section 10 and, the Appropriate Government, is of the opinion, whether on an application made to it in this behalf or otherwise, that the dispute is of such nature that any other establishment group or class of establishments of a similar nature is likely to be interested in or affected by such dispute, the Appropriate Government may, at any time of making the reference or at any time thereafter but before the submission of award, include in that reference such establishment group or class of establishments, whether or not at the time of such inclusion any dispute exists or is apprehended in that establishment group or class of establishments [Section 10(5)]

Form of Award

The award of a National Tribunal must be in writing and it must be signed by its Presiding Officer [Section 16(2)].

Publication of Award

According to the provisions of Section 17(1), every award of a National Tribunal must be published within a period of thirty days from the date of its receipt by the Appropriate Government and it must be published in such manner as it thinks fit.

It is stated in Section 17(2) that, "'Subject to the provisions of Section 17-A, the award published under Section 17(1) shall be final and shall not be called into question by any court in any manner whatsoever."

Period for Submitting of an Award

An order referring an industrial dispute to the National Tribunal under Section 10 shall specify the period within which such National Tribunal shall submit its award on such dispute to the Appropriate Government [Section 10(2-A)].

Where such industrial dispute is connected with an individual workman, no such period shall exceed three months [Proviso to Section 10(2-A)]. But where the parties to an industrial dispute apply in the prescribed manner, whether jointly or separately, to the National

Tribunal for extension of such period or for any other reason, and the Presiding Officer of such National Tribunal considers it necessary or expedient to extend such period, he may for reasons to be recorded in writing, extend such period by such further period as he may think fit [Proviso to Section 10(2-A)].

In computing any period specified in this section, the period, if any, for which the proceedings before the National Tribunal had been stayed by any injunction or order of a Civil Court shall be excluded [Proviso to Section 10(2-A)].

It is also further provided in the Section 10(2-A) that no proceedings before the National Tribunal shall lapse merely on the ground that any period specified under this sub-section had expired without such proceeding being completed.

On the Death of Parties, Proceedings do not Lapse

The provisions made in Section 10(8) of this Act relates to the proceedings pending on the death of the parties to the dispute. Section 10(8) lays down that -
"No proceedings pending before National Tribunal in relation to an industrial dispute shall lapse merely by reason on the death of any of the parties to the dispute being a workman, and such National Tribunal shall complete such proceedings and submit its award to the Appropriate Government."

Barring the Other Authorities under this Act for Adjudication of an Industrial Dispute Pending before the National Tribunal

Where any reference has been made under Section 10(1-A) to a National Tribunal [Please see the provisions of Section 10(1-A)] given under the heading, 'Reference of disputes to National Tribunal'], then notwithstanding anything contained in this Act, no Labour Court or Tribunal shall have jurisdiction to adjudicate upon any matter which is under adjudication before the National Tribunal, and accordingly,

(a) if the matter under adjudication before the National Tribunal is pending in a proceeding before a Labour Court or the Tribunal, the proceeding before the Labour Court or the Tribunal, as the case may be, insofar as it relates to such matter shall be deemed to have been quashed on such reference to the National Tribunal; and

(b) it shall not be lawful for the Appropriate Government to refer the matter under adjudication before the National Tribunal to any Labour Court or Tribunal for adjudication during the pendency of the proceeding in relation to such matter before the National Tribunal.

In this sub-section, which is mentioned above, the expressions, 'Labour Court' or 'Tribunal' includes any Court or Tribunal or any other authority constituted under any law relating to investigation and settlement of industrial disputes in force in any state [Explanation to Section 10(6)].

(4) Voluntary Reference to Arbitration

Section 10-A of the Industrial Disputes Act, 1947, provides for the voluntary reference of disputes to arbitration. Where any industrial dispute exists or is apprehended and the employer and the workmen agree to refer the dispute to arbitration, they may do so by an agreement in writing in the form prescribed by the rules and signed in the manner laid down in the rules. However, the reference to the arbitration must be made before the dispute has been referred to any authority under Section 10. The definition of 'Arbitrator' and the provisions relating to voluntary reference of a dispute to arbitration are discussed as below:

Definition of 'Arbitrator' and Provisions relating to Voluntary Reference of a Dispute to Arbitration

Arbitrator [Section 2(aa)]

In the Industrial Disputes Act, 1947, the definition of 'Arbitrator' is given in Section (aa) and it is only stated that **'Arbitrator' includes an umpire**. However, the provisions relating appointment of an umpire and to voluntary reference of dispute to arbitration have been made in Section 10-A, which is as follows:

(a) Time to making Voluntary Reference of Dispute to Arbitration and who can make such reference: Where any industrial dispute exists or is apprehended and the employer and the workmen agree to refer the dispute to arbitration, they may, at any time before the dispute has been referred under Section 10 to a Labour Court or Tribunal or National Tribunal, by a written agreement, but save as aforesaid refer the dispute to arbitration [Section 10-A(1)].

Thus, the reference to arbitration must be made before the dispute has been referred to any authority under Section 10. Such reference to arbitration can be made by the employer and the workmen on the agreement amongst themselves where any industrial dispute exists or is apprehended.

(b) To whom Arbitration Reference can be made: Section 10-A(1) makes it amply clear that voluntary reference of dispute to arbitration shall be made to such person or persons including the Presiding Officer of a Labour Court, Industrial Tribunal or National Tribunal as an arbitrator or arbitrators as may be specified in the arbitration agreement.

(c) Appointment of an Umpire: The parties to the dispute can select any person as an arbitrator or persons as arbitrators. But, where an arbitration agreement provides for a reference of the dispute to an even number of arbitrators, then, that agreement shall provide for the appointment of another person as an umpire. The umpire thus appointed shall enter upon the reference if the arbitrators are equally divided in their opinion, and the award of the umpire shall prevail and shall be deemed to be the arbitration award for the purposes of this Act [Section 10-A(1-A)].

(d) Form of Arbitration Agreement: An arbitration agreement referred to in Section 10-A(1) shall be in such form and shall be signed by the parties thereto in such manner as may be prescribed [Section 10-A(2)]

(e) Provisions relating to Forwarding a Copy of the Arbitration Agreement to the Appropriate Government and the Conciliation Officer: Section 10-A(3) states that, "A copy of the arbitration agreement shall be forwarded to the Appropriate Government and the conciliation officer and the Appropriate Government shall, within one month from the date of the receipt of such copy, publish the same in the Official Gazette."

(f) Opportunity to Employers and Workmen who are not Parties to the Arbitration Agreement but are involved in the Dispute to represent their Case : Where an industrial dispute has been referred to arbitration and the Appropriate Government is satisfied that the persons making the reference represent the majority of each party, the Appropriate Government may, within one month, issue a notification in such manner as may be prescribed, and when any such notification is issued, the employers and workmen who are not parties to the arbitration agreement but are involved in the dispute, shall be given an opportunity of representing their case before the arbitrator or arbitrators, as the case may be [Section 10-A(3-A)]

(g) Duty of the Arbitrators: It is the duty of the arbitrator or arbitrators to investigate the dispute and then to submit the arbitration award duly signed to the Appropriate Government. Section 10-A(4) lays down that, **"The arbitrator or arbitrators shall investigate the dispute and submit to the Appropriate Government, the arbitration award signed by the arbitrator or arbitrators, as the case may be."**

(h) Prohibition of Continuance of Strike or Lock-out: When a dispute is referred to arbitration, the Appropriate Government may prohibit the continuance of any strike or lock-out by issuing an order. Section 10-A[4-A] states that, "where an industrial dispute has been referred to arbitration and notification has been issued under Section 10-A(3-A), the Appropriate Government may, by order, prohibit the continuance of any strike or lock-out in connection with such dispute which may be in existence on the date of the reference."

(i) Arbitration Act, 1940, not to apply: According to Section 10-A(5), "Nothing in the Arbitration Act, 1940 (10 of 1940), shall apply to arbitration under this section." Thus, when a dispute is referred to arbitration under Section 10-A, the provisions of the Arbitration Act, 1940, do not apply to arbitration under Section 10-A of the Industrial Disputes Act, 1947.

3.5 Procedure and Powers of the Authorities [Section 11]

We have already considered the duties of various authorities appointed by the Appropriate Government or the Central Government, as the case may be, under this Act. The procedure to be followed and powers given to the authorities are also explained in Chapter IV of this Act. Let us consider them briefly. Section 11 of this Act provides for the procedure and powers of Conciliation Officers, Boards, Courts and Tribunals.

Section 1: Procedure and Powers of Conciliation Officers, Boards, Courts and Tribunals:

1. Subject to any rules that may be made in this behalf, an arbitrator, a Board, Court, Tribunal or National Tribunal shall follow such procedure as the arbitrator or other authority concerned may think fit.

2. A Conciliation Officer or a member of a Board or Court or the Presiding Officer of a Labour Court, Tribunal or National Tribunal may, for the purpose of inquiry into any existing or apprehended industrial dispute, after giving reasonable notice, enter the premises occupied by the establishment to which the disputes relate.

3. Every Board, Court, Labour Tribunal and National Tribunal shall have the same powers as are vested in a Civil Court under the Code of Civil Procedure, 1908, when trying a suit in respect of the following matters, namely:

    (a) Enforcing the attendance of any person and examining him on oath;

    (b) Compelling the production of documents and material objects;

    (c) Issuing summons for the examination of witness(es);

    (d) In respect of such other matters as may be prescribed, and every inquiry or investigation by a Board, Court, Labour Court, Tribunal and National Tribunal shall be deemed to be a judicial proceeding, within the meaning of Sections 193 and 228 of the Indian Penal Code.

4. A Conciliation Officer may enforce the attendance of any person for the purpose of examination of such person or call for and inspect any document which he has ground for considering to be relevant to the industrial dispute or to be necessary for the purpose of verifying the implementation of any award or carrying out any other duty imposed on him under this Act, and for the aforesaid purposes, a Conciliation Officer shall have the same powers as are vested in a Civil Court under the Code of Civil Procedure, 1908, in respect of enforcing the attendance of any person and examining him or of compelling the production of documents.

5. A Court, Labour Court, Tribunal or National Tribunal may, if it thinks fit, appoint one or more persons having special knowledge of the matter under consideration as assessor or assessors to advise it in the proceeding before it.

6. All Conciliation Officers, members of a Board or Court and the Presiding Officers of a Labour Court, Tribunal or National Tribunal shall be deemed to be public servants within the meaning of Section 21 of the Indian Penal Code.

7. Subject to any rules made under this Act, the costs of, and incidental to any proceeding before a Labour Court, Tribunal or National Tribunal shall be in the discretion of that Labour Court, Tribunal or National Tribunal and the Labour Court, Tribunal or National Tribunal, as the case may be, shall have full powers to determine by and to when and to what extent and subject to what conditions, if

any, such costs are to be paid, and to give all necessary directions for the purposes aforesaid and, such costs may, on an application made to the Appropriate Government by the person entitled, be recovered by the Government in the same manner as an arrear of land revenue.

8. Every Labour Court, Tribunal or National Tribunal shall be deemed to be a Civil Court for the purposes of Ssections 345, 346 and 348 of the Code of Criminal Procedure, 1973.

Section 11-A makes amply clear the powers of Labour Courts, Tribunals and National Tribunals to give appropriate relief in case of discharge or dismissal of workmen. Section 11-A reads as follows:

Section 11-A: Power of Labour Courts, Tribunal and National Tribunals to give appropriate relief in case of discharge or dismissal of workman:

Where in industrial dispute relating to the discharge or dismissal of a workman has been referred to a Labour Court, Tribunal or National Tribunal for adjudication and, in the course of the adjudication proceedings, the Labour Court, Tribunal or National Tribunal, as the case may be, is satisfied that the order of discharge or dismissal was not justified, it may, by its award, set aside the order of discharge or dismissal and direct reinstatement of the workman on such terms and condition, if any, as it thinks fit, or give such other relief to the workman including the award of any lesser punishment in lieu of discharge or dismissal as the circumstances of the case may require.

Provided that in any proceeding under this section, the Labour Court, Tribunal or National Tribunal, as the case may be, shall rely only on the materials on record and shall not take any fresh evidence in relation to the matter.

3.6 Strikes and Lock-outs

3.6.1 Strikes

Lock-outs and strikes are the weapons in the hands of employers and workmen, respectively, to compel one other to agree to their demand(s).

Strike has been defined in Section 2(q) of this Act to mean cessation of work by a body of persons employed in any industry acting in combination or a concerted refusal or a refusal under a common understanding of any number who are or have been so employed to continue to work or to accept employment. Strike is a powerful weapon in the hands of employees for collective bargaining. The employees through this mechanism can in a way compel the employers to sit across with them for settling their disputes in the form of collective bargaining. When all other methods to resolve the industrial disputes fail, this weapon of strike is used as a last resort. The right to go on strike has been given to the workmen, but this Act imposes certain restrictions on the rights of workmen. This Act prohibits strikes under certain circumstances. It also makes separate provisions for public utility service and private enterprises.

The important points of strike are as follows:

1. A strike is a weapon which is used by employees or workmen acting together to force their employer to agree to the demands made by them.

2. A strike implies a stoppage of work by a number of employees acting together. But mere absence from work on personal grounds does not amount to cessation or stoppage or refusal of work. There should be premeditation or plan to cease or to refuse to work in a body of workmen.

3. The duration or stoppage or cessation of work is immaterial. If the workmen acting together cease their work even for an hour or a part thereof, it can be called a strike.

4. When workmen go on strike against the provisions of this Act, such strike is considered illegal.

5. Even a partial refusal of work by a body of workmen may constitute a strike.

6. A strike can be a 'stay-in strike' or 'go-slow strike.'

7. In certain industries, overtime work is considered essential and it is a legal obligation. While in certain industries, overtime work is done habitually and is customary. Refusal of overtime work in such cases is considered as against the conditions of service. If overtime work is refused, then, it may be considered as a strike.

From the definition and the important points mentioned above, we come to know that the following two factors must exist to constitute a strike.

(a) The workmen must be absent from work either in a body or in a group. They must refuse to work when they are expected to do under legal or contractual obligation for their employer.

(b) The cessation or refusal to do the work is voiced either in concerted form of all workmen or in a group of workmen. Mere absence from duty or work on any personal ground does not amount to cessation or refusal of work. There must exist some form of predetermination or some plan to cease or refuse to do the work in a body of workmen.

Important Provisions Relating to Strikes

(A) Provisions relating to Prohibition of Strike [Section 22]

1. No person employed in a public utility service shall go on strike, in breach of contract –

    (a) Without giving a notice of strike to the employer, as hereinafter provided, within six weeks before striking; or

    (b) Within fourteen days on giving such notice, or

(c) Before the expiry of the date of strike specified in such notice as aforesaid; or

(d) During the pendency of any conciliation proceeding before a conciliation officer and seven days after the conclusion of such proceedings [Section 22(1)].

2. The notice of strike under the provisions mentioned above in Section 22(1) shall not be necessary where there is already in existence a strike in public utility services. But, it is very essential for the employer to send an intimation of such strike to such authority as may be specified by the Appropriate Government, on the day on which the strike is declared, either generally or for a particular area or for a particular class of public utility services [Section 22(3)].

The notice of strike referred to in Section 22(1) must be given by such number of persons to such person or persons and in such manner as may be prescribed [Section 22(4)].

3. If on any day an employer receives from any person employed by him any such notices as are referred to in Section 22(1), he must within five days thereof, report to the Appropriate Government or to such authority as that Appropriate Government may prescribe the number of such notices receive on that date [Section 22(6)].

(B) General Prohibition of Strike [Section 23]

No workman who is employed in any industrial establishment will go on strike in breach of contract under the following circumstances:

1. During the pendency of conciliation proceedings before a Board and seven days after the conclusion of such proceeding.

2. During the pendency of proceedings before a Labour Court, an Industrial Tribunal or National Tribunal and two months after the conclusion of such proceedings.

3. During the pendency of arbitration proceedings before an arbitrator and two months after the conclusion of such proceedings, where a notification has been issued under Section 10-A(3-A), or

4. During any period in which a settlement or award is in operation, in respect of any of the matters covered by the settlement or award.

(C) Illegal strikes [Section 24]:

1. A strike shall be illegal if it is commenced or declared in contravention of Sections 22 or 23 or if it is continued in contravention of an order made under Section 10(3) or under Section 10-A(4-A) [Section 24(1)].

2. Where a strike in pursuance of an industrial dispute has already commenced and is in existence at the time of the reference of the dispute to a Board, an arbitrator, a Labour Court, Tribunal or National Tribunal, the continuance of such strike shall

not be deemed to be illegal, provided that such strike was not at its commencement in contravention of the provisions of this Act or the continuance thereof was not prohibited under Section 10(3) or under Section 10-A(4-A) [Section 24(2)].

3. Any strike declared in consequence of an illegal lock-out shall not be deemed to be illegal [Section 24(3)].

3.6.2 Lock-outs

A 'lock-out' has been defined in Section 2(1) of this Act. A Lock-out means the temporary closing of a place of employment, or the suspension of work, or the refusal by an employer to continue to employ any number of workmen employed by him. Thus, a lock-out is resorted to by the given employer to compel the employees to accept his/her terms of working.

A lock-out is a coercive weapon available to the employer to impose his terms and conditions. In short, it is an antithesis of a strike. But it must be remembered that lock-out should not be misunderstood as closure. Closure and lock-out are two different terms.

Characteristics of Lock-outs

From the above mentioned definition of lock-out and the discussion we had so far, we can gather its following important characteristics. They are -

(1) Lock-out is an act of management and it is generally intended to put some pressure on the workers in order to make them agree to the terms and conditions of work of their employer.

(2) Mere suspension of work on account of shortage of raw materials, coal, supply of energy, water etc., does not amount to a lock-out.

(3) Lock-out indicates the temporary closure of the place of business and not the closure of the business itself.

(4) Lock-out is generally caused by strike, fear of disorder, fear of destruction of the properties of the firm, company etc. Most of these causes are the results of industrial disputes.

(5) Lock-out indicates the temporary closing of a place of employment, or the suspension of work, or the refusal of an employer to continue to employ any number of persons employed by him.

(6) Lock-out and discharge do not mean one and the same thing. In a lock-out, the relationship between an employer and his employees continues. But, in the case of discharge, this relationship is cut off.

(7) Lock-out does not indicate closure. Closure implies discontinuation of the business.

Important Provisions Relating to Lock-outs

The important provisions relating to lock-out made in this Act are as follows:

(A) Provisions relating to Prohibition of Lock-out [Section 22]

1. It is mentioned in Section 22(2) that, "No employer carrying on any public utility service shall lock-out any of his workmen –

    (a) Without giving them notice of lock-out as hereinafter provided, within six weeks before locking-out; or

    (b) Within fourteen days of giving such notice; or

    (c) Before the expiry of the date of lock-out specified in an such notice as aforesaid; or

    (d) During the pendency of any conciliation proceedings before a Conciliation Officer, and seven days' after the conclusion of such proceedings."

2. The notice of lock-out under this Section 22 shall not be necessary where there is already in existence a lock-out of any public utility service. However, the employer shall send the intimation of such lock-out on the day on which it is declared, to such authority, as may be specified by the Appropriate Government either generally or for a particular area or for a particular class of public utility services [Section 22(3)].

3. The notice of lock-out referred to in Section 22(2) is required to be given in such manner as may be prescribed [Section 22(5)].

4. If an any day an employer gives to any persons employed by him any such notices as are referred to in Section 22(2), he shall within five days thereof report to the Appropriate Government or to such other authority as that Government may prescribe, the number of such notices given on that date [Section 22(6)].

(B) Provisions relating to General Prohibition of lock-out [Section 23]

According to the provisions of Section 23, No employer shall declare a lock-out –

1. During the pendency of conciliation proceedings before a Board and seven days after the conclusion of such proceedings;

2. During the pendency of proceedings before a Labour Court, Tribunal or National Tribunal and two months after the conclusion of such proceedings;

3. During the pendency of arbitration proceedings before an arbitrator and two months after the conclusion of such proceedings, where a notification has been issued under Section 10-A(3-A); or

4. "During any period in which a settlement or award is in operation, in respect of any of the matters covered by the settlement or award."

(C) Provisions relating to Illegal Lock-out [Section 24]:
1. A lock-out shall be illegal, if (a) it is commenced or declared in contravention of Sections 22 or 23 which are mentioned above, or (b) it is continued in contravention of an order made under Section 10(3) or Section 10-A(4-A) [Section 24(1)].
2. Where a lock-out in pursuance of an industrial dispute has already commenced and is in existence at the time of reference of the dispute to a Board, an arbitrator, a Labour Court, Tribunal or National Tribunal, the continuance of such lock-out shall not be deemed to be illegal, provided that such lock-out was not at its commencement in contravention of the provisions of this Act, or the continuance thereof was not prohibited under Section 10(3) or under Section 10-A(4-A) [Section 24(2)].
3. Any lock-out declared in consequence of an illegal strike shall not be deemed to be illegal [Section 24(3)].

3.6.3 Prohibition of Strikes and Lock-outs in Public Utility Services [Section 22]

The provisions relating to prohibition of strikes and lock-outs in Public Utility Services in Section 22 is as follows –

No person employed in a public utility service shall go on strike in breach of contract (a) without giving to the employer notice of strike, as hereinafter provided, within six weeks before striking, or (b) within fourteen days of giving such notice; or (c) before the expiry of the date of strike specified in any such notice as aforesaid, or (d) during the pendency of any conciliation proceeding before a Conciliation Officer and seven days after the conclusion of such proceedings [Section 22(1)].

No employer carrying on any public utility service shall lock-out any of his workmen (a) without giving them notice of lock-out; as hereinafter provided, within six weeks before locking-out; or (b) within fourteen days of giving such notice, or (c) before the expiry of the date of lock-out specified in any such notice as aforesaid, or (d) during the pendency of any conciliation proceedings before a Conciliation Officer and seven days after the conclusion of such proceedings [Section 22(2)].

The notice of a strike or lock-out under Section 22 shall not be necessary where there is already in existence a strike or lock-out, as the case may be, in the public utility service, but the employer shall send a intimation of such strike or lock-out on the day on which it is declared; to such authority as may be specified by the Appropriate Government either generally or for a particular area or for a particular class of public utility services [Section 22(3)].

The notice of strike referred to in Section 22(1) shall be given by such number of persons to such person or persons and in such manner as may be prescribed [Section 22(4)].

The notice of lock-out referred to Section 22(2) shall be given in such manner as may be prescribed [Section 22(5)].

If on any day, an employer receives from any persons employed by him any such notices as are referred to in Section 22(1) or gives to any person employed by him any such notices as are referred to in Section 22(2), he shall within five days thereof report to the Appropriate Government or to such authority as that Government may prescribe, the number of such notice received or given on that day [Section 22(6)].

3.6.4 General Prohibition of Strikes and Lock-outs [Section 23]

Section 23 of this Act makes provisions for the general prohibition of Strikes and Lockouts. It says that no workman who is employed in any industrial establishment shall go on strike in breach of contract and no employer of any such workmen shall declare a lock-out - (a) during the pendency of conciliation proceedings before a Board and seven days after conclusion of such proceedings, or (b) during the pendency of proceeding before a Labour Court, Tribunal or National Tribunal and two months after the conclusion of such proceedings, or (bb) during the pendency of arbitration proceeding before an arbitrator and two months after the conclusion of such proceedings, where a notification has been issued under Section 10-A(3-A) or (c) during any period in which a settlement or award is in operation in respect of any of the matters covered by the settlement or award.

3.6.5 Illegal Strikes and Lock-outs [Section 24]

A strike or lock-out shall be illegal - (i) if it is commenced or declared in contravention of Sections 22 or 23 or (ii) if it is continued in contravention of an order made under sub-section (3) of Section 10 or sub-section 4(A) of Section 10-A [Section 24(1)].

Where a strike or lock-out in pursuance of an industrial dispute has already commenced and is in existence at the time of the reference of the dispute to a board, an arbitrator, a Labour Court, Tribunal or National Tribunal, the continuance of such strike or lock-out shall not be deemed to be illegal [Section 24(2)].

Provided that such strike or lock-out was not at its commencement in contravention of the provisions of this Act or the continuance thereof was not prohibited under Section 10(3) or 10-A(4-A) [Proviso to Section 24(2)].

A lock-out declared in consequence of an illegal strike or a strike declared in consequence of an illegal lock-out shall not be deemed to be illegal [Section 24(3)].

Thus, lock-outs and strikes declared in public utility services in the following circumstances are held illegal.

Strikes and lock-outs declared or commenced without giving proper notice in a prescribed manner or during the pendency of conciliation proceedings before a conciliation officer and after seven days after the conclusion of such proceedings. Then,

Strikes and lock-outs whether declared or commenced in public utility service are illegal if commenced or declared during the pendency of (a) conciliation proceedings before a Board and seven days after the conclusion of such proceedings; (b) Proceedings before Labour Court, an Industrial Tribunal or National Tribunal and two months after the conclusion of such proceedings (c) during any period in which a settlement or award is in operation in respect of any matters covered by the settlement or award.

3.6.6 Distinction between 'Strike' and 'Lock-out'

Strike	Lock-out
1. 'Strike' means a cessation of work by a body of persons employed in any industry acting in combination, or a concerted refusal, or a refusal under a common understanding of any number of persons who are or have been so employed to continue to work or to accept employment [Section 2(q)].	1. 'Lock-out' means the temporary closing of a place of employment, or the suspension of work, or the refusal by an employer to continue to employ any number of persons employed by him [Section 2(1)].
2. A strike is a weapon used by the employees or workmen acting together to force their employer to agree to the demands made by them.	2. Lock-out is an act resorted to by the management. It is the employer's weapon which is used by him to put pressure on the workers to make them agree to his terms and conditions as regards work. Lock-out can be described as an antithesis of a strike.
3. A strike implies a stoppage or cessation of work by the employees acting together. A strike can be 'stay-in strike' or 'Go-slow' strike.	3. Lock-out indicates the temporary closure of the place of business by an employer; but not the closure of the business itself.
4. In the case of a strike, an employer is not liable to pay wages for the period of strike.	4. In the case of a lawful lock-out, no compensation is payable by an employer. But, if it is illegal, an employer is liable to pay compensation for the period of lock-out to his employees.
5. A strike declared in consequence of an illegal lock-out, such strike is not deemed to be illegal [Section 24 (3)].	5. A lock-out declared in consequence of an illegal strike, such lock-out is not deemed to be illegal [Section 24(3)].
6. Any workman who commences, continues or otherwise acts in furtherance of a strike which is illegal, is punishable with imprisonment for a term which may extend upto one month, or with a fine which may extend upto ₹ Fifty, or, with both [Section 26(1)].	6. Any employer who commences, continues or otherwise acts in furtherance of a lock-out which is illegal, is punishable with imprisonment for a term which may extend upto one month or with a fine which may extend upto ₹ One Thousand or, with both [Section 26(2)].

3.7 Lay-off and Retrenchment

The provisions relating to 'lay-off' and 'retrenchment' have been included in Chapter V-A of this Act. However, both the definitions of the aforesaid terms are given in Section 2 of this Act.

3.7.1 Lay-off

Section 2(kkk) of this Act defines lay-off and, accordingly, 'lay-off' means the refusal, failure or inability of an employer to provide or to give employment to a workman whose name is borne on the muster rolls of his industrial establishment and who has not been retrenched. Such failure, refusal or inability to provide employment to a workman may be due to one of the following causes, such as –

(1) The accumulation of stocks.

(2) Shortages of coal, power, fuel or raw materials.

(3) The breakdown of machinery.

(4) Natural calamity.

(5) Any other connected reason –

A workman is deemed to have been laid off for any day if he presents himself for work at the establishment at the appointed time for the purpose and during the normal working hours on that day and is not given employment by the employer within two hours of his so presenting himself, but if the workman, instead of being given an employment at the commencement of any shift for any day is asked to present himself for the purpose during the second half of the shift for the day and is given employment, then, he shall be deemed to have been laid off only for one-half of that day. It is further provided in this section that if he is not given any such employment even after so remaining present he shall not be deemed to have been laid-off for the second half of the shift for the day and shall be entitled to full basic wages and dearness allowance for that part of the day.

3.7.2 Retrenchment

The term 'retrenchment' is defined in Section 2(oo) of the Industrial Disputes Act as follows:

'Retrenchment' means the termination by the employer of the services of a workman for any reason whatsoever, otherwise than as punishment inflicted by way of disciplinary act.

To retrench means to end, cease or to conclude. However, retrenchment does not include (i) voluntary retirement of a workman, or (ii) retirement of a workman on reaching the age of superannuation if the contract of the employment between the employer and the workman concerned contains a stipulation in that behalf, or (iii) termination of service of a workman on the ground of continued ill health or (iv) termination of service of the workmen as a result of the non-renewal of the contract of employment between the employer and the workmen concerned on its expiry or of such contract being terminated under a stipulation in that behalf contained therein.

Thus, it seems that it is only when the services of a workman are dispensed with on the ground of surplus labour, then, the termination of services of such workman may be called retrenchment.

3.7.3 Right of Workman Laid-off for Compensation [Section 25-C]

Section 25-C of this Act provides the workman concerned with the right to receive lay-off compensation. It is given to a workman to relieve the hardship on the grounds of human public policy. The principle of social justice is followed in awarding lay-off compensation. The provisions regarding the payment of compensation to a workman who is laid off are contained in Section 25-C, is reproduced as follows:

The important provisions of Section 25-C can be summarised as follows:

(1) For entitlement of compensation, the workman should not be a *badli* or casual workman and his name must appear on the muster-rolls of the industrial establishment.

(2) The workman must have completed not less than one full year of continuous service.

(3) When the above mentioned conditions are fulfilled, the workman, whether laid-off continuously or intermittently, shall be paid compensation by his employer for all days during which he is laid-off, of course, except for such weekly holidays as may intervene.

(4) The rate at which the compensation is to be paid shall be equal to fifty per cent of the total basic wages as well as dearness allowance that would have been payable to the workman had he not been laid-off.

(5) Compensation shall not be payable to a workman during any period of twelve months after the expiry of the first forty-five days if there is an agreement to that effect between the employer and the workmen.

(6) Where a workman is laid-off for a period of forty-five days during the period of twelve months, the employer can retrench the workman, according to the provisions contained in Section 25-F at any time after the expiry of the first forty-five days of lay-off.

(7) When the employer retrenches the workman, any compensation paid to the workman for having been laid-off during the preceding twelve months may be set-off against the compensation payable for retrenchment of the workman.

3.7.4 Conditions Precedent to Retrenchment of Workmen [Section 25-F]

We have already studied the meaning of the term 'retrenchment'. Now, let us consider the conditions precedent to retrenchment of workmen under this Act.

No workman employed in an industry who has been in continuous service for not less than one year under an employer shall be retrenched by the employer until –

(1) The workman has been served one month's notice in writing indicating the reasons for retrenchment and the period of notice has expired or the workman has been paid in lieu of such notice, wages for the period of such notice.

(2) The workman has been paid at the time of retrenchment, compensation which shall be equivalent to fifteen days average pay for every completed year of continuous service or any part thereof of six months; and

(3) Notice in the prescribed manner is served on the Appropriate Government or such authority as may be specified by the Appropriate Government by notification in the Official Gazette [Section 25-F].

3.7.5 Procedure for Retrenchment

Section 25-G of this Act makes clear the procedure for retrenchment. This section applies the rule of 'Last come First go' to retrenchment. Section 25-G states that where any workman in an industrial establishment, who is a citizen of India, is to be retrenched and he belongs to a particular category of workmen in that establishment, in the absence of any agreement between the employer and the workman in this behalf, the employer shall ordinarily retrench the workman who was the last person to be employed in that category, unless for reasons to be recorded, the employer retrenches any other workman.

3.7.6 Re-employment of Retrenched Workman [Section 25-H]

The provisions relating to re-employment of retrenched workman is made in Section 25-H of this Act as under:

Where any workmen are retrenched and the employer proposes to take into his employment any persons, he shall, in such manner as may be prescribed, give an opportunity to the retrenched workmen who are citizens of India, to present themselves for re-employment and, such retrenched workmen, who offer themselves for re-employment shall have preference over other persons.

3.7.7 Difference between Lock-out and Lay-off

	Lock-out		Lay-off
1.	Lock-out means the temporary closing of a place of employment or the suspension of work or the refusal by an employer to continue to employ any number of persons employed by him.	1.	Lay-off means the failure, refusal or inability of an employer on account of shortage of coal, power, fuel or raw materials or the accumulation of stock or the breakdown of machinery or natural calamity or of any other connected reasons to provide employment to a workman whose name is borne on the muster-rolls of this industrial establishment and who has not been retrenched.

Lock-out	Lay-off
2. Lock-out is resorted to by an employer to pressurise the workmen to accept his demand(s).	2. Lay-off is really not connected with the economic reasons because of which it becomes difficult for an employer to provide employment and such reasons are therefore beyond his control.
3. Lock-out arises due to an industrial dispute. It continues during the period of dispute.	3. Lay-off is not concerned or connected with an industrial dispute.
4. When lock-out is to be declared, the employer is not bound to pay any compensation to the workmen.	4. When the workmen are laid off, the employer has to pay compensation to those workmen who are laid-off.
5. When lock-out is to be declared, the employer has to fulfil certain conditions as those prescribed in Sections 22 and 23 of this Act.	5. No such conditions are required to be fulfilled before the declaration of lay-off.
6. When lock-out is declared, workman is not required to remain present at the factory doors or at the doors of establishment, at the commencement of working hours.	6. When workmen are laid-off, the laid-off workmen have to remain present for work at the time of the commencement of working hours.
7. In the case of lock-out, lock-out in excess of 45 days in a year does not give an employer any right or option to retrench the workmen.	7. The employer gets an option to retrench the workmen if lay-off continues for more than forty five days in a year.
8. When lock-out is declared, the workmen loose their full amount of wages.	8. When workmen are laid-off, they lose half the amount of their wages.
9. When lock-out is declared, no alternative employment is provided to the workmen concerned.	9. When workmen are laid-off, the laid-off workmen may be provided or offered an alternative employment.

3.7.8 Difference between Retrenchment and Lock-out

Retrenchment	Lock-out
1. The term 'retrenchment' as used in this Act means the termination by the employer of the service of a workman for any reason whatsoever, otherwise than as punishment inflicted by way of disciplinary action. It does not include –	1. Lock-out means the temporary closing down of an employment place or suspension of work or the refusal by an employer to continue to employ any number of persons employed by him.

Retrenchment	Lock-out
(a) Voluntary retirement of a workman. (b) Retirement of a workman on reaching superannuation age. (c) Termination of service of workman as a result of non-renewal of the contract of employment. (d) Termination of services on the ground of continued ill health of a workman.	
2. Retrenchment is done to remove surplus labour.	2. Lock-out is coercive and is declared by employer for compelling the workmen to accept his/her demand(s).
3. Workmen may be retrenched independent of an industrial dispute.	3. Lock-out is declared because of an industrial dispute.
4. Retrenchment is permanent.	4. Lock-out is temporary.
5. Retrenchment puts an end to the relationship between an employer and his workmen.	5. In the case of lock-out, the relationship between the employer and his workmen continues.

3.7.9 Distinction between 'Retrenchment' and 'Lay-off'

Retrenchment	Lay-off
1. By retrenchment is meant the termination of service of a workman by an employer for any reason, whatsoever, otherwise than as punishment inflicted by way of disciplinary action. Retrenchment does not include voluntary retirement, because of reaching the age of superannuation, termination of services either because of continued ill health of a workman or because of non-renewal of employment contract.	1. Lay-off means the failure, refusal or inability of an employer to provide employment to the workmen employed by him on account of the following reasons: (a) Storage of coal, power, fuel, raw materials. (b) Accumulation of stock. (c) Breakdown of machinery. (d) Natural calamity. (e) Any other connective reason. The names of workmen who are laid off must appear on the muster-rolls and they must not be retrenched.

Retrenchment	Lay-off
2. Workmen are retrenched to remove surplus labour.	2. Workmen are laid off because of the reasons mentioned above which are beyond the control of the given employer.
3. Retrenchment is permanent.	3. Lay-off is temporary.
4. In retrenchment, the relationship between the employer and his workmen comes to an end.	4. In lay-off, the relationship between the employer and his workmen is suspended temporarily.

3.8 Closure of an Industrial Undertaking [Section 25 FFA]

The provisions made in Section 25-FFA of this Act regarding the notice to be given for closing down of any undertaking and, accordingly, an employer who intends to close down an undertaking shall serve, at least sixty days before the date on which the intended closure is to become effective, a notice, in the prescribed manner on the Appropriate Government stating clearly the reason(s) for the intended closure of the undertaking:

Provided that nothing in this section shall apply to:

(1) An undertaking in which

    (a) Less than fifty workmen are employed, or

    (b) Less than fifty workmen were employed on an average per working day in the preceding twelve months,

(2) An undertaking set up for the construction of buildings, bridges, roads, canals, dams or for other construction work or project [Section 25-FFA(i)].

Notwithstanding anything contained in sub-section (1), the Appropriate Government may, if it is satisfied that owing to such exceptional circumstances as accident to the undertaking or death of the employer concerned or the like it is necessary so to do, by order, direct that provisions of sub-section (1) shall not apply in relation to such undertaking for such period as may be specified in the order [Section 25-FFA(2)]

3.8.1 Compensation to be paid to Workmen in Case of Closing Down of an Undertaking [Section 25-FFF]

By closure of an undertaking is meant the closing down of industrial activity and, as a consequence, workmen employed in such undertaking are rendered jobless. When an undertaking is closed, compensation is required to be paid to the workmen working in such undertaking. Provisions have been made in Section 25-FFF of this Act as regards the compensation to be paid to workmen in the case of closing down of an undertaking. These provisions are as follows:

Where an undertaking is closed down for any reason whatever, every workman who has been in continuous service for not less than one year in that undertaking immediately before such closure shall subject to the provisions of sub-section (2) be entitled to notice and compensation in accordance with the provisions of Section 25-F as if the workman has been retrenched [Section 25-FFF(i)].

It is also provided that where the undertaking is closed down on account of unavoidable circumstances beyond the control of the employer concerned, the compensation to be paid to the workman under clause (b) of Section 25-F shall not exceed his average pay for three months [Proviso to Section 25-FFF(i)].

An undertaking which is closed down for reason(s), merely of:
(1) Financial difficulties including financial loss; or
(2) Accumulation of undisposed stocks, or
(3) The expiry of the period of the lease or licence granted to it; or
(4) In case where the undertaking is engaged in mining operations, exhaustion of the minerals in the area in which such operations are carried on, shall not be deemed to have been closed down on account of unavoidable circumstances beyond the control of the employer within the meaning of the proviso to this sub-section.

This section further states that notwithstanding anything contained in sub-section (1) where an undertaking engaged in mining operations is closed down by reason(s) merely of exhaustion of the minerals in the area in which such operations are carried on, no workman referred to in that sub-section shall be entitled to any notice or compensation in accordance with the provisions of Section 25-F, if –
(a) The employer provides the workman with alternative employment with effect from the date of closure at the same remunerations as he was entitled to receive, and on the same terms and conditions of service as were applicable to him, immediately before the closure,
(b) The service of workman has not been interrupted by such alternative employment; and
(c) The employer is, under the terms of such alternative employment or otherwise, legally liable to pay to the workman, in the event of his retrenchment, compensation on the basis that his service has been continuous and has not been interrupted by such alternative employment [Section 25-FFF(1-A)].

For the purposes of sub-sections (1) and (1-A), the expressions 'minerals' and 'mining operations' shall have the meanings respectively assigned to them in clause (a) and (b) of Section 3 of the Mines and Minerals (Regulation and Development) Act, 1957 [Section 25- FFF(1-B)].

Where any undertaking set up for the construction of building, bridges, canals, dams or other construction work is closed down on account of the completion of the work within two years from the date on which the undertaking had been set up, no workman employed therein shall be entitled to any compensation under clause (b) of Section 25-F but if the construction work is not so completed within two years, he shall be entitled to notice and compensation under that section for every completed year of continuous service or any part thereof in excess of six-months [Section 25-FFF(2)].

3.8.2 Procedure of Closing Down on Undertaking [Section 25-O]

The provisions relating to the procedure of closing down an undertaking, the powers of the Appropriate Government, compensation to be paid to the workmen etc., have been made in Section 25-O of this Act, which is as follows:

1. An employer who intends to close down an undertaking of an industrial establishment to which this Chapter applies shall, in the prescribed manner, apply, for prior permission at least ninety days before the date on which the intended closure is to become effective, to the Appropriate Government, stating clearly the reasons for the intended closure of the undertaking and copy of such application shall also be served simultaneously on the representatives of the workman in the prescribed manner [Section 25-O(1)] It is also provided that nothing in this sub-section shall apply to an undertaking set up for the construction of buildings, bridges, roads, canals, dams or for other construction work [Proviso to Section 25-O(1)].

2. Where an application for permission has been made under sub-section (1), the Appropriate Government, after making such inquiry as it thinks fit and after giving a reasonable opportunity of being heard to the employer, the workmen and the persons interested in such closure may, having regard to the genuineness and adequacy of the reasons stated by the employer, the interests of the general public and all other relevant factors, by order and for the reasons to be recorded in writing, grant or refuse to grant such permission and a copy of such order shall be communicated to the employer and the workmen [Section 25-O(2)].

3. Where an application has been made under sub-section (1) and the Appropriate Government does not communicate the order granting or refusing to grant permission to the employer within a period of sixty days from the date on which such application is made, the permission applied for shall be deemed to have been granted on the expiration of the said period of sixty days [Section 25-O(3)].

4. An order of the Appropriate Government granting or refusing to grant permission shall, subject to the provisions of sub-section (5), be final and binding on all the parties and shall remain in force for one year from the date of such order [Section 25-O(4)].

5. The Appropriate Government may either on its own motion or on the application made by the employer or any workman, review its order granting or refusing to grant permission under sub-section (2) or refer the matter to a Tribunal for

adjudication [Section 25-O(5)]. It is provided that where a reference has been made to a Tribunal under this sub-section, it shall pass an award within a period of thirty days from the date of such reference [Proviso to Section 25-O(5)].

6. Where no application for permission under sub-section (1) is made within the period specified therein, or where the permission for closure has been refused, the closure of the undertaking shall be deemed to be illegal from the date of closure and the workmen shall be entitled to all the benefits under any law for the time being in force of if the undertaking had not been closed down [Section 25-O(6)].

7. Notwithstanding anything contained in the foregoing provisions of this section, the Appropriate Government may, if it is satisfied that owing to such exceptional circumstances as accident in the undertaking or death of employer or the like it is necessary so to do, by order, direct that the provisions of sub-section (I) shall not apply in relation to such undertaking for such period as may be specified in the order [Section 25-O(7)].

8. Where an undertaking is permitted to be closed down under sub-section (2) or where permission for closure is deemed to be granted under sub-section, (3), every workman who is employed in that undertaking immediately before the date of application for permission under this section, shall be entitled to receive compensation which shall be equivalent to fifteen days' average pay for every completed year of continuous service or any part thereof in excess of six months [Section 25-O(8)].

3.9 Penalties

The provisions of penalties for various offences are made in this section of this as follows:

(1) Penalty for Closure [Section 25-R]

Any employer who closes down an undertaking without complying with the provisions of sub-section (1) of Section 25-O shall be punishable with imprisonment for a term which may extend upto six months or with fine which may extend upto five thousand rupees or, with both [Section 25(1)].

Any employer, who contravenes an order refusing to grant permission to close down an undertaking under sub-section (2) or Section 25-O or a direction given under Section 25-P shall be punishable with imprisonment for a term which may extend upto one year, or with fine which may extend upto five thousand rupees, or with both, and where the contravention is a continuing one, with a further fine which may extend upto two thousand rupees for every day during which such contravention continues after the conviction [Section 25-R(2)].

(2) Penalty for Committing Unfair Labour Practices [Section 25-U]

No employer or workman or a trade union, whether registered under the Trade Union Act, 1926, or not shall commit any unfair labour practice [Section 25-T]. Unfair labour practice relates to those practices as specified in the Fifth Schedule [Section 2(ra)]. Any person who commits any unfair labour practice is punishable with imprisonment for a term which may extend upto six months or with fine which may extend upto Rupees one thousand or with both [Section 25-U].

(3) Penalty for Illegal Strikes and Lock-outs [Section 26]

Any workman who commences, continues or otherwise acts in furtherance of a strike which is not legal under this Act is punishable with imprisonment for a period which may be extended upto one month or with a fine which may be extended upto fifty rupees or with both [Section 26(1)].

Any employer who commences, continues or otherwise acts in furtherance of a lock-out which is not legal under this Act, is punishable with imprisonment for a term which may extend to one month or with a fine which may be imposed upto rupees one thousand or with both [Section 26(2)].

The remedy which is indicated in this Section 26 is the statutory remedy. No other relief outside this Act can be available on general principles of jurisprudence. The relief, therefore, of compensation by proceedings in arbitration is contrary to law.

(4) Penalty for Instigation [Section 27]

The terms 'Instigation' or 'Incitation' have some deeper meaning than a mere asking a person to do any particular act. These words or terms seem to convey the meaning "to good or urge forward or to encourage the doing of an act. Any person who instigates or incites others to take part in, or otherwise acts in furtherance of a strike or lock-out which is not legal under this Act, is punishable with imprisonment for a term which may extend to six months or with a fine which may also be imposed up to Rupee one thousand or, with both.

(5) Penalty for giving financial aid to Illegal Strikes and Lock-outs [Section 28]

Any person who knowingly applies or expends any money in direct furtherance or supports any illegal strikes or lock-out is punishable with imprisonment for a term which may be extended upto six months or with fine which may be extended upto one thousand rupees or, with both.

(6) Penalty for Breach of Settlement or Award [Section 29]

Any person who commits a breach of term of any settlement or award, which is binding on such person under this Act, is punishable with imprisonment for a period which may extend upto six months or with a fine of ₹ .... or, with both; and where the breach is a continuing one, with a further fine which may extend upto Rupees two hundred for every day during which the breach continues after the conviction for the first breach and the Court trying the offence, if it imposes a fine on the offender, may direct that the whole or any part of the fine realised from him shall be paid, by way of compensation, to any person who, in the opinion of the Court, has been injured by such breach.

This Section 29 of this Act covers strikes in violation of settlement.

(7) Penalty for Disclosing Confidential Information [Section 30]

Any person who purposely or wilfully discloses any such information as is referred to in Section 21 of this Act in contravention of its provisions, on complaint made by or on behalf of the trade union or individual whose business is affected, is punishable with imprisonment for a term which may extend upto six months, or with a fine which may extend upto Rupees one thousand or, with both [Section 30].

(8) Penalty for Closure without Notice [Section 30-A]

Any employer who closes down any undertaking without complying with the provisions of Section 25-FFA of this Act is punishable with imprisonment for a period which may be extended upto six months, or with a fine which may extend upto Rupees five thousand or, with both [Section 30-A].

(9) Penalty for other Offences [Section 31]

Any employer who contravenes the provisions of Section 33 of this Act is punishable with the imprisonment for a period which may extend upto six months or with fine which may extend upto Rupees one thousand or, with both [Section 31(1)].

Any person who contravenes any provisions of this Act or any rule made thereunder is punishable, if not other penalty elsewhere is provided by or under this Act for such contravention, with fine which may extend upto Rupees one hundred [Section 31(2)].

(10) Offences Committed by Companies, Association of Persons, etc.

According to Section 32 of this Act, "Where a person committing an offence under this Act is a company, or other body corporate, or an association of persons (whether incorporated or not), every director, manager, secretary, agent or other officer or person concerned with the management thereof shall, unless he proves that the offence was committed without his knowledge or consent, be deemed to be guilty of such offence."

(11) Cognisance of Offences [Section 34]

(a) No Court shall take cognisance of any offence punishable under this Act or of the abetment of any such offence, save on complaint made by or under the authority of the Appropriate Government [Section 34(1)].

(b) No Court inferior to that of [a Metropolitan Magistrate or a Judicial Magistrate of the First Class] shall try any offence punishable under this Act [Section on 34(2)].

The Factories Act, 1948

3.10 Introduction

Labour legislation, in essence, has socio-economic dimensions to it. This is so, since it relates to those problems that plague the labour force, both at an individual and collective level *vis-à-vis* his/her working conditions. In other words, it touches not only his social aspects of his life but also goes to embrace his economic well-being, as well. Of late, we are witness to an era where large scale industrialisation bringing with its own set of problems – namely, one that affects the working class people, in the form of, long working hours, industrial fatigue, industrial hazards, bad environmental conditions at work place, insanitation and, thereby to various diseases etc.

The problems created by rapidly growing industrialisation can broadly be classified under various heads, such as, working conditions, industrial safety, making payments of wages to the workers, industrial relations, social security etc. In order to minimise their severity and to protect the interest of the workers, various Acts relating to labour have been passed. The Factories Act, 1948, is one of such Acts.

In the early days of modern industrial system, there were no legal restrictions on the employers and, thus, they were free to use their labour in any manner they pleased. The result was the exploitation of workers in many ways. That apart, the conditions in factories were also intolerable and inhuman. The heart-rending conditions of workers evoked the sympathies of many social workers and leaders.

The manufacturers of Lancashire also pressed the Government to pass factory legislation in India because they thought that the absence of such legislation might give the Indian manufacturers an unfair advantage. Besides this, the rapid growth of industries and its attendant ills, namely, deteriorating conditions of workers, exploitation etc., pointed to the need of legislation for regulating the working conditions in factories.

The passing of the Indian Factories Act, 1881, was a watershed development in labour legislation. This Act provided for *inter alia* the prohibition of employment of children below seven years of age and prescribed for nine hours' work for a day. Thus, though the children working in the factories got protection to a certain extent, the conditions of the adult workers could not improve and they continued to suffer. Moreover, in the absence of proper factory inspection, the Factories Act, 1881, remained almost a dead letter.

In pursuance of the recommendations made in the First Labour Conference held in Berlin in 1890, a commission was appointed by the Government of India to investigate into various labour problems and considering the recommendations of that commission, the Indian Factories Act, 1891, was passed. The Indian Factories Act, 1911, was passed thereafter, which mandated twelve-hour a day work for adult male workers.

The Indian Factories Act, 1911, was amended in 1923, 1926 and 1931 in order to incorporate certain changes relating to conditions of workers working in factories. Thus, the Amendment Acts of 1891, 1911, 1922 etc., amongst others, widened the scope of the definition of factory, placed limitations on hours of work of women employees, prohibited employment of children and women in some dangerous processes in factories and also restricted the number of work hours for all adult workers.

Thereafter, some minor amendments were made by the Acts of 1926 and 1931. Meanwhile, the Royal Commission on Labour was appointed in 1929 which conducted a comprehensive inquiry into various labour problems in India and suggested certain recommendations. On the basis of the recommendations made by the Royal Commission on Labour, the factory legislation was thoroughly overhauled by the Indian Factories Act, 1934.

The primary object of the aforesaid Act was to protect workers employed in factories against industrial and occupational hazards. It introduced several new things, for example, classification of factories into seasonal and perennial; introduction of a third group of non-adult adolescent workers; the principle of spreadover, regulation of over-time, working hours of workers etc. This Act too was amended several times, the more important of it being the amendments of 1940, 1945, 1946 and 1947. These enactments definitely strengthened the protective provision of the Act as regards the employment of children in factories and also introduced the following three important features:

(1) Annual holidays with pay;

(2) A 48-hour week; and

(3) Canteen for workers.

Thereafter, in 1948, the whole of the legislation was again recast and the Factories Act, 1948, was enacted. The said Act was amended several times and, amongst them, the following were the most important.

Certain sections of the Factories Act, 1948, were replaced and an entirely new chapter on "annual leave with wages for Chapter VIII of the Act was substituted by an Amendment Act, 1954." In 1956, it was amended wherein it was mandated to have 240 days' work in a calendar year as the minimum attendance necessary to qualify for leave with wages. Lately, by an Amendment Act, 1987, some sections were amended. Some provisions of the Amendment Act, 1987, came into force with effect from 1st December, 1987, and others from 1st June, 1988.

3.11 Objects and the Scope of the Act

We have already considered herein the certain objects of various Factories Acts passed before 1948. The preamble of the Factories Act, 1948, lays down the basic object of the Act in the following words:

"Whereas it is expedient to consolidate and amend the law regulating labour in the factories."

Thus, to regulate the labour in the factories and to help improve their condition is the basic object behind passing this Act.

Objects can be enumerated as follows:

(1) To protect the workers employed in factories against industrial and occupational hazards.

(2) To make elaborate provisions regarding the workers' health, safety and welfare for protecting the workers' interest.

(3) To make provisions for restricting the working hours in the factories.

(4) To make provisions regarding the employment of young persons.

(5) To make provisions regarding the annual leave with wages.

(6) To appoint necessary staff for the proper implementation of the Act.

(7) To make every necessary effort for improving the conditions of workers in the factories and protecting their interests.

The Factories Act, 1948, widened the definition of the term 'factory', introduced certain definitions of new words, expressions etc., abolished the distinction between seasonal and non-seasonal-factories, extended widely the basic provisions of health, safety and welfare to all workers, raised the minimum age for the admission of children and reduced the maximum permissible daily hours of work of children, fixed the hours of work in respect of adults etc.

The Factories Act, 1948, extends to the whole of India. It came into force on 1st April, 1949. Section 116 of this Act provides that unless otherwise provided this Act shall apply to factories belonging to the Central or any State Government.

The Act covers all industrial establishments employing ten or more workers where power is used and twenty or more workers where power is not used. Other factories can also be brought within the purview of this Act through a special notification.

3.12 Definitions

In Section 2 of the Act, definitions of different words, expressions and concepts are given which are as under.

(1) Adult [Section 2(a)]

'Adult' means a person who has completed his eighteenth year of age.

(2) Adolescent [Section 2(b)]

'Adolescent' means a person who has completed his fifteenth year of age but has not completed his eighteenth year.

(3) Calendar Year [Section 2(bb)]

'Calender Year' means the period of twelve months beginning with the first day of January in any year.

(4) Child [Section 2(c)]

'Child' means a person who has not completed his fifteenth years of age.

(5) Competent Person [Section 2(ca)]

'Competent person' in relation to any provision of this Act means a person or an institution recognised as such by the Chief Inspector for the purpose of carrying out tests, examinations and inspections required to be done in the factory under the provisions of this Act having regard to:

(a) the qualifications and experience of the person and facilities available at his disposal; or

(b) the qualifications and experience of the persons employed in such institution and facilities available therein, with regard to the conduct of such tests, examinations and inspections, and more than one person or institution can be recognised as a competent person in relation to a factory.

(6) Hazardous Process [Section 2(cb)]

'Hazardous process' means and includes any process or any activity in relation to an industry specified in the first schedule where, unless special care is taken, raw materials used therein or the intermediate or finished products, byproducts, wastes or effluents thereof would:

(i) cause material impairment to the health of persons engaged in or connected therewith, or

(ii) result in the pollution of the general environment.

It is further provided that the State Government may amend the First Schedule by way of addition, omission or variation of any industry specified in the said schedule, by proper notification in the Official Gazette.

(7) Young Person [Section 2(d)]

'Young person' means a person who is either child or an adolescent.

Section 67 of this Act provides that no person may be employed in a factory if he has not completed his fourteenth year of age. Considering the provision thus made, workers who are young person must be those who have completed fourteen years of age but not completed their eighteenth year of age.

(8) Day [Section 2(e)]

'Day' means a period of twenty four hours beginning at midnight.

In one case (Chick V/s. Smith), it was held that no fraction of time is admissible in law except in cases where it is very essential to distinguish. Day denotes the period from midnight to midnight.

In this Act, references to time of day are references to Indian Standard Time, being five and half hours ahead of Greenwich Mean Time [Section 3].

It is provided that for any area in which Indian Standard Time is not ordinarily observed, the State Government is competent to make rules:

(a) Specifying the area;

(b) Defining the local mean time ordinarily observed therein; and

(c) Permitting such time to be observed in all or any of the facilities situated in the area.

(9) Week [Section 2(f)]

'Week' means a period of seven days beginning at midnight on Saturday night or such other night as may be approved in writing for a particular area by the Chief Inspector of Factories.

(10) Power [Section 2(g)]

'Power' means electrical energy or any other form of energy which is mechanically transmitted and is not generated by human or animal energy.

(11) Prime Mover [Section 2(h)]

'Prime mover' means any engine, motor or any other appliance which generates or otherwise provides power.

(12) Transmission Machinery [Section 2(i)]

'Transmission machinery' means any shaft, wheel, pulley, drum, system of pulleys, coupling, clutch, driving belt or any other appliance or device by which the motion of a prime mover is transmitted to or received by any machinery or any other appliance.

(13) Machinery [Section 2(j)]

'Machinery' includes prime movers, [which include generating or otherwise providing power], transmission machinery and all other appliances whereby power is generated, transformed, transmitted or applied.

(14) Manufacturing process [Section 2(k)]

'Manufacturing process' means any process for:

(a) making, altering, repairing, ornamenting, finishing, packing, oiling, washing, cleaning, breaking up, demolishing, or otherwise treating or adapting any article or substance with a view to its use, sale, transport, delivery or disposal, or

(b) pumping oil, water, sewage or any other substance, or

(c) generating, transforming or transmitting power, or

(d) composing types for printing, printing by letters press, lithography, photogravure or any other similar process or book binding; or

(e) constructing, reconstructing, repairing, refitting, finishing or breaking up ships or vessels or

(f) preserving or storing any article in cold storage.

The abovementioned definition makes clear the meaning of the manufacturing process. In deciding whether or not a particular business or process is a manufacturing process, the circumstances of each particular case must be considered. To constitute a manufacturing process, it is very essential that there must be some sort of transformation of articles.

(15) Worker [Section 2(l)]

'Worker' means any person employed, directly or by or through any agency, including a contractor, with or without the knowledge of the principal employer, whether for remuneration or not, in any manufacturing process or in cleaning any part of the machinery or premises used for a manufacturing process or in any other kind of work incidental to or connected with the manufacturing process or the subject of manufacturing process but the term 'worker' does not include any member of the armed forces of the union.

Before 1976, persons employed by contractors or agents were not considered as workers. But the Factories (Amendment) Act, 1976, widened the scope of the definition of 'worker' and, accordingly, any person employed by an agency or a contractor with or without the knowledge of the principal employer is also a worker. Even the Supreme Court also expressed the view in the Central Railway Workshop V/s Vishwanath case that the definition of the term 'worker' is sufficiently wide as it includes not only persons employed in a manufacturing process but also all those person who are employed in cleaning any part of machinery or premises used for manufacturing process. But, here, it must be remembered that where all workers within the meaning of this definition under this Act would be employees, but all employees would not be workers.

The expression 'employed' in the definition of Worker [Section 2(l)] under this Act indicates that the relationships of servant and master must exist. It is immaterial whether the worker employed in the process of manufacturing is paid his wages or not or is paid wages on piece rate or time-rate basis.

Whether a particular person is a worker or not is decided upon the terms of contract between him and the employer. The term "worker' does not include an independent contractor or his coolies or servants as they are not under the control and supervision of the employer.

In different cases, the following persons were declared to be 'workers'.
(a) Any apprentice or an honorary employee.
(b) Any person engaged in a manufacturing process [Section 2(k)] whether for wages or not.
(c) Any worker doing clerical job satisfying the test as laid down in the definition.
(d) Any person selling manufactured articles in the premises of the factory.
(e) Piece-rate worker who is a regular and is under an obligation to work either for fixed period or between fixed hours as per contract of employment of service [Maharashtra State V/s Waji].
(f) Time office clerk and time keeper in a workshop.
(g) It was decided in one case [Rahtas Industries V/s. Lakhan] that a person who was engaged in a paper factory and used to receive raw materials like, rags and waste papers is a worker.

But the following persons were held that they were not workers:
(a) A piece-rate worker who used to go to the factory at his sweet will was not considered as worker.
(b) The employees of a sole selling agent of the products of a factory were not held to be its workers [Crown V/s Narayan].
(c) Selling agents occupying a room in a factory.
(d) Partners working in the canteen.

(16) Factory [Section 2(m)

'Factory' means any premises including the precincts thereof:
(a) Whereon ten or more workers are working or were working on any day of the preceding twelve months and in any part of which a manufacturing process is being carried on with the aid of power or is ordinarily so carried on or
(b) Whereon twenty or more workers are working or were working on any day of the preceding twelve months and in any part of which a manufacturing process is being carried on without the aid of power, or is ordinarily so carried on - but it does not include a mine which is subject to the operation of the Mines Act, 1952, or a mobile unit belonging to the armed forces of the Union a railway running shed or a hotel restaurant or any eating house or place or poly house or green house engaged in activity of floriculture or high value crops.

In short, a 'factory' is any premises whereon ten or more persons are engaged if power is used or twenty or more persons are engaged in any manufacturing process if power is not used. The mine, a mobile unit of the Armed forces of the Union, a railway running shed, a hotel restaurant or any eating place are excluded.

(17) Occupier [Section 2(n)]

The term 'occupier' is defined in Section 2(n) of the Factories Act, 1948, as follows:

'Occupier' of a factory is the person who has ultimate control over the affairs of the factory. Provided that –
(a) In the case of a firm or any other association of individuals, any one of the individual partners or members thereof shall be deemed to be the occupier;
(b) If it is a company, any one of the directors shall be deemed to be the occupier;
(c) In the case of a factory which is owned and/or controlled by the Central Government or any State Government or any local authority, the person or persons appointed to manage the affairs of the factory by the Central Government or the State Government or the local authority, as the case may be, shall be deemed to be the occupier.

It is provided further that in the case of a ship which is being repaired or on which maintenance work is being carried out in a dry dock which is available for hire.

3.13 Authorities

(A) The Inspecting Staff

The inspecting staff, so far as the Factories Act, 1948, is concerned includes inspectors and certifying surgeons. Provisions relating to the appointments, powers, duties etc., of the inspecting staff have been made in Chapter II of this Act by including three sections, i.e., 8th, 9th and 10th. Section 8 provides for the appointments of factory inspectors; while Section 9 deals with the powers of the inspectors. Section 10 makes provisions for the appointment of certifying surgeons and their duties are also made clear in it.

Now, let us study these sections in detail.

Appointments of Inspectors:

The Factories Act envisages the following five types of inspectors;

(1) Inspectors, (2) Chief Inspectors, (3) Additional Chief Inspectors, (4) Joint Chief Inspectors, and (5) Deputy Chief Inspectors.

Section 8(1) of this Act provides that the State Government may, by notification in the Official Gazette, appoint such persons who possess the prescribed qualifications as the inspectors for the purposes of this Act. The State Government may assign to them such local limits as it may think proper.

Appointment of Chief Inspector

The State Government, by giving notification in the Official Gazette, may appoint any person to be a Chief Inspector who shall, in addition to the powers conferred on him under this Act, exercise the powers of an Inspector throughout the State [Section 8(2)]

Appointments of Additional Chief Inspectors, Joint Chief Inspectors and Deputy Chief Inspectors

The State Government may also, by notification in the Official Gazette, appoint as many additional Chief Inspectors, Joint Chief Inspectors and Deputy Chief Inspectors and other officers as it thinks fit to assist the Chief Inspector and to exercise such of the powers of the Chief Inspector as may be specified in the notification [Section 8(2-A)].

Every Additional Chief Inspector, Joint Chief Inspector, Deputy Chief Inspector and other officers appointed under sub-section (2–A) of this section shall, in addition to the powers of the Chief Inspector specified in the notification by which he is appointed, exercise the power of an Inspector throughout the State [Section 8(2–B)].

Disabilities for Appointment as Inspector

No person shall be appointed under all sub-sections of Section 8 mentioned above or having been so appointed, shall continue to hold office, or who is or becomes directly or indirectly interested in a factory or in any of the processes or any business carried on therein or in any patent or machinery connected therewith [Section 8(3)].

Every District Magistrate shall be an Inspector for his/her district [Section 8(4)].

Appointments of Additional Inspectors

The State Government may, by notification in the Official Gazette, appoint such public officers as it thinks fit to be additional Inspectors for all or any of the purposes of this Act, within such local limits as it may assign to them respectively [Section 8(5)].

In any area where there is more than one Inspector, the State Government may, by notification as aforesaid, declare the powers which such Inspectors shall respectively exercise and the Inspectors to whom the prescribed notices are to be sent [Section 8(6)].

Every Chief Inspector, Additional Chief Inspector, Joint Chief Inspector, Deputy Chief Inspector, Inspector and all other officers appointed under this Section 8 shall be deemed to be the public servant within the meaning of the Indian Penal Code and shall be officially subordinate to such authority as the State Government may specify in this behalf [Section 8(7)].

The meaning of all the above provisions of Section 8 is crystal clear. However, certain points may need to be noted. They are:

(1) For the purposes of sub-section 4 of Section 8 of this Act, the act of a District Magistrate as an Inspector is an executive act only and not a judicial act.

(2) Chief Inspector can exercise powers of an Inspector. If any complaint is filed by Chief Inspector, it is deemed as the complaint filed by an Inspector.

(3) It is the State Government which decides the jurisdiction of the inspectors and powers to be exercised by these public officers appointed under Section 8 of this Act by notification in the Official Gazette.

(4) No person can be appointed under Section 8 of this Act and, if so appointed, shall continue to hold office, who is directly or indirectly interested in any of the affairs of a factory [Section 8(3)]

(5) If in any area, there are more inspectors than one, the State Government, may declare the powers which such inspectors shall respectively exercise and the inspector to whom the prescribed notices are to be sent. In B. Rice and Flour Mills V/s Inspectors of Factories case, it was held that where the Chief Inspector was the only authority to sanction prosecution for offences, the sanction by the Additional Inspector of Factories would not be legal.

Powers of the Inspectors

It is mentioned in Section 8(6) that "in any area where there are more Inspectors than one, the State Government may, by notification as aforesaid, declare the powers which such Inspectors shall respectively exercise and the Inspector to whom the prescribed notices are to be sent."

The Inspectors are vested with the following powers under this Act. They are:

(1) Powers of the Inspectors under Section 9

Under Section 9 of this Act, an Inspector may, subject to any rules made in this behalf and within the local limits for which he is appointed to exercise the following powers:

(a) Enter, with such assistants who are persons in service of the Government or any local or public authority, or with any expert as he thinks proper and fit, any place which is used, or which he has reasons to believe is used, as factory.

(b) Make examinations of premises, plants, machinery, buildings, article or substance.

(c) Enquire into any accident or any dangerous occurrence, whether resulting in bodily injury or disability or not and take on the spot or otherwise statements of any person or persons which he may consider necessary for such inquiry.

(d) Require the production of any prescribed register or any paper record or any other document relating to the factory.

(e) Seize or take copies of, any register, record or any other document or any portion thereof; as he may consider necessary in respect of any offence under this Act, which he has reason to believe, has been committed.

(f) Direct the occupier of the factory that any premises or any part of the premises or anything lying therein, shall be left undisturbed, whether generally or in particular respects, for so long as is necessary for the purpose of any examination under clause (b) of this section.

(g) Take measurements, photographs and also make such recordings as he considers necessary for the purpose of any examination under clause (b) of this section, taking with him any necessary instrument or instruments and equipments too.

(h) In case of any article or any substance found in any premises or in any part thereof, being an article or substance which appears to him as having caused or is likely to cause danger to the health or safety of the workers employed, direct it to be dismantled or subject it to any process or test, but not so as to damage or destroy it unless the same is, in the circumstances necessary, for carrying out the purposes of this Act, and take possession of any such article or substance or even a part thereof, and detain it for so long as is necessary for such examination.

(i) Exercise such other powers as may be prescribed.

It is further provided that no person shall be compelled under this section to answer any question or give any evidence tending to incriminate himself.

(2) Power to require medical examination [Section 75]

Where an Inspector is of the opinion that any person working in a factory without a certificate of fitness is a young person, or a young person working in a factory with a certificate of fitness is no longer fit to work in the capacity stated in the certificate, he has the power to serve the notice to the manager of the factory requiring that such person or young person, as the case may be, shall be examined by a certifying surgeon and, if the Inspector so directs, such young person or persons shall not be employed or permitted to work in any factory until he has been so examined and has been given a certificate of fitness or a fresh certificate of fitness, as the case may be, under Section 69, or issued him a certificate by the certifying surgeon examining him that he is not a young person.

(3) Power to take Samples [Section 91]

An Inspector may at any time during normal working hours of a factory, after informing the occupier, or manager of the factory, or any other person in-charge of the factory, as the case may be, take a sufficient sample of any substance or article used or intended to be used in the factory for examination.

(4) Power of Survey and Examination [Section 91-A]

Under Section 91-A, power of survey and examination, subject to the proper notice in writing issued to the occupier or manager of the factory, has been given to the Chief Inspector, the Director-General of Health Services and the Director-General of Factory

Advice Service and Labour Institutes or, any other such officer as may be authorised by the State Government in this behalf. After receiving such notice from the authorised officer or person, the occupier or the manager of the factory is bound to offer all facilities for undertaking such survey.

(B) Certifying Surgeon

The provisions relating to appointment, power, disqualifications and duties have been made in Section 10 of this Act, which are as follows:

Appointment of Certifying Surgeon

Under Section 10 of this Act, the State Government may appoint qualified medical practitioners as the certifying surgeons within such local limits or for such factory or class or description of factories as the State Government may assign to them respectively [Section 10 (1)].

Power of the Certifying Surgeon to authorise any Qualified Medical Practitioner to Act as a Certifying Surgeon

The certifying surgeon may, with the prior approval of the State Government, authorise any qualified medical practitioner to exercise any of his powers granted to the certifying surgeon under this Act for such period as the certifying surgeon may specify. This can be done subject to such conditions as the State Government may think fit to impose, and references in this Act to any medical practitioner when so authorised [Section 10 (2)].

(3) Disqualifications of a Certifying Surgeon

It is provided in the sub-section (3) of Section 10 that no person shall be appointed to be or authorised to exercise the powers of a certifying surgeon, or having been so appointed or authorised, continue to exercise such powers, who is or becomes the occupier of a factory or is or has become directly or indirectly interested therein or in any process or business carried on therein or in any patent or machinery connected therewith or is otherwise in the employment of the factory.

It is further provided that the State Government may exempt any person or class of persons from the provisions of sub-section (3) of Section 10 in respect of any factory or class or description of factories. The State Government does it so by issuing an order in writing and subject to such conditions as may be specified in the order [Proviso to Section 10(3)].

It must be remembered here that in this section, a 'Qualified Medical Practitioner' means a person holding a qualification granted by an authority specified in the Schedule to the Indian Medical Degrees Act, 1916, or in the Schedule to the Indian Medical Council Act, 1933. [Explanation to Section 10].

Duties of a Certifying Surgeon

The Certifying Surgeon shall carry out all such duties as may be prescribed in connection with:

    (a) the examination and certification of young persons under various sections of this Act;

(b) the examination of persons who are engaged in factories in such dangerous occupations or processes as may be prescribed;

(c) the exercising of such medical supervision as may be prescribed for any factory or class or description of factories, where:

(i) cases of illness have occurred which it is reasonable to believe are due to the nature of the manufacturing process carried on, or other conditions or work prevailing therein;

(ii) by reason of any change in the manufacturing process carried on or in the substances used therein or by reason of the adoption of any new manufacturing process, there is a likelihood of injury to the health of workers employed in that manufacturing process;

(iii) young persons who are or are about to be, employed in any work which is likely to cause any injury to their health [Section 10(4)]

3.14 Provisions Relating to Workers' Health

One of the outstanding features of the Factories Act, 1948, is the provision for health, safety and welfare of the workers.

This Act makes various provisions in regard to matters relating to health as well as safety and welfare of the workers. These provisions impose certain obligations upon occupiers or managers of factories to protect workers from accidents and to secure for them conditions conducive to their health, safety and welfare in the premises where they work.

It is obligatory for the managers or the occupiers to maintain necessary inspecting staff and to make necessary provision for maintaining the health, cleanliness, etc., and also provide certain amenities like, ventilation, light, drinking water, latrines and urinals, etc.

Sections 11 to 20 (Chapter III) of this Act contain provisions as regards health of workers. Now, let us briefly study these provisions.

[I] Cleanliness [Section 11]

(1) Every factory shall be kept clean and free and fresh from effluvia or outflow of bad and injurious gases which may arise from any drain, privy or any other nuisance, and, in particular –

(a) accumulations of dirt and refuse shall be removed daily by sweeping or by any other effective method from the floors and the benches of workrooms, and also from staircases and passages, and the same shall be disposed off in a suitable manner;

(b) the floor of every workroom shall be cleaned at least once in every week by washing, using disinfectant wherever necessary or by some other effective method;

(c) where a floor is liable to become wet in the course of any manufacturing process, to such extent as is capable of being drained, effective means of drainage shall be provided for and maintained;

(d) all inside walls as well as partitions, all ceilings or tops of all rooms and all walls, sides and tops of passages and staircases shall:

    (i) where they are painted otherwise than with washable paint or varnished, must be re-painted or re-vanished at least once in every period of five years.

    (ii) where they are painted with washable water paint, must be re-painted with at least one coat of such paint at least once in every period of three years and must be washed properly at least once in every period of six months.

    (iii) where they are painted or varnished or where they have smooth impervious surfaces, must be cleaned at least once in every period of fourteen months by such methods as may be prescribed.

    (iv) all doors and frames of the windows and other wooden as well as metallic framework and shutters shall be kept painted or varnished and such painting or varnishing shall be carried out at least once in every period of five years.

    (v) the dates on which the processes required by the abovementioned clause (d) of this section are carried out shall be entered in the prescribed register maintained for this purpose.

(2) If, in view of the nature of operations carried on in a factory or class or description of factories or any part of a factory or class or description of factories, it is not possible for the occupier to comply with all or any of the provision of sub-section 1 of Section 11 mentioned hereinabove, the State Government may, by order in writing, exempt such factory from any or all the provisions of that sub-section and specify alternative methods for keeping the factory in a clean state.

Thus, it is expected that the compound surrounding of every factory as well as all its rooms, roofs, shutters, window cases etc., must be maintained in a sanitary and clean condition, free of dust, rubbish, dirt and loathsome dirt [filth] or debris, etc.

[II] Disposal of Wastes and Effluents [Section 12]

(1) Effective arrangements are required to be made in every factory for the treatment of wastes and effluents due to the maintaining process carried on therein, so as to render them innocuous (harmless), and for their disposal.

(2) The State Government may make rules prescribing arrangements to be made under sub-section (1) of this Section or requiring that arrangements made in accordance with sub-section (l) shall be approved by any such authority as may be prescribed.

Here, it must be remembered that any factory coming under the purview of this Act can be prosecuted even if plans for arrangements of wastes and effluents have neither been approved nor disapproved.

[III] Ventilation and Temperature [Section 13]

(1) Effective and suitable provisions are required to be made in every factory to which this Act is made applicable for securing and maintaining in every workroom:

(a) an adequate ventilation by the circulation of fresh air; and

(b) such a temperature as will secure to workers therein reasonable conditions of comfort and prevent any injury to health;

And, in particular:

(i) walls and roofs must be of such material and designed in such a way so that the reasonable temperature shall not be exceeded but shall be kept as low as is practicable.

(ii) where the nature of the work carried on in the factories involves, or is likely to involve, the production of excessively high temperatures, such adequate measures as are practicable are required to be introduced to protect the workers therefrom, by separating the process which produces such temperatures from the workroom, by insulating the hot parts or, by any other effective means.

(2) The State Government is authorised to prescribe a standard of adequate ventilation and reasonable temperature for any factory or class or description of factories or parts thereof and direct that proper measuring instruments, at such places and in such position as may be specified in this behalf, shall be provided for and such records as may be prescribed, shall be maintained.

(3) If it appears to the Chief Inspector that excessively high temperatures in any factory, highly injurious to the health of workers working therein can be reduced by adopting suitable measures, he may serve on the occupier, without any prejudice to the rules made under sub-section (2) of Section 13, an order in writing specifying the measures which, in his opinion, should be adopted, and requiring those measures to be carried out before a specified date.

[IV] Dust and Fumes [Section 14]

(1) In every factory in which, by reason of the manufacturing process carried on, there is given off any dust or fumes or any other impurity of such a nature and to such an extent as is likely to be injurious to the health of workers working therein or offensive to workers employed therein, or any dust in substantial quantities, effective measures must be introduced to prevent its inhalation and accumulation in any workroom, and if any exhaust applicable is necessary for this purpose, it shall

be applied as near as possible to the point of origin of the dust, fumes or other impurity, and such point shall be enclosed as far as possible.

(2) In any factory, no stationary internal combustion engine shall be operated unless the exhaust is conducted into the open air, and no other internal combustion engine shall be operated in any room unless effective measures have been introduced to prevent such accumulation of fumes and other impurity therefrom as they are likely to be injurious to workers employed in the room.

[V] Artificial Humidification [Section 15]

(1) In respect of all factories in which the humidity of the air is artificially increased, the State Government may make rules -

   (a) prescribing standard of humidification;

   (b) regulating the methods used for artificially increasing the humidity of the air;

   (c) directing prescribed tests for determining the humidity of the air to be correctly carried out and properly recorded.

   (d) prescribing methods to be adopted for securing adequate ventilation and cooling of the air and thereby the workrooms.

(2) In any factory in which the humidity of the air is artificially increased, the water used for the purpose shall be taken from a public supply, or any other source of drinking water, or shall be effectively purified before it is so used in the factory.

(3) If it appears to an Inspector that the water used in a factory for increasing humidity which is required to be effectively purified under sub-section (2) of Section 15 mentioned hereinabove is not effectively purified, he may serve on the manager of the factory an order in writing, specifying the measures which in his opinion should be adopted, and requiring them to be carried out before the date specified in such order.

It must be noted that humidification is employed in many factories in India. It is employed, more so in, cotton textile factories, in some cigarette-making factories. In this regard, the State Government is empowered to make necessary rules in respect of all factories in which humidity of the air is artificially created or increased.

[VI] Overcrowding [Section 16]

(1) No room in any factory shall be overcrowded to an extent which is injurious to the health of the workers employed therein.

(2) There shall be at least 9.9 cubic metres of space for every worker employed for all those factories in existence at the time of the commencement of this Act and 14.2 cubic metres of space for every worker employed in the factories built after the commencement of this Act. In calculating the space of 9.9 cubic metres or 14.2 cubic metres, no account shall be taken of any space which is more than 4.2 metres above the level of the floor of the room.

(3) If the Chief Inspector by order in writing so requires, there shall be posted in each workroom of a factory, a notice specifying the maximum number of workers who may, in compliance with the provisions of this Act, be employed in the room.

(4) The Chief Inspector may exempt, by issuing the order in writing, subject to such conditions, if any, as he may think fit to impose, any workroom from the provisions of Section 16 of this Act, if he is satisfied that the compliance therewith in respect of the room is not necessary in the interest of the health of the workers employed therein.

[VII] Lighting [Section 17]

(1) In every part of a factory where workers work or pass or loiter, there must be provided and maintained sufficient and suitable lighting, natural or/and artificial.

(2) In every factory, all glazed windows and skylights used for the purposes of lighting of the workroom must be kept clean on both the surfaces - inner as well as outer, and free from any obstruction.

(3) In every factory, effective provisions must be made, so far as is practicable, for the prevention of:
  (a) glare, either directly from a source of light or by reflection from a smooth surface or polished surface or from both,
  (b) the formation of shadows to such an extent as to cause eyestrain or the risk of accident to any worker working therein.

(4) The State Government may prescribe standards of sufficient and suitable lighting facilities for factories or for any class or description of factories or for any manufacturing process.

[VIII] Drinking Water [Section 18]

(1) In every factory, effective arrangements are required to be made to provide and maintain at suitable points conveniently situated for all workers employed therein a sufficient supply of wholesome drinking water.

(2) All such points must be legibly marked 'drinking water' in such a language so that the majority of the workers employed therein may understand and such points shall not be situated within six metres of any washing place, latrines and urinals, spitoons and open drains carrying sewage or effluent or any other source of contamination unless a shorter distance is approved in writing by the Chief Inspector.

(3) In every factory wherein more than two hundred and fifty workers are ordinarily employed, provisions shall be made for cooling the drinking water during hot weather by any effective means and for the distribution thereof.

(4) In respect of all factories or any class or description of factories, the State Government may make rules for securing compliance with the provision of all the sub-sections of Section 18 mentioned hereinabove and for the examination by prescribed authorities of the supply and distribution of drinking water in all factories.

[IX] Latrines and Urinals [Section 19]

(1) In every factory –
   (a) Sufficient latrine and also urinal accommodation of prescribed types must be provided for and, one which is conveniently situated and accessible to workers at all times while they are at the factory.
   (b) Separate enclosed accommodation is required to be provided – both for male and female workers.
   (c) Such accommodation must be adequately lighted and properly ventilated. No latrine or urinal shall, unless specially exempted in writing by the Chief Inspector, communicate with any workroom except through an intervening open space or passage which is adequately ventilated.
   (d) All such accommodation must be maintained in a clean and sanitary condition at all times.
   (e) Sweepers must be employed whose primary duty would be to keep latrines, urinals and washing places clean.

(2) In every factory wherein more than two hundred and fifty workers are ordinarily employed –
   (a) all latrine and urinal accommodations shall be of prescribed sanitary types only;
   (b) the floors and internal walls, up to the height of ninety centimetres, of the latrines and urinals and also of the sanitary blocks shall be laid in glazed tiles or otherwise finished to provide a smooth polished impervious surface.
   (c) Without prejudice to the provisions of clause (d) and (e) of Section 19(1), the floors, portions of walls and blocks so laid or finished and sanitary pans of the latrines and urinals shall be thoroughly washed and cleaned at least once in every seven days with suitable detergents or disinfectants or, with both.

(3) The State Government may prescribe the number of latrines and urinals to be provided in any factory in proportion to the number of female and male workers ordinarily employed therein and provide for such further matters in respect of sanitation in factories, including the obligation of workers in this regard as the State Government considers it necessary in the interest of the health of workers employed therein.

[X] Spittoons [Section 20]

(1) In every factory, there must be provided a sufficient number of spittoons at convenient places and they must be maintained in a clean and hygienic condition.

(2) The State Government may make rules prescribing the type and the number of spittoons to be provided and their location in any factory and provide for such further matters relating to their maintenance in a clean and hygienic condition.

(3) No person shall spit within the premises of a factory except in the spittoons provided for that purpose and a notice containing this provision and the penalty for its violation must be prominently displayed at suitable places in the premises of the factory.

(4) Whoever spits in contravention of sub-section (3) of Section 20 shall be punishable with fine not exceeding Rupees five.

It is obvious that the intention of the sub-section (4) of Section 20 is to enforce and promote discipline amongst the employees of any factory and, therefore, the provision is made that anyone spitting in contravention of sub-section (3) of Section 20 will do so at the cost of punishment.

3.15 Provisions Relating to Safety of Workers

One of the outstanding features of the Factories Act, 1948, is the provision for safety of the workers. In this Act, various provisions have been made in regard to the matters relating to safety of the workers. Special provisions have also been made in respect of young persons, women and children.

Section 23 prohibits young persons from working on dangerous machineries; while Section 22 prohibits women and children from working on any moving part of machinery. Sections 21 to 41 [Chapter IV] of this Act contain provisions relating to the safety of the workers and the provisions of these sections are absolute and obligatory in their character and the occupier or manager of every factory is bound to follow them. Let us now consider the provisions of this Act as regards the safety of the workers.

1. Fencing of Machinery [Section 21]

If dangerous parts of the machinery installed in a factory are not securely fenced, the chances of causing accidents are more. Therefore, it is provided in Section 21 that all dangerous parts of the machinery must be securely fenced. For example, moving parts of prime movers and flywheels connected to every prime movers and flywheels connected to every part of an electric generator, a motor or rotary convertor etc. Section 21 of this Act states that -

(a) In every factory, the following needs to be securely fenced, namely –
  (i) every moving part of a prime mover and every fly-wheel connected to a prime mover, whether the prime mover or flywheel is in the engine house or not;
  (ii) the headrace and tailrace of every water-wheel and water turbine;
  (iii) any part of a stock-bar which projects beyond the head stock of a lathe; and
  (iv) unless they are in such position or of such construction as to be safe to every person employed in the factory as they would be. If they were securely fenced, the following, namely –
    (i) every part of an electric generator, motor, or rotary convertor
    (ii) every part of transmission machinery; and
    (iii) every dangerous part of any other machinery,

shall be securely fenced by safeguards of substantial construction which shall be constantly maintained and kept in position while the parts of machinery they are fencing are in motion or in use. It is also provided that for the purpose of determining whether any part of machinery is in such position or is of such construction as to be safe as aforesaid, account shall not be taken of any occasion when –

    (i)   it is necessary to make an examination of any part of the machinery aforesaid while it is in motion or, as a result of examination, to carry out lubrication or other adjusting operation while the machinery is in motion, being an examination or operation which it is necessary to be carried out while that part of the machinery is in motion, or

    (ii) in the case of any part of a transmission machinery used in such process as may be prescribed (being a process of a continuous nature the carrying on of which shall be, or is likely to be, substantially interfered with by the stoppage of that part of the machinery), it is necessary to make an examination of such part of the machinery while it is in motion or, as a result of such examination, to carry out any mounting or shipping of belts or lubrication or other adjusting operation while the machinery is in motion, and such examination or operation is made or carried out in accordance with the provisions of sub-section (1) of Section (22) [Section 21(1)].

(b) The State Government may by rules prescribe such further precautions as it may consider necessary in respect of any particular machinery or part thereof, or exempt subject to such condition as may be prescribed for securing the safety of the workers, any particular machinery or part thereof from the provisions of this section [Section 21(2)].

2. Work on or near machinery in motion [Section 22]

Section 22(1) provides for the examination of machinery which is in motion by a specially trained adult male worker only. He must wear tight fitting clothing while conducting such an examination. While Section 22(2) places restrictions on women and young persons in respect of cleaning, lubricating or adjusting any part of the machinery in motion which may expose them to risk of injury for any moving part of machinery. Section 22(1) states that, "Where in any factory it becomes necessary to examine any part of machinery referred to in Section 21, while the machinery is in motion, or, as a result of such examination, to carry out –

(a) in a case referred to in clause (i) of the proviso to sub-section (1) of Section 21, lubrication or other adjusting operation; or

(b) in a case referred to in clause (ii) of the proviso aforesaid, any mounting or shipping of belts or lubrication or other adjusting operation, while the machinery is in motion such examination or operation shall be made or carried out only by a specially trained adult male worker wearing tight fitting clothing (which shall be supplied by the occupier) whose name has been recorded in the register prescribed in this behalf and who has been furnished with a certificate of his appointment, and while he is so engaged –

(i) such worker shall not handle a belt at a moving pulley unless –
- the belt is not more than fifteen centimetres in width;
- the pulley is normally for the purpose of drive and not merely a fly-wheel or balance wheel (in which case, a belt is not permissible);
- the belt joint is either laced or flush with the belt;
- the belt, including the joint and the pulley rim, are in good repair;
- there is reasonable clearance between the pulley and any fixed plant or structure;
- secure foothold and, where necessary, secure handhold, are provided for the operator, and
- any ladder in use for carrying out any examination or operation aforesaid is securely fixed or lashed or is firmly held by a second person.

(ii) without prejudice to any other provision of this Act relating to the fencing of machinery, every set screw, bolt and key on any revolving shaft, spindle, wheel or pinion, and all spur, worn and other toothed or friction gearing in motion with which such worker otherwise be liable to come into contact, shall be securely fenced to prevent such contact.

According to Section 22(2), "No woman or young person shall be allowed to clean, lubricate or adjust any part of a prime mover or of any transmission machinery while the prime mover or transmission machinery is in motion, or to clean, lubricate or adjust any part of any machine if the cleaning, lubrication or adjustment thereof would expose the woman or young person to risk of injury from any moving part either of that machine or of any adjacent machinery.

Section 22(3) makes it clear that, "The State Government may, by notification in the Official Gazette, prohibit, in any specified factory or class or description of factories, the cleaning, lubricating or adjusting by any person of specified parts of machinery when those parts are in motion."

3. Employment of young persons on dangerous machines [Section 23]

The provisions of Section 23 put restrictions on young persons to work on any dangerous machine unless they have been specially instructed as to the dangers and precautions to be taken. Section 23 is as follows:

(a) No young person shall be required or allowed to work on any machine to which this section applies, unless he has been fully instructed as to the dangers arising in connection with the machine and the precautions to be observed, and
   (i) has received sufficient training at work on the machine, or
   (ii) is under adequate supervision by a person who has a thorough knowledge and experience of the machine [Section 23(1)].

(b) Sub-section (1) shall apply to such machines as may be prescribed by the State Government, being machines which in its opinion are of such a dangerous character that young persons ought not to work at them unless the foregoing requirements are complied with [Section 23(2)].

Thus, the State Government is required to specify the machines which are dangerous in its opinion for young persons to work under Section 23(2).

4. **Striking gear and devices for cutting off power [Section 24]**
   (a) In every factory –
      (i) suitable striking gear or other efficient mechanical appliance shall be provided for and maintained and used to move driving belts to and from fast and loose pulleys which form part of the transmission machinery, and such gear or appliances shall be so constructed, placed and maintained as to prevent the belt from creeping back on to the fast pulley;
      (ii) driving belts when not in use shall not be allowed to rest or ride upon shafting in motion [Section 24(1)].
   (b) In every factory, suitable devices for cutting off power in case of emergencies from running machinery shall be provided and maintained in every workroom [Section 24(2)].

It is provided that in respect of factories in operation before the commencement of this Act, the provisions of this sub-section shall apply only to those workrooms in which electricity is used as power [Proviso to Section 24(2)].

   (c) When a device, which can inadvertently shift from 'off' to 'on' position, is provided in a factory to cut off power, arrangements shall be provided for locking the device in safe position so as to prevent accidental starting off of the transmission machinery or other machines to which the device is fitted [Section 24(3)].

Thus, Section 24 seeks to provide additional safeguards as regards transmission machinery. According to the provisions of this section, in every factory, suitable devices for cutting-off power from running machinery (in case of emergencies) must be provided for and maintained in every workroom. Driving belts when not in use are not allowed to rest or ride upon shaft in motion.

Further, it is also provided in Section 24(3) that when a device, which can inadvertently shift from off to on position, is provided, arrangements must be made for locking up the device in a safe position. Obviously, these provisions have been made to prevent accidental starting of the transmission machinery or other machines to which such device is fitted.

5. **Provisions of the Act relating to Self-acting machines [Section 25]**

According to the provisions of Section 25, moving parts of any self-acting machine must not be allowed to come within forty-five centimetres of any fixed structure which is not the part of the machine and thus, traversing part is not allowed to run within forty-five centimetres from any fixed structure.

Section 25 says that, "No traversing part of a self-acting machine in any factory and no material carried thereon shall, if the space over which it runs is a space over which any person is liable to pass, whether in the course of his employment or otherwise, be allowed to run on its outward or inward traverse within a distance of forty-five centimetres from any fixed structure which is not part of the machine."

It is also provided that the Chief Inspector may permit the continued use of a machine installed before the commencement of this Act which does not comply with the requirements of this section on such conditions for ensuring safety as he may think fit to impose.

6. Casting of the New Machinery [Section 26]

All machinery driven by power and installed in any factory after the commencement of this Act, i.e., 1st April 1949, certain parts like screw, bolts, key etc., on any revolving shaft, spindle etc., must be sunk, encased properly or otherwise effectively guarded. If the provisions of Section 26 which are given below are not complied with, the person concerned shall be liable to be punished with imprisonment for a term that may extend upto three months or with a fine upto Five Hundred Rupees or, with both. Section 26(3) empowers the State Government to make rules specifying further safeguards to be provided in respect of any other dangerous part of any particular machine or any class of machines.

Section 26 is as follows:

(a) In all machinery driven by power and installed in any factory after the commencement of this Act, –

   (i) every set screw, bolt or key on any revolving shaft, spindle, wheel or pinion shall be so sunk, encased or otherwise effectively guarded as to prevent danger;

   (ii) all spur, worm and other toothed or friction gearing which does not require frequent adjustment while in motion, shall be completely encased, unless it is so situated as to be as safe as it would be if it were completely encased [Section 26(1)].

(b) Whoever sells or lets on hire or, as agent of a seller or hirer, causes or procures to be sold or let on hire for use in a factory any machinery driven by power which does not comply with the provisions of sub-section (1) or any rules made under sub-section (3) shall be punishable with imprisonment for a term which may extend upto three months or with fine which may extend upto five hundred rupees or, with both [Section 26(2)].

(c) The State Government may make rules specifying further safeguards to be provided in respect of any other dangerous part of any particular machine or class or description of machines [Section 26(3)].

7. Prohibition of Employment of Women and children near Cotton openers [Section 27]

Women and children are not allowed to work near cotton openers except in certain cases as mentioned in Section 27.

"No woman or child shall be employed in any part of a factory for pressing cotton in which a cotton-opener is at work" [Section 27]. It is also provided that if the feed-end of a cotton-opener is in a room separated from the delivery-end by a partition extending to the roof or to such height as the Inspector may in any particular case specify in writing, women and children may be employed on the side of the partition where the feed-end is situated [Proviso to Section 27].

8. Provisions relating to Hoists and Lifts [Section 28]

Every hoist and lift in every factory must be so constructed as to be safe and must be properly maintained. The hoist of lifts must be examined at least once in every six months. The rules, requirements as to how the safety is to be secured are given in Section 28. It states that, in every factory –

(a) every hoist and lift shall be
   (i) of good mechanical construction, sound material and adequate strength;
   (ii) properly maintained, and shall be thoroughly examined by a competent person at least once in every period of six months and a register shall be kept containing the prescribed particulars of every such examination.

(b) every hoistway and liftway shall be sufficiently protected by an enclosure fitted with gates, and the hoist or lift and every such enclosure shall be so constructed as to prevent any person or thing from being trapped between any part of the hoist or lift and any fixed structure or moving part;

(c) the maximum safe working load shall be plainly marked on every hoist or lift, and no load greater than such load shall be carried thereon;

(d) the cage of every hoist or lift used for carrying persons shall be fitted with a gate on each side from which access is afforded to a landing;

(e) every gate referred to in clause (b) or clause (d) shall be fitted with inter-locking or other efficient device to secure that the gate cannot be opened except when the cage is at the landing and that the cage cannot be moved unless the gate is closed [Section 28(1)].

The following additional requirements shall apply to hoists and lifts used for carrying persons and installed or reconstructed in a factory after the commencement of this Act, namely:

(a) where the cage is supported by rope or chain, there shall be at least two ropes or chains separately connected with the cage and balance weight, and each rope or chain with its attachments shall be capable of carrying the whole weight of the cage together with its maximum load;

(b) efficient devices capable of supporting the cage together with its maximum load in the event of breakage of the ropes, chains or attachments shall be provided for and maintained;

(c) an efficient automatic device shall be provided and maintained to prevent the cage from over-running [Section 28(2)]

The Chief Inspector may permit the continued use of a hoist or lift installed in a factory before the commencement of this Act which does not fully comply with the provisions of sub-section (1) upon such conditions for ensuring safety as he may think fit to impose [Section 28(3)].

The State Government may, if in respect of any class or description of hoist or lift, is of opinion that it would be unreasonable to enforce any requirement of sub-sections (1) and (2) by order direct that such requirement shall not apply to such class or description of hoist or lift [Section 28(4)].

For the purposes of this section, no lifting machine or appliance shall be deemed to be a hoist or lift unless it has a platform or cage, the direction or movement of which is restricted by guides [Explanation to Section 28].

9. Provisions relating to lifting machines, chains, ropes and lifting tackles [Section 29]

The provisions in respect of lifting machines, chains, ropes and lifting tackles as to how the safety is to be secured in their respect have been made in Section 29 which are as follows:

(a) In any factory, the following provisions shall be complied with, in respect of every lifting machine (other than a hoist and lift) and every chain, rope and lifting tackle for the purpose of raising or lowering persons, goods or materials –

(i) all parts including the working gear, whether fixed or movable of every lifting machine and every chain, rope or lifting tackle shall be –
- of good construction, sound material and adequate strength and free from defects;
- properly maintained; and
- thoroughly examined by a competent person at least once in every period of twelve months, or at such intervals as the Chief Inspector may specify in writing, and a register shall be kept containing the prescribed particulars of every such examination;

(ii) no lifting machine and no chain, rope or lifting tackle shall, except for the purpose of test, be loaded beyond the safe working load which shall be plainly marked thereon together with an identification mark and duly entered in the prescribed register; and where this is not practicable, a table showing the safe working loads of every kind and size of lifting machine or chain, rope or lifting tackle in use shall be displayed in prominent positions on the premises;

(iii) while any person is employed or working on or near the wheel track of a travelling crane in any place where he would be liable to be struck by the crane, effective measures shall be taken to ensure that the crane does not approach within [six metres] of that place [Section 29(1)].

(b) The State Government may make rules in respect of any lifting machine or any chain, rope or lifting tackle used in factories –

   (i) prescribing further requirements to be complied with, in addition to those set out in this section;

   (ii) providing for exemption from compliance with all or any of the requirements of this section, where in its opinion, such compliance is unnecessary or impracticable [Section 29(2)].

(c) For the purposes of this section, a lifting machine or a chain, rope or lifting tackle shall be deemed to have been thoroughly examined if a visual examination supplemented, if necessary, by other means and by the dismantling of parts of the gear, has been carried out as carefully as the conditions permit in order to arrive at a reliable conclusion as to the safety of the parts examined [Section 29 (3)].

Explanation: In this Section, –

   (i) 'lifting machine' means a crane, crab, winch, teagle, pulley, block, gin, wheel, transporter or runway;

   (ii) 'lifting tackle' means any chain sling, rope sling, hook, shackle, swivel, coupling, socket, clamp, tray or similar appliance, whether fixed or movable, used in connection with the raising or lowering of persons, or loads by use of lifting machines [Explanation to Section 29].

10. Provisions relating to Revolving Machinery [Section 30]

In every factory, wherein grinding is carried on, the maximum safe working speed of every revolving machinery connected therewith is required to be notified. All the steps must be taken to see to it that the safe speed is not exceeded under any circumstances. Section 30 reproduced below outlines the provisions of the section relating to revolving machinery.

(a) In every factory, in which the process of grading is carried on, there shall be permanently affixed to or placed near each machine in use, a notice indicating the maximum safe working peripheral speed of every grindstone or abrasive wheel, the speed of the shaft or spindle upon which the wheel is mounted, and the diameter of the pulley upon such shaft or spindle necessary to secure such safe working peripheral speed [Section 30(1)].

(b) The speed indicated in notices under sub-section (1) shall not be exceeded [Section 30(2)].

(c) Effective measures shall be taken in every factory to ensure that the safe working peripheral speed of every revolving vessel, cage, basket, flywheel, pulley, disc or similar appliance driven by power is not exceeded [Section 30(3)].

11. Provisions relating to pressure plant [Section 31]

(a) If in any factory, any plant or machinery or any part thereof is operated at a pressure above atmospheric pressure, effective measures shall be taken to ensure that the safe working pressure of such plant or machinery or part is not exceeded [Section 31(1)].

(b) The State Government may make rules providing for the examination and testing of any plant or machinery such as is referred to in sub-section (1) and prescribing such other safety measures in relation thereto as may in its opinion being necessary in any factory or class or description of factories [Section 31(2)].

(c) The State Government may, by rules, exempt, subject to such conditions as may be specified therein, any part of any plant or machinery referred to in sub-section (1) from the provisions of this section [Section 31(3)].

Thus, these provisions of Section 31 imply that in any factory, if any operation is carried on at a pressure higher than the atmospheric pressure, effective measures and necessary steps must be taken to see to it that the safe pressure, i.e., safe working pressure is not exceeded. In this regard, the State Government is empowered to make necessary rules providing for the examination and testing of any plant, machinery and also providing for additional safety measures.

12. Provisions relating to Floors, Stairs and Means of Access [Section 32]

In every factory –

(a) all floors, steps, stairs, passages and gangways shall be of sound construction and properly maintained and shall be kept free from obstructions and substances likely to cause persons to slip and where it is necessary to ensure safety, steps, stairs, passages and gangways shall be provided with substantial hand-rails;

(b) there shall, so far as is reasonably practicable, be provided and maintained safe means of access to every place at which any person is at any time required to work;

(c) When any person has to work at a height from where he is likely to fall, provision shall be made, so far as is reasonably practicable, by fencing or otherwise, to ensure the safety of the person so working.

Thus, it has been provided under Section 32 that all floors, steps, stairs, passages, gangways must be of sound construction and properly maintained. They must be kept free from obstructions and substances which are likely to cause persons to slip. Handrails must also be provided for, wherever necessary. Also, safe means of access must be provided wherein the workers carry on any work.

13. Provisions relating to Pits, Sumps, Opening in Floors etc. [Section 33]

Pits, sumps etc., in every factory must be securely covered or fenced off from the viewpoint of safety of the workers. Hence, the provisions relating to pits, sumps etc., have been made in Section 33 of this Act, which is as follows:

(a) In every factory, fixed vessel, sump, tank, pit or an opening in the ground or in a floor which, by reasons of its depth, situation, construction or contents, is or may be a source of danger, shall be either securely covered or securely fenced [Section 33(1)].

(b) The State Government may, by order in writing, exempt, subject to such conditions as may be prescribed, any factory or class or description of factories in respect of any vessel, sump, tank, pit or opening from compliance with the provisions of this section [Section 33(2)].

14. Provisions relating to excessive weights [Section 34]

Certain restrictions are put on lifting or carrying of excessive weights by the workers. The State Government is empowered to prescribe the maximum weights which may be lifted or carried or moved by the workers. No worker shall be to be asked to carry any load so heavy as to cause him injury. It is provided in Section 34 that –

(a) No person shall be employed in any factory to lift, carry or move any load as heavy as likely to cause him/her injury [Section 34(1)].

(b) The State Government may make rules prescribing the maximum weights which may be lifted, carried or moved by adult men, adult women, adolescents and children employed in factories or in any class or description of factories or in carrying on any specified process [Section 34(2)].

Insofar as excessive weights are concerned, the Maharashtra Government has included Rule 66 pertaining to the excessive weights in the Maharashtra Factories Rules, 1963, which is given as below:

(i) In any factory, no person, shall unaided by another person or mechanical device, lift by hand or carry overhead, or over the back or shoulders, any material, article, tool or appliance exceeding the maximum limit in weight set out in the following schedule.

SCHEDULE

Persons	Maximum weight of material, article, tool or appliance (kgs)
(a) Adult male	55
(b) Adult female	30
(c) Adolescent male	30
(d) Adolescent female	20
(e) Male Child	16
(f) Female Child	13

(ii) In any factory, no person in conjunction with other person, unaided by mechanical device, shall lift by hand or carry overhead or over the back of shoulders, any material, article, tool or appliance if the weight thereof exceeds the sum of weight permissible for each person separately, as fixed by the Schedule to sub-rule (1)].

15. Protection of Eyes [Section 35]

When workers work on machines, there is always present a risk of injury to the eyes from fragments thrown-off while in the process of manufacturing and from excessive light, if any, and hence, it has been provided for in Section 35 that in every factory, screen or suitable goggles must be provided for the protection of workers' eyes, according to the rules made by the State Government in this behalf. It is laid down in Section 35 that, "In respect of any such manufacturing process carried on in any factory as may be prescribed, being a process which involves –

(a) risk of injury to the eyes from particles or fragments thrown-off in the course of the process or

(b) risk to the eyes by reason of exposure to excessive light, the State Government may by rules require that effective screens or suitable goggles shall be provided for the protection of persons employed on, or in the immediate vicinity of, the process."

16. Precautions against dangerous fumes, gases etc [Section 36]

Section 36 pertains to the precautions which must be taken against dangerous fumes, gases etc. Section 36(1) prohibits an entry by any person into any chamber, tank, vat, pit, pipe etc., where any gas, fume, dust is present or is likely to be present which may be dangerous to such person.

While Section 36(2) implies that all practicable measures or steps must be taken for removal of gas, fumes, dust etc. The provisions of Section 36 are given as follows –

(a) No person shall be required or allowed to enter any chamber, tank, vat, pipe, flue or other confined space in any factory in which any gas, fume, vapour or dust is likely to be present to such an extent as to involve risk to persons being overcome thereby, unless it is provided with a manhole of adequate size or other effective means of egress [Section 36(1)].

(b) No person shall be required or allowed to enter any confined space as is referred to in sub-section (1), until all practicable measures have been taken to remove any gas, fume, vapour or dust, which may be present so as to bring its level within the permissible limits and to prevent any ingress of such gas, fume, vapour or dust and unless –

(i) a certificate in writing has been given by a competent person, based on a test carried out by himself that the space is reasonably free from dangerous gas, fume, vapour or dust; or

(ii) such person is wearing suitable breathing apparatus and a belt securely attached to a rope, the free end of which is held by a person outside the confined space [Section 36(2)].

17. Precautions regarding the use of portable electric light [Section 36–A]

(a) no portable electric light or any other electric appliance of voltage exceeding twenty-four volts shall be permitted for use inside any chamber, tank, vat, pit, pipe, flue or other confined space unless adequate safety devices are provided; and

(b) if any inflammable gas, fume or dust is likely to be present in such chamber, tank, vat, pit, pipe, flue or other confined space, no lamp or light other than that of flame-proof construction shall be permitted to be used in the factory.

18. Provisions relating to precautions against explosive or inflammable gas, dust etc [Section 37]

In any factory, where a manufacturing process produces any inflammable gas, dust, fume etc., it has been made compulsory under Section 37 to take necessary steps to enclose the machine or plant used in the manufacturing process, in order to prevent the accumulation of substances and to exclude all possible sources of ignition.

19. Precautions in case of Fire [Section 38]

From the viewpoint of safety of the workers, the safety precautions to be taken in case of fire are mentioned in Section 38. They are as follows -

(a) In every factory, all practicable measures shall be taken to prevent outbreak of fire and its spread, both internally and externally, and to provide and maintain –

   (i) safe means of escape for all persons in the event of a fire, and

   (ii) the necessary equipment and facilities for extinguishing fire [Section 38(1)].

(b) Effective measures shall be taken to ensure that in every factory all the workers are familiar with the means of escape in case of fire and have been adequately trained in the routine to be followed in such cases [Section 38(2)].

It is further stated in Section 38(4) that, "Notwithstanding anything contained in clause (a) of sub-section (1) or sub-section (2), if the Chief Inspector, having regard to the nature of the work carried on in any factory, the construction of such factory, special risk to life or safety, or any other circumstances, is of the opinion that the measures provided in the factory, whether as prescribed or not, for the purposes of clause (a) of sub-section (1) or sub-section (2), are inadequate, he may, by order in writing, require that such additional measures as he may consider reasonable and necessary, be provided in the factory before such date as is specified in the order."

In this regard, as the State Government is vested with the rule-making power, it may make rules in respect of any factory or class or description of factories, requiring the measures to be adopted to give effect to the provisions of Section 38 mentioned above [Section 38(3)].

20. Power to require specifications of defective parts or test of stability [Section 39]

If it appears to the Inspector that any building or part of building or any part of the ways, machinery or plant in a factory is in such a condition that it may be dangerous to human life or safety, he may serve on the occupier or manager or, both of the factory, an order in writing requiring him before a specified date –

(a) to furnish such drawings, specifications and other particulars as may be necessary to determine whether such building, ways, machinery or plant can be used with safety, or

(b) to carry out such tests in such manner as may be specified in the order and to inform the Inspector of the results thereof [Section 39].

21. Safety of Buildings and Machinery [Section 40]

The provisions of Section 40 insofar as the safety of building and machinery are as follows -

(a) If it appears to the Inspector that any building or part of a building or any part of the ways, machinery or plant in a factory is in such a condition that it is dangerous to human life or safety, he may serve on the occupier or manager or both of the factory, an order in writing specifying the measures which in his opinion should be adopted, and requiring them to be carried out before specified date [Section 40(1)].

(b) If it appears to the Inspector that the use of any building or part of a building or any part of the ways, machinery or plant in a factory involves imminent danger to human life or safety he may serve on the occupier or manager or both of the factory, an order in writing prohibiting its use until it has been properly repaired or altered [Section 40(2)].

Thus, these two sections of the Act, i.e., Sections 39 and 40 relate to safety provisions of buildings and machinery. Section 39 for its application contemplates a possibility of danger; while Section 40 contemplates danger which is imminent, if not already existing. If any building or any machinery is in a dangerous or a defective condition, the Inspector of Factories is empowered to ask for holding tests to determine how the buildings and machinery can be made safe. If there is any immediate danger, the use of such buildings or machinery can be prohibited until they have been properly repaired or altered.

22. Provisions relating to maintenance of buildings [Section 40–A]

If it appears to the Inspector that the use of any building or part of a building in a factory is in such a state of disrepair as is likely to lead to conditions detrimental to the health and welfare of the workers, he may serve on the occupier or manager or both of the factory, an order in writing specifying the measures which in his opinion should be taken and requiring the same to be carried out before such date as is specified in the order.

23. Provisions relating to the employment of safety officers by the occupier [Section 40-B]

In every factory –

(a) wherein one thousand or more workers are ordinarily employed, or

(b) wherein, in the opinion of the State Government, any manufacturing process or operation is carried on, which process or operation involves any risk of bodily injury, poisoning or disease, or any other hazard to health, to the person employed in the factory, the occupier shall, if so required by the State Government by notification in the Official Gazette, employ such number of Safety Officers as may be specified in that notification [Section 40-B(1)].

(c) The duties, qualifications and conditions of service of Safety Officers shall be such as may be prescribed by the State Government [Section 40-B(2)].

24. Power to make rules to supplement this Chapter [Section 41]

Section 41 is the general section which empowers the State Government to require such additional safety devices to be taken as it may deem necessary and proper. Section 41 states that, "The State Government may make rules requiring the provision in any factory or any class or description of factories of such further devices and measures for securing the safety of persons employed therein as it may deem necessary."

3.16 Provisions Relating to Welfare of Workers

The provisions relating to workers' health and safety are definitely important. But, the provisions relating to the welfare of workers is no less important. The provisions relating to the welfare of workers have been incorporated in Sections 42 to 50 of Chapter V of the Factories Act, 1948. Now, let us consider the provisions made in this Act as regards the welfare of the workers.

(1) Provisions relating to washing facilities [Section 42]

The provisions of Section 42 relating to washing facilities are as follows:

(a) "In every factory –
  (i) adequate and suitable facilities for washing shall be provided and maintained for the use of the workers therein;
  (ii) separate and adequately screened facilities shall be provided for the use of male and female workers;
  (iii) such facilities shall be conveniently accessible and shall be kept clean." [Section 42(1)].

(b) The State Government may, in respect of any factory or class or description of factories or of any manufacturing process, prescribe standards of adequate and suitable facilities for washing [Section 42(2)].

(2) Provisions of Section 43 relating to facilities for storing and drying of wet clothing

"The State Government may in respect of any factories or class or description of factories, make rules requiring the provision therein of suitable places for keeping clothing not worn during working hours and for the drying of wet clothing" [Section 43].

Thus, the State Governments are empowered to make rules for providing suitable places for keeping clothings of workers which are not worn by them during the working hours in the factory and also for the drying of wet clothings in respect of any factory or class of factories.

(3) Provisions of Section 44 in respect of facilities for sitting

(a) Provisions relating to sitting arrangements for workers who are obliged to work in standing position

In every factory suitable arrangements for sitting shall be provided and maintained for all workers obliged to work in a standing position, in order that they may take advantage of any opportunities for rest which may occur in the course of their work [Section 44(1)].

(b) Provisions relating to sitting arrangements for workers doing the work which can be done in a sitting position

If, in the opinion of the Chief Inspector, the workers in any factory engaged in a particular manufacturing process or working in a particular room are able to do their work efficiently in a sitting position, he may, by order in writing, require the occupier of the factory to provide before a specified date such seating arrangements as may be practicable for all workers so engaged or working [Section 44(2)].

(c) Exemption granted under this Section 44

The State Government may, by notification in the Official Gazette, declare that the provisions of sub-section (1) shall not apply to any specified factory or class or description of factories or to any specified manufacturing process [Section 44(3)].

(d) Provisions of Section 45 relating to first-aid appliances

Certain provisions have been made in Section 45 of this Act in respect of making the first-aid appliances to the workers. These provisions are given as below:

(a) At least one first-aid box with prescribed contents must be provided for every one hundred and fifty workers

There shall in every factory be provided and maintained, so as to be readily accessible during all working hours first-aid boxes or cupboards equipped with the prescribed contents, and the number of such boxes or cupboards to be provided and maintained shall not be less than one for every one hundred and fifty workers ordinarily employed at any one time in the factory [Section 45(1)].

It is also provided nothing except the prescribed contents shall be kept in a first-aid box or cupboard [Section 45(2)].

(b) A first-aid box must be kept in the charge of a responsible person

Each first-aid box or cupboard shall be kept in the charge of a separate responsible person who holds a certificate in first-aid treatment [recognised by the State Government] and who shall always be readily available during the working hours of the factory [Section 45(3)].

The following Rule 77 of the Maharastra Factories Rules, 1963, pertains to the notice regarding the first-aid.

A notice containing the names of the persons working within the precincts of the factory who are trained in first-aid treatment and who are in-charge of the first-aid boxes or cupboards shall be pasted in every factory at a conspicuous place and near each such box or cupboard. The notice shall also indicate work room where the said person shall be available. The name of the nearest hospital and its telephone number shall also be mentioned prominently in the said notice.

(c) Provision for an ambulance room in a factory where more than five hundred workers are employed

In every factory wherein more than five hundred workers are ordinarily employed, there shall be provided and maintained an ambulance room of the prescribed size, containing the prescribed equipment and in the charge of such medical and nursing staff as may be prescribed and those facilities shall always be made readily available during the working hours of the factory [Section 45(4)].

(5) Provisions of Section 46 relating to canteens

According to the provisions of Section 46, canteen facilities must be provided in a factory wherein more than two hundred fifty workers are ordinarily employed. The State Governments are empowered to make rules in this respect. What may be provided in these rules is made clear in Section 46(2). Let us now consider the provisions relating to canteens as given in this Act.

(a) The State Government may make rules requiring that in any specified factory wherein more than two hundred and fifty workers are ordinarily employed, a canteen or canteens shall be provided and maintained by the occupier for the use of the workers [Section 46(1)]

(b) Without prejudice to the generality of the foregoing power, such rules may provide for –
  (i) the date by which such canteen shall be provided;
  (ii) the standards in respect of construction, accommodation, furniture and other equipment of the canteen;
  (iii) the foodstuffs to be served therein and the charges which may be made thereof;
  (iv) the constitution of the managing committee of the canteen and representation of the workers in the management of it;
  (v) the items of expenditure in the running of the canteen which are not to be taken into account in fixing the cost of foodstuffs and which shall be borne by the employer;
  (vi) the delegation to the Chief Inspector, subject to such conditions as may be prescribed, of the power to make rules under clause (c) [Section 46(2)].

(6) Provisions of Section 47 relating to shelters, rest rooms and lunch rooms

(a) To every factory, wherein more than one hundred and fifty workers are ordinarily employed, adequate and suitable shelters or rest rooms and a suitable lunch room, with provision for drinking water, where workers can eat meals brought by them, shall be provided and maintained for the use of the workers [Section 47(1)].

It is provided that any canteen maintained in accordance with the provisions of Section 46 shall be regarded as part of the requirements of this sub-section [Proviso 1 to Section 47(1)].

It is provided further that where a lunch room exists, no worker shall eat any food in the workroom [Proviso 2 to Section 47(1)].

(b) The shelters or rest rooms or lunch rooms to be provided under sub-section (1) shall be sufficiently lighted and ventilated and shall be maintained in a cool and clean condition [Section 47(2)].

(c) The State Government may –

   (i) prescribe the standards in respect of construction, accommodation, furniture and other equipment of shelters, rest rooms and lunch rooms to be provided, under this section;

   (ii) by notification in the Official Gazette, exempt any factory or class or description of factories from the requirements of this section [Section 47(3)].

(7) Provisions of Section 48 relating to creches

(a) Provision of a suitable room or rooms for the use of children in a factory wherein more than thirty women workers are ordinarily employed

In every factory wherein more than thirty women workers are ordinarily employed, there shall be provided and maintained a suitable room or rooms for the use of children under the age of six years of such women [Section 48(1)].

(b) Rooms must be adequately lighted and ventilated

Such rooms shall provide adequate accommodation, shall be adequately lighted and ventilated, shall be maintained in a clean and sanitary condition and shall be under the charge of women trained in the care of children and infants [Section 48(2)].

(c) Powers of the State Government to make rules in respect of the creches to be provided under this Section 48

The State Government may make rules –

   (i) prescribing the location and the standards in respect of construction, accommodation, furniture and other equipment of rooms to be provided under this section;

   (ii) requiring the provision in factories to which this section applies of additional facilities for the care of children belonging to women workers, including suitable provision of facilities for washing and changing their clothing;

(iii) requiring the provision in any factory of free milk or refreshment or, both for such children;

(iv) requiring that facilities be given in any factory for the mothers of such children to feed them at the necessary intervals [Section 48(3)]

(8) Provisions of Section 49 in respect of the employment of welfare officers

(a) Employment of welfare officers

In every factory wherein five hundred or more workers are ordinarily employed, the occupier shall employ in the factory such number of welfare officers as may be prescribed [Section 49(1)]

(b) Duties, qualifications, conditions of service of welfare officers

The State Government may prescribe the duties, qualifications and conditions of service of officers employed under the sub-section (1) of Section 49 [Section 49(2)].

(9) Power of the State Government to make rules to supplement this chapter [Section 50]

The State Government may make rules –

(a) exempting, subject to compliance with such alternative arrangement for the welfare of workers as may be prescribed, any factory or class or description of factories from compliance with any of the provisions of this Chapter [Section 50(1)]

(b) requiring in any factory or class or description of factories that representative of the workers employed in the factory shall be associated with the management of the welfare arrangements of workers.

In this regard, the Maharashtra Government has made the rule, i.e., Rule 92, which provides for exemption from the provisions of Section 48 (creches) under clause (a) of this Section 50. We have already considered the aforesaid rule while discussing the provisions of Section 48 relating to creches.

3.17 Provisions of Chapter VIII relating to Annual Leave with Wages

The Factories Act, 1948, provides for weekly holidays, compensatory holidays as well as annual leave with wages according to certain rules. We have already considered the provisions relating to weekly and compensatory holidays in detail. Now, let us consider the provisions relating to annual leave with wages.

Chapter VIII containing the Sections from 78 to 84 of the Factories Act, 1948, provides for annual leave with wages. These provisions are given as below.

Application of Chapter VIII:

(1) The provisions of this Chapter shall not operate to the prejudice of any right to which a worker may be entitled under any other law or under the terms of any award, agreement (including settlement) or contract of service [Section 78(1)].

It is also provided that if such award, agreement (including settlement) or contract of service provides for a longer annual leave with wages than provided in this Chapter, the quantum of leave, which the worker shall be entitled to, shall be in accordance with such award, agreement or contract of service, but in relation to matters not provided for in such award, agreement or contract of service or matters which are provided for less favourably therein, the provisions of Sections 79 to 82, so far as may be, shall apply [Proviso to Section 78(1)].

(2) The provisions of this Chapter shall not apply to workers in any factory of any railway administered by the Government, who are governed by leave rules approved by the Central Government [Section 78(2)].

Rules relating to Annual Leave with Wages:

Section 79 provides for the rules relating to annual leave with wages which are given as below:

[1] Provisions or rules relating to leave entitlement [Section 79(1)]

Every worker who has worked for a period of two hundred and forty days or more in a factory during a calendar year shall be allowed during the subsequent calendar year, leave with wages for a number of days calculated at the rate of –

(a) if an adult, one day for every twenty days of work performed by him during the previous calendar year;

(b) if a child, one day for every fifteen days of work performed by him during the previous calendar year.

[2] Computation of period of the two hundred forty days for the purpose of leave entitlement

In Explanation 1 to Section 79(1) and the provision of Section 79(2) how the period of two hundred forty days is to be computed is made clear.

(a) For the purpose of this sub-section 1 of Section 79 –

(i) any days of lay-off, by agreement or contract or as permissible under the standing orders;

(ii) in the case of a female worker, maternity leave for any number of days not exceeding twelve weeks; and

(iii) the leave earned in the year prior to that in which the leave is enjoyed; shall be deemed to be days on which the worker has worked in a factory for the purpose of computation of the period of two hundred and forty days or more, but he shall not earn leave for these days. [Explanation 1 to Section 79(1)]

The leave admissible under this sub-section shall be exclusive of all holidays whether occurring or at either end of the period of leave. [Explanation 2 to Section 79(1)] **[II]** A worker whose service commences otherwise than on the first day of January shall be entitled to leave with wages at the rate laid down in clause (i) or, as the case may be, clause (ii) of sub-section (1) if he has worked for two-third of the total number of days in the remainder of the calendar year [Section 79(2)].

[3] Leave with wages and discharge, superannuation, dismissal, death of a worker, quitting of employment by a worker.

If a worker is discharged or dismissed from service or quits his employment or is superannuated or dies while in service, during the course of the calendar year, he/she or his/her heir or nominee, as the case may be, shall be entitled to wages in lieu of the quantum of leave to which he was entitled immediately before his discharge, dismissal, quitting of employment, superannuation or death, as the case may be, calculated at the rates specified in sub-section (1), even if he had not worked for the entire period specified in sub-section (1) or subsection (2) making him eligible to avail of such leave, and such payment shall be made –
   (a) where the worker is discharged or dismissed or quits employment before the expiry of the second working day from the date of discharge, dismissal or quitting; and
   (b) where the worker is superannuated or dies while in service, before the expiry of two months from the date of such superannuation or death [Section 79(3)].

[4] Provisions of Section 79(4) relating to treatment of fraction of leave

Section 79(4) states that, "in calculating leave under this section, fraction of leave of half a day or more shall be treated as one full day's leave and fraction of less than half a day shall be omitted."

[5] Provisions of Section 79(5) relating to treatment of unavailed leave

"If a worker does not in any one calendar year take the whole of the leave allowed to him under sub-section (1) or sub-section (2), as the case may be, any leave not taken by him shall be added to the leave to be allowed to him in the succeeding calendar year." [Section 79(5)].

It is also provided that the total number of days of leave that may be carried forward to a succeeding year shall not exceed thirty in the case of an adult or forty in the case of a child [Proviso 1 to Section 79(5)].

It is further provided that, a worker, who has applied for leave with wages but has not been given such leave in accordance with any scheme laid down in sub-sections (8) and (9) [or in contravention of sub-section (10)] shall be entitled to carry forward the leave refused without any limit [Proviso 2 to Section 79(5)].

[6] Application in writing to be made by a worker within a specified time

A worker may at any time apply in writing to the manager of a factory not less than fifteen days before on which he wishes his leave to begin, to take all the leave or any portion thereof allowable to him during the calender year [Section 79(6)]

It is also provided that the application shall be made not less than thirty days before the date on which the worker wishes his leave to begin, if he is employed in a public utility service as defined in clause (n) of Section 2 of the Industrial Disputes Act, 1947 (XIV of 1947) [Proviso 1 to Section 79(6)].

It is provided further that the number of times in which leave may be taken during any year shall not exceed three [Proviso 2 to Section 79(6)].

[7] Provisions of Section 79(7) relating to an application for leave covering a period of illness

The provisions of Section 79(7) imply that an application for leave covering a period of illness may not be made within the time specified in Section 79(6). According to Section 79(7), "If a worker wants to avail himself of the leave with wages due to him to cover a period of illness, he shall be granted such leave even if the application for leave is not made within the time specified in sub-section (6), and in such a case wages as admissible under Section 81 shall be paid not later than fifteen days, or in the case of a public utility service not later than thirty days from the date of the application for leave."

[8] Provisions relating to the scheme for granting the leave under Section 79(8)

Section 79(8) provides that, "For the purpose of ensuring the continuity of work, the occupier or manager of the factory, in agreement with the Works Committee of the factory constituted under Section 3 of the Industrial Disputes Act, 1947 (XIV of 1947), or a similar Committee constituted under any other Act or if there is no such Works Committee or a similar Committee in the factory in agreement with the representatives of the workers therein chosen in the prescribed manner, may lodge with Chief Inspector a scheme in writing whereby the grant of leave allowable under this section may be regulated."

[9] Display of the scheme for granting the leave

A scheme lodged under sub-section (8) shall be displayed at some conspicuous and convenient places in the factory and shall be in force for a period of twelve months from the date on which it comes into force, and may thereafter be renewed with or without modification for a further period of twelve months at a time, by the manager in agreement with the Works Committee or a similar Committee, or as the case may be, in agreement with the representatives of the workers as specified in sub-section (8), and a notice of renewal shall be sent to the Chief Inspector before it is renewed [Section 79(9)].

[10] Provisions relating to refusal of leave under Section 79(10)

"An application for leave which does not contravene the provisions of Section 10(6) shall not be refused unless refusal is in accordance with the sub-scheme for the time being in operation under sub-sections (8) and (9) of Section 79."

[11] Provisions of Section 79(11) relating to payment of wages to a worker for leave period even though the worker is discharged or he quits service

"If the employment of a worker is entitled to leave under Section (1) or sub-section (2), as the case may be, is terminated by the occupier before he has taken the entire leave to which he is entitled, or if he has applied for leave and having not been granted such leave, the worker quits employment before he has taken the leave, the occupier of the factory shall pay him the amount payable under the Section 80 in respect of the leave not taken, and such payment shall be made, where the employment of the worker is terminated by the occupier, before the expiry of the second working day after such termination and where a worker who quits the employment, on or before the next pay day."

[12] Provisions of Section 79(12) relating to unavailed leave and computation of period of notice

The unavailed leave of a worker shall not be taken into consideration in computing the period of any notice required to be given before discharge or dismissal.

Provisions of Section 80 relating to Wages during Leave Period:

(a) For the leave allowed to him under Section 78 or Section 79, as the case may be, shall be entitled to wages at a rate equal to the daily average of his total full time earnings for the days on which he actually worked during the month immediately preceding his leave, exclusive of any overtime and bonus but inclusive of dearness allowance and the cash equivalent of the advantage accruing through the concessional sale to the worker of food grains and other articles [Section 80(1)].

It is also provided that in the case of a worker who has not worked on any day during the calendar month immediately preceding his leave, he shall be paid at a rate equal to the daily average of his total full time earnings for the days on which he actually worked during the last calendar month preceding his leave, in which he actually worked, exclusive of any overtime and bonus but inclusive of dearness allowance and the cash equivalent of the advantage accruing through the concessional sale to the workers of foodgrains and other articles [Proviso to Section 80(1)].

(b) Section 80(2) makes it clear that, "the cash equivalent of the advantage accruing through the concessional sale to the worker of food grains and other articles shall be computed as often as may be prescribed on the basis of the maximum quantity of food grains and other articles admissible to a standard family."

'Standard family' means a family consisting of worker, his or her spouse and two children below the age of fourteen years requiring in all three adult consumption units. [Explanation 1 to Section 80(2)].

'Adult consumption unit' means the consumption unit of a male above the age of fourteen years and the consumption unit of a female above the age of fourteen years and that of a child below the age of fourteen years shall be calculated at the rates of 0.8 and 0.6, respectively, of one adult, consumption unit. [Explanation 2 to Section 80(2)]

(3) **Power of the State Government to make rules under Section 80(3):** The State Government may make rules prescribing –

- (a) the manner in which the cash equivalent of the advantage accruing through the concessional sale to a worker of food grains and other articles shall be computed, and
- (b) the registers that shall be maintained in a factory for the purpose of securing compliance with the provisions of this section.

3.18 Penalties

There are Sections from 92 to 106-A included in the Chapter X of the Factories Act of 1948 and these Sections make clear the provisions of this Act relating to penalties for certain offences and procedural matters.

(1) Provisions of Section 92 relating to general penalty for offences

In any factory, if there is any contravention of any of the provision of this Act or any rules made thereunder, subject to other express provisions made in the Act and also subject to the provisions of Section 93 which are given below, the penalties punishments for such contravention are given in Section 92. The provisions of Section 92 are as follows:

"Save as otherwise expressly provided in this Act and subject to the provisions of Section 93, if in, or in respect of, any factory there is any contravention of the provisions of this Act or of any rules made thereunder or of any order in writing given thereunder, the occupier and manager of the factory shall each be guilty of an offence and punishable with imprisonment for a term which may extend to two years or with fine which may extend to one lakh rupees or with both, and if the contravention is continued after conviction, with a further fine which may extend to one thousand rupees for each day on which the contravention is so continued [Section 92].

It is also provided that, "Where contravention of any of the provisions of Chapter IV or any rule made thereunder under Section 87 has resulted in an accident causing death or serious bodily injury, the fine shall not be less than twenty five thousand rupees in the case of an accident causing death and five thousand rupees in the case of an accident serious bodily injury" [Proviso to Section 92].

In this Section and in Section 94 "serious bodily injury" means an injury which involves, or in all probability will involve, the permanent loss of the use of, or permanent injury to, any limb or the permanent loss of, or injury to, sight or hearing, or the fracture of any bone, but shall not include, the fracture of bone or joint (not being fracture of more than one bone or joint) of any phalanges of the hand or foot [Explanation to Section 92].

(2) Provisions of Section 93 making clear the liability of owner of premises in certain circumstances

(a) Where in any premises separate buildings are leased to different occupiers for use as separate factories, the owner of the premises shall be responsible for the provision and maintenance of common facilities and services, such as approach road, drainage, water-supply, lighting and sanitation [Section 93 (1)].

(b) The Chief Inspector shall have, subject to the control of the State Government power to issue orders to the owners of the premises in respect for the carrying out of the provisions of sub-section (1) of Section 93 [Section 93 (2)].

(c) Where in any premises, independent or self-contained, floors or flats are leased to different occupiers for use as separate factories, the owner of the premises shall be liable as if he were the occupier or manager of a factory, of an contravention of the provisions of this Act in respect of –

  (i) latrines, urinals and washing facilities in so far as the maintenance of the common supply of water for these purposes is concerned;

  (ii) fencing of machinery and plant belonging to the owner and not specifically entrusted to the custody or use of an occupier;

(iii) safe means of access to the floors of flats, and maintenance and cleanliness of staircases and common passages;

(iv) precautions in case of fire;

(v) maintenance of hoists and lifts; and

(vi) maintenance of any other common facilities provided in the premises [Section 93 (3)].

(d) The Chief Inspector shall have, subject to the control of the State Government power to issue orders to the owners of the premises in respect of carrying out the provisions of sub-section (3) of Section 93 [Section 93 (4)].

(e) The provisions of sub-section (3) relating to the liability of the owner shall apply where in any premises independent rooms with common latrines, urinals and washing facilities are leased to different occupiers for use as separate factories [Section 93 (5)].

It is also provided that "the owner shall be responsible also for complying with the requirements relating to the provisions and maintenance of latrines, urinals and washing facilities" [Proviso to Section 93 (5)].

(f) The Chief Inspector shall have, subject to the control of the State Government, the power to issue orders to the owner of the premises referred to in Section 93 (5) in respect of carrying out the provisions of Section forty six or Section forty eight [Section 93 (6)].

(g) Where in any premises, portions of a room or a shed are leased to different occupiers for use as separate factories, the owner of the premises shall be liable for any contravention of the provisions of –

(i) Chapter III except Sections 14 and 15;

(ii) Chapter IV except Sections 22, 23, 27, 34, 35 and 36.

Provided that, in respect of the provisions of Sections 21, 24 and 32 the owner's liability shall be only in so far as such provisions relate to things under his control.

Provided further that, the occupier shall be responsible for complying with the provisions of Chapter IV in respect of plant and machinery belonging to or supplied by him.

(iii) Section 42 [Section 93 (7)].

(h) The Chief Inspector shall have, subject to the control of the State Government power to issue order to the owner of the premises in respect of carrying out the provision of sub-section (7) of Section 93 [Section 93 (8)].

(i) In respect of sub-sections (5) and (7) while computing for the purposes of any of the provisions of this Act the total number of workers employed, the whole of the premises shall be deemed to be a single factory [Section 93 (9)].

(3) Enhanced penalty provided under Section 94 after previous conviction

(a) If any person who has been convicted of any offence punishable under Section 92 is again guilty of an offence involving a contravention of the same provision, he shall be punishable on a subsequent conviction with imprisonment for a term which may extend to three years or with fine which shall not be less than ten thousand rupees but which, may extend to two lakh rupees or with both [Section 94 (1)].

It is also provided that "The court may, for any adequate and special reasons to be mentioned in the judgement, impose a fine of less than ten thousand rupees [Proviso 1 to Section 94 (1)].

It is also provided further that "Where contravention of any of the provisions of Chapter IV or any rule made thereunder or under Section 87 has resulted in an accident causing death or serious bodily injury, the fine shall not be less than thirty-five thousand rupees in the case of an accident causing death and ten thousand rupees in the case of an accident causing, serious bodily injury" [Proviso 2 to Section 94 (1)].

(b) For the purposes of sub-section (1), no cognizance shall be taken of any conviction made more than two years before the commission of the offence for which the person is subsequently being convicted [Section 94 (2)].

(4) Penalty imposed under Section 95 for obstructing the Inspector

"Whoever wilfully obstructs an Inspector in the exercise of any power conferred on him by or under this Act, or fails to produce on demand by an Inspector any registers or other documents in his custody kept in pursuance of this Act or of any rules made thereunder or conceals or prevents any workers in a factory from appearing before, or being examined by, an Inspector, shall be punishable with imprisonment for a term which may extend to six months or with fine which may extend to ten thousand rupees or with both."

(5) Penalty for wrongfully disclosing results of analysis under Section 91

"Whoever, except in so far as it may be necessary for purposes of a prosecution for any offence punishable under this Act, publishes or discloses to any person the results of an analysis made under Section 9l, shall be punishable with imprisonment for a term which may extend to six months or with fine which may extend to ten thousand rupees or with both" [Section 96].

(6) Penalty for contravention of the provisions of Section 41-B, 41-C and 41-H

(a) Whoever is to comply with or contravenes any the provisions of Sections 41-B, 41-C or 41-H or the rules made thereunder, shall, in respect of such failure or contravention, be punishable with imprisonment for a term which may extend to seven years and with fine which may extend to two lakh rupees, and in case the failure or contravention continues, with additional fine which may extend to five thousand rupees for every day during which such failure or contravention continues after the conviction for the first such failure or contravention [Section 96-A (1)].

(b) If the failure or contravention referred to in sub-section (1) continues beyond a period of one year after the date of conviction, the offender shall be punishable with imprisonment for a term which may extend to ten years [Section 96-A (2)].

(7) Provisions of Section 97 relating to offences by workers

(a) Subject to the provisions of Section 111, if any worker employed in a factory contravenes any provision of Act or rules or order made thereunder, imposing any duty or liability on workers, he shall be punishable with fine which may extend to five hundred rupees.

(b) Where a worker is convicted of an offence punishable under sub-section (1) the occupier or manager of the factory shall not be deemed to be guilty of an offence in respect of that contravention, unless it is proved that he failed to take all reasonable measures for its prevention.

(8) Penalty for using false certificate of fitness under Section 98

"Whoever knowingly uses or attempts to use, as a certificate of fitness granted to himself under Section 70, a certificate granted to another person under that Section, or who, having procured such a certificate, knowingly allows it to be used, or an attempt to use it to be made, by another person, shall be punishable with imprisonment for a term which may extend to two months or with fine which may extend to one thousand rupees or with both.

(9) Penalty for permitting double employment of child under Section 99

If a child works in a factory on any day on which he has already been working in another factory, the parent or guardian of the child or the person having custody of or control over him obtaining any direct benefit from his wages, shall be punishable with fine which may extend to one thousand rupees, unless it appears to the Court that the child so worked without the consent or convenience of such parent, guardian or person.

Section 100 relating to determination of occupier in certain cases is deleted with effect from 1st December 1987.

RECENT AMENDMENTS IN THE FACTORIES ACT, 1947

- Narendra Modi Government has recently cleared proposals to amend Factories Act, 1948.
- The Union Cabinet has approved 54 changes in the Factories Act, 1948.
- The Government will now table the proposed amendments in the Parliament and given the majority it enjoys, it won't be facing any problem to get them approved.

Important Amendments in the Factories Act, 1948

(a) The amendment is expected to allow women for night duty with adequate safety and also ensure provision for transport after work.

(b) The proposed amendments also aimed to increase the overtime hours from the current limit of 50 hours per quarter to 100 hours per quarter.

(c) With the approval of State government, the amendment also proposes this limit to be increased to a maximum of 125 hours per quarter.

(d) Ensuring safer working conditions for employees working in hazardous environment as well as provision of Canteen facilities.

(e) Factories employing 200 or more workers would have to provide canteen facilities instead of the present provision of 250 workers.

(f) It also provides for shelters or restrooms and lunchrooms in factories in which 75 or more workers are employed instead of the present stipulation of 150 workers.

(g) The changes also aim to prohibit pregnant women and physically handicapped people from being assigned to machinery-in-motion.

(h) Reducing the eligibility for entitlement of annual leave-with-wages to 90 days from the existing 240 days.

(i) Double overtime of workers to 100 hours per quarter from 50 hours per quarter.

(j) Ensuring safer working conditions for employees working in hazardous environment.

(k) Provision of Canteen facilities in factories having 75 or more workers.

Questions for Discussion

1. Explain the machinery for settlement of Industrial Disputes.
2. Explain the powers of authorities under the Industrial Disputes Act, 1946.
3. What is strike? Explain the various provisions relating to strike.
4. Describe the provisions relating to worker's health (under the Factories Act, 1948).
5. Discuss the various provisions relating to safety of workers (under the Factories Act, 1948).
6. Explain the various provisions relating to welfare of workers (under the Factories Act, 1948).
7. Write short notes:
    (a) Lockout
    (b) Lay-off
    (c) Retrenchment
    (d) Working hours of adults (Factories Act, 1948)
    (e) Penalties (Factories Act, 1948)
    (f) Provisions regarding leave with wages (Factories Act, 1948).

Questions from Previous Pune University Examinations

1. What do you understand by provisions regarding Leave with Wages? **April 2011**

Ans.: Refer to Article 3.17 of this Chapter.

2. Explain various Authorities, their Powers and Duties under I. D. Act, 1946. **April 2011**

Ans.: Refer to Article 3.5 of this Chapter.

3. "Welfare is a basic Need for any Factory". Discuss the statement with various Welfare Provisions under Factories Act, 1948. **October 2011**

Ans.: Refer to Article 3.16 of this Chapter.

4. What are the Various Health Provisions under the Factories Act, 1948? **April 2012**

Ans.: Refer to Article 3.14 of this Chapter.

Industrial Relations and Labour Law   The Industrial Disputes Act, 1946 and Factories Act, 1948

5. Define the term Strike. Explain various Provisions relating to Strikes.

October 2012

Ans. : Refer to Article 3.6.1 of this Chapter.

6. What are the Various Welfare Provisions under the Factories Act, 1948 ?

April 2014

Ans. : Refer to Article 3.16 of this Chapter.

7. Write Short Notes :

(A) Lay-off and Retrenchment.   **October 2010**

Ans. : Refer to Article 3.7 of this Chapter.

(B) Strike and Lock-out.   **April 2011, October 2011**

Ans. : Refer to Article 3.6 of this Chapter.

(C) Welfare Provisions.   **April 2011**

Ans. : Refer to Article 3.16 of this Chapter.

(D) Provisions of Leave with Wages.   **April 2012**

Ans. : Refer to Article 3.17 of this Chapter.

(E) Provisions relating to Cleanliness.   **October 2012**

Ans. : Refer to Article 3.14 (Point I) of this Chapter.

(F) Provisions relating to Overcrowding.   **October 2012**

Ans. : Refer to Article 3.14 (Point VI) of this Chapter.

(G) Provisions relating to Washing Facilities.   **October 2012**

Ans. : Refer to Article 3.16 (Point 1) of this Chapter.

✳✳✳

Chapter 4...

The Payment of Wages Act, 1936 and The Minimum Wages Act, 1948

Contents ...

The Payment of Wages Act, 1936

- 4.1 Introduction
- 4.2 Object, Scope and Extent of Application of the Act
- 4.3 Subject-matter of the Act
- 4.4 Definitions
- 4.5 Responsibility for Payment of Wages
- 4.6 Fixation of Wage Period
- 4.7 Time of Payment of Wages
- 4.8 Wages to be Paid to Persons who are Terminated from Service
- 4.9 Wages must be Paid on a Working Day Duly
- 4.10 Wages must be Paid in Currency Notes or Current Coins or in Both
- 4.11 Deductions from Wages
- 4.12 Unauthorised Deductions Not Allowed
- 4.13 What Shall Not be a Deduction?
- 4.14 Authorised Deductions
- 4.15 Amount of Deductions or Limit on Deductions [Section 7 (3)]
- 4.16 Maintenance of Records [Section 13 A]
- 4.17 Enforcement of the Act
- 4.18 Appointment of Inspectors, their Rights, Functions etc. under the Act for the Purposes of Enforcement of the Act
- 4.19 Penalties

The Minimum Wages Act, 1948

4.20 Introduction
4.21 Objects, Scope and Application of the Act
4.22 Outline of the Minimum Wages Act, 1948
4.23 Definitions
4.24 Fixing of Minimum Rates of Wages
4.25 Minimum Rate of Wages
4.26 Procedure for Fixing and Revising Minimum Wages
4.27 Wages in Kind
4.28 Payment of Minimum Rate of Wages
4.29 Fixing the Hours for a Normal Working Day
4.30 Provisions related to Overtime
4.31 Wages of Workers who Works for less than Normal Working Day
4.32 Wages for Two or More Classes of Work
4.33 Minimum Time Rate Wages for Piece Work
4.34 Maintenance of Registers and Records
4.35 Appointment of Inspectors and their Powers
4.36 Penalties
- Questions for Discussion
- Questions from Previous Pune University Examinations

Payment of Wages Act, 1936

4.1 Introduction

Before 1936, there was no law regulating the wages of Indian labour. Delay in making payment of wages, deductions from wages on various grounds and so on were general practices among the employers. Many of the industrial disputes were due to such practices. But there was no control on the employers who were powerful and who used to harass their workers. Therefore, the Royal Commission on Labour was appointed to consider the question of the desirability of passing legislation regulating the payment of wages and the measures to check unfair deductions. The recommendations of the Royal Commission on Labour formed the basis of the Payment of Wages Act, 1936.

4.2 Object, Scope and Extent of Application of the Act

The Act is applicable to the whole of India and came into force on and from 28th March, 1937. The Act is adapted in Independent India on and from 15th August, 1947 by the Indian (Adaptation of Existing Indian Laws) Order, 1947 made by the Governor - General in exercise of the power conferred by Sections 9 and 18 of the Indian Independence Act of 1947 and later by the Article 372 of the Constitution of India. This Act has been amended fifteen times since its passing. The last amendment was done in 2005 by the Payment of Wages (Amendment) Act, 2005 (41 of 2005) and it received the assent of the President of India on 5th September, 2005.

The basic object of the Payment of Wages Act of 1936 is to regulate the payment of wages to certain classes of persons employed in factories, industries etc. to which this Act is applicable and to make payment of wages in particular form and at regular intervals without making any unauthorised deductions.

The preamble to the Payment of Wages Act, 1936 clearly lays down the main object of the Act which is as follows:

"An Act is passed to regulate the payment of wages to certain classes of persons in the industry".

This Act requires the employers to make timely payments of Wages to persons employed in their industries. It also protects the workers against arbitrary fines imposed by their employers and unauthorised deductions made from their wages. Thus, the Act is basically enacted –

(1) for the purpose of safeguarding the wages of the workers under certain conditions as laid down in the Act and

(2) for the purpose of the making regular payment of wages to the workers without unauthorised deductions.

Section 1 of this Act makes the scope and the application of the Act very clear. Section 1 is as follows:

(1) This Act may be called the Payment of Wages Act, 1936 [Section 1 (1)].

(2) It extends to the whole of India [Section 1 (2)].

(3) It shall come into force on such date as the Central Government may, by notification in the Official Gazette, appoint [Section 1 (3)]. It was brought into force on 28th March, 1937.

(4) It applies in the first instance to the payment of wages to persons employed in any factory, to persons employed (otherwise than in a factory) upon or in railway by the railway administration or, either directly or through a sub-contractor, by a person fulfilling a

contract with a railway administration and to persons employed in an industrial or other establishment specified in sub-clauses (a) to (g) of clause (ii) of Section 2 [Section 1 (4)].

(5) The State Government may, after giving three months' notice of its intention of doing so, by notification in the Official Gazette, extend the provisions of this Act or any of them to the payment of wages to any class of persons employed in any establishment or class of establishments specified by the Central-Government under sub-clause (h) of clause (ii) of Section 2 [Section 1 (5)].

Provided that, in relation to any such establishment owned by the Central Government, no such notification shall be issued except with the concurrence of that Government [Proviso to Section 1 (5)].

By amending this Act, Section 1 (6) was substituted which is as follows:

(6) "This Act applies to wages payable to an employed person in respect of a wage period if such wages for that wage period do not exceed Eighteen Thousand Five Hundred Rupees (₹ 18,000) per month or such other high sum which, on the basis of figures of the Consumer Expenditure Survey published by the National Survey Organisation, the Central Government may, after every five years, by notification in the Official Gazette, specify". Thus, wages averaging less than ₹ 18,000 per month are covered or protected by this Act w.e.f. 11-9-2012.

Originally, this limit was ₹ 400/- only. The limit was raised from ₹ 400/- to ₹ 1,000/- by the Payment of Wages (Amendment) Act of 1976 and then to ₹ 1,600/- by the Payment of Wages (Amendment) Act of 1982. Thereafter, it was increased upto ₹ Ten Thousand Now, it is ₹ 18,000/-. Thus, at present this Act does not apply to persons whose wages exceed ₹ 18,000/- per month. It must also be noted that this Act is not applicable to all the employees in various industries in India, but it covers only certain classes of persons employed in industries specified in Section 1 (4), (5) and (6) of the Act.

4.3 Subject-Matter of the Act

From the provisions of Section 1 (4) and (5) which have been given above, the subject-matter of the Act is understood which is as follows:

In the first, this Act applies to the payment of wages

(1) to persons in any factory to which this Act is applicable

(2) to persons employed otherwise than in a factory or railway by a railway administration or

(3) to persons employed either directly or through a sub-contractor, by a person fulfilling a contract with a railway administration.

The State Governments are empowered to extend this Act or any part of this Act, by notification in the Official Gazette of giving three month's notice, to the payment of wages of any class of persons employed in any industrial establishment or to any class of persons employed in any class or group of industrial establishments.

Section 24 of the Act makes clear the power of the Central Government in this respect. The powers conferred upon the State Government as above shall be powers of the Central Government in relation to

(a) railways,

(b) air-transport services,

(c) mines and

(d) oil-fields

The Central Government by notification in the Official Gazette has extended this Act to:

(i) The payment of wages to all classes of persons employed in coal-mines (*w.e.f.* 15th January, 1948, vide Gazette of India, 1948, Pt. I.S.I. p. 44);

(ii) The payment of wages to all classes of persons employed in mines, other than coal-mines, to which the Indian Mines Act, 1923, applies (*w.e.f.* 15th June, 1951, vide Gazette of India, 1951, Pt. II, S.3, p. 537);

(iii) The payment of wages to all classes of persons employed in mines to which the Mines Act, 1952 applies in certain parts of India and to the payment of wages to all classes of persons employed in mines to which the Mines Act, 1952 applies in the rest of India except the State of Jammu Kashmir (Vide Gazette of India, 1952, Pt. II. S.3, p. 1171)

(iv) The payment of wages to all classes of persons employed in mines to which the Mines Act, 1952 applies [*w.e.f.* 1st February, 1959, Vide Gazette of India, 1959, Pt. II, Sec. 3 (ii), p. 2979]; and

(v) The payment of wages to all classes of persons employed in oil-fields in the whole of India except the State of Jammu and Kashmir, and the State of Assam to which this Act has already been extended separately [*w.e.f.* 14th September, 1962, Vide Gazette of India, 1962, Pt. II. sec, 3 (ii), p. 3002].

4.4 Definitions

The definitions of various terms or words used are given in Section 2 of this Act which are as follows.

(1) Appropriate Government [Section 2 (1)]:

"Appropriate Government" means in relation to railways, air transport services, mines and oil fields, the Central Government and, in relation to all other cases, the State Government.

(2) Employed Person [Section 2 (i-a)]

"Employed person" includes the legal representative of a deceased employed person.

(3) Employer [Section 2 (i-b)]

'Employer' includes the legal representative of a deceased employer.

(4) Factory [Section 2 (i-c)]

"Factory" means a factory as defined in clause (m) of Section 2 of the Factories Act, 1948 and includes any place to which the provisions of that Act have been applied under sub-section (1) of Section 85 thereof.

A factory under the Factories Act of 1948 [Section 2 (m)] means and includes any premises including the precincts thereof –

(a) whereon ten or more workers are working, or were working on any day of the preceding twelve months, and in any part of which a manufacturing process is being carried on with the aid of power, or is ordinarily so carried on;

(b) whereon twenty or more workers are working, or were working on any day of the preceding twelve months, and in any part of which a manufacturing process is being carried on without the aid of power, or is ordinarily so carried on, but it does not include a mine subject to the operation of the Mines Act, 1952, or a mobile unit belonging to the armed forces of the Union, a railway running shed or a hotel, restaurant or eating place;

For computing the number of workers for the purposes of this Section 2 (m), all workers in different groups and relays in a day shall be taken into account. [Explanation 1 to Section 2 (m) of the Factories Act, 1948].

Moreover for the purposes of this Section 2 (m), the mere fact that an Electronic Data Processing Unit or a Computer Unit is installed in any premises or part thereof, shall not be construed to make it a factory, if no manufacturing process is being carried on in such premises or part thereof. [Explanation II to Section 2 (m) of the Factories Act 1948].

According to Section 2 (1-b) of the Payment of Wages Act, 1936, a factory also includes any place to which the provisions of the Factories Act, 1948 have been applied under Section 85 (1), thereof which says that the State Government may, by notification in the Official Gazette, declare that all or any of the provisions of this Act shall apply to any place wherein a manufacturing process is carried on with or without the aid of power or is so ordinarily carried on, notwithstanding that:

(i) the number of persons employed therein is less than ten, if working with the aid of power and less than twenty if working without the aid of power;

(ii) the persons working therein are not employed by the owner thereof but are working with the permission of, or under agreement with such owner;

Provided that, the manufacturing process is not being carried on by the owner only with the help of his family. This means where the manufacturing process is carried on by the owner with the help of his family, then sub-clause (ii) which is mentioned above would not apply. This must be noted that for the purpose of this Section 85 of the Factories Act, 1948, owner includes a lessee or mortgagee with possession of the premises.

(5) Industrial or Other Establishment [Section 2 (ii)]

Industrial or other establishment means any:

(a) tramway service or motor transport service engaged in carrying passengers or goods or both by road for hire or reward; (aa) air transport service, other than such service belonging to, or exclusively employed in the military, naval or air force of the Union of the Civil Aviation Department of the Government of India.

(b) dock; wharf or jetty;

(c) inland vessel, mechanically propelled;

(d) mine, quarry or oil-field;

(e) plantation;

(f) workshop or other establishment in which articles are produced, adapted or manufactured, with a view to their use, transport or sale;

(g) establishment in which any work relating to the construction, development or maintenance of buildings, roads, bridges or canals or relating to operations connected with navigation, irrigation or the supply of water, or relating to the generation, transmission and distribution of electricity or any other form of power is being carried on;

(h) any other establishment or class of establishments which the Appropriate Government may, having regard to the nature thereof, the need for protection of persons employed therein and other relevant circumstances, specify by notification in the Official Gazette.

Thus, all the above mentioned establishments are industrial establishments and the Appropriate Government has the right to declare any establishment as industrial or other establishment for the purpose of this Act by giving notification in the Official Gazette. In one case, it was held that where the printing work in the printing press was carried on at one place and its composition work at the other place, the latter place also was declared as the industrial establishment within the definition of this Act.

(6) Mine [Section 2 (ii-a)]

'Mine' has the meaning assigned to it in clause (j) of sub-section (1) of Section 2 of the Mines Act, 1952.

According to Section 2 (1) (j) of the Mines Act, 1952 "mines" means any excavation where any operation for the purpose of searching for or obtaining minerals has been or is being carried on and includes:

(a) all borings, bore holes and oil wells;

(b) all shafts, in or adjacent to and belonging to a mine whether in the course of being sunk or not;

(c) all levels and inclined planes in the course of being driven;

(d) all open cast workings;

(e) all conveyors or aerial ropeways provided for the bringing into or removal from a mine of minerals or other articles or for the removal of refuse therefrom;

(f) all edits, levels, planes, machinery, works, railways, tramways and sidings, in or adjacent to and belonging to a mine;

(g) all workshops and stores situated within the precincts of a mine and under the same management and used solely for purpose connected with that mine or a number of mines under the same management;

(h) all power stations for supplying electricity solely for the purpose of working the mine or number of mines under the same management;

(i) any premises for the time being used for depositing refuse from a mine, or in which any operation in connection with such refuse is being carried on, being premises exclusively occupied by the owner of the mine;

(j) unless exempted by the Central Government by notification in the Official Gazette, any premises or part thereof, in or adjacent to and belonging to a mine, on which any process ancillary to the getting, dressing or preparation for sale of minerals or of coke is being carried on.

(7) Plantation [Section 2 (iii)]

'Plantation' has the meaning assigned to it in clause (f) of Section 2 of the Plantations Labour Act, 1951.

According to Section (2) (f) of the Plantation Labour Act, 1951 "Plantation" means any plantation to which the Plantation Labour Act, 1951 whether wholly or in part, applies and includes offices, hospitals, dispensaries, schools, and any other premises and for any purpose connected with such plantation, but does not include any factory on the premises to which the provisions of the Factories Act, 1948 apply".

(8) Prescribed [Section 2 (iv)]

'Prescribed' means prescribed by rules made under this Act.

(9) Railway Administration [Section 2 (v)]

'Railway Administration' has the meaning assigned to it in Section 3 (6) of the Indian Railways Act, 1890.

According to Section 3 (6) of the Indian Railways Act, 1890 "Railway Administration" means the Manager of the railway and includes the "Government".

(10) Wages [Section 2 (vi)]

'Wages' means all remuneration (whether by way of salary, allowances or otherwise) expressed in terms of money or capable of being so expressed which would, if the terms of employment, expressed or implied, were fulfilled, be payable to a person employed in respect of his employment or of work done in such employment, and includes:

(a) any remuneration payable under any award or settlement between the parties or order of a Court;

(b) any remuneration to which the person employed is entitled in respect of overtime work or holidays or any leave period;

(c) any additional remuneration payable under the terms of employment whether called a bonus or by any other name.

(d) any sum which by reason of the termination of employment of the person employed is payable under any law, contract of instrument which provides for the payment of such sum, whether with or without deductions, but does not provide for the time within which the payment is to be made;

(e) any sum to which the person employed is entitled under any scheme framed under any law for the time being in force;

The expression 'Wages' does not include the following:

(i) any bonus (whether under a scheme of profit sharing or otherwise) which does not form part of the remuneration payable under the terms of employment or which is not payable under any award or settlement between the parties or order of a Court;

(ii) the value of any house-accommodation, or of the supply of light, water, medical attendance or other amenity or of any service excluded from the computation of wages by a general or special order of the Appropriate Government;

(3) any contribution paid by the employer to any Pension or Provident Fund, and the interest which may have accrued thereon;

(4) any travelling allowance or the value of any travelling concession;

(5) any sum paid to the employed person to defray special expenses entailed on him by the nature of this employment; or

(6) any gratuity payable on the termination of employment in cases other than those specified in sub-clause (d).

Provisions

4.5 Responsibility for Payment of Wages

Every employer shall be responsible for the payment to persons employed by him of all wages required to be paid under this Act [Section 3].

Provided that in the cases of persons employed in factories, industrial or other establishments or in railways otherwise than by a contractor, following persons shall be responsible for making the payment.

(a) In factories, the person who is appointed as the manager of the factory under Section 7 (1) (f) of the Factories Act, 1948.

(b) In industrial or other establishment, if there is a person responsible to the employer for the supervision and the control of the industrial or other establishment.

(c) In railways, otherwise than the factories, if the employer is the railway administration and the railway administration has nominated a person in this behalf for the local area concerned;

Thus, Section 3 of the Payment of Wages Act fixes the responsibility on the particular person to make payment to the persons employed in factories, industrial or other establishment.

4.6 Fixation of Wage Period

Every person responsible for the Payment of Wages (for example, in the case of factories, the manager appointed under the Factories Act, 1948, in the case of industrial or other establishment, a person responsible to the employer for the supervision and control of the industrial or other establishment as the case may be etc.) shall fix wage periods in respect of which such wages shall be payable [Section 4 (1)]. However, wage-period shall not exceed one month [Section 4 (2)].

4.7 Time of Payment of Wages

Provisions relating to the time of paying wages are as follows:

The wages of every person employed upon or in any railway, factory, industrial establishment or any other establishment upon or in which less than one thousand persons are employed, shall be paid before the expiry of the seventh day and if the number of persons employed is more than one thousand, wages shall be paid before the expiry of the tenth day after the last day of the wage-period in respect of which wages are payable [Section 5 (a) and (b)].

It is also provided that in the case of persons employed on a wharf, dock or jetty or in a mine, the balance of wages found due to completion of the final tonnage account of the ship or wagons loaded or unloaded, as the case may be, shall be paid before the expiry of seventh day from the day of such completion [Proviso to Section 5 (1)].

4.8 Wages to be Paid to Persons who are Terminated from Service

Where the employment of any person is terminated by the employer or on behalf of the employer, the wages earned by such person whose employment is terminated shall be paid before the expiry of the second working day from the day on which this employment is terminated [Section 5 (2)]. However, it is provided in this section that where the employment of any person in an establishment is terminated due to the closure of the establishment for any reason other than a weekly or other recognised holiday, the wages earned by him shall be paid before the expiry of the second day from the day on which his employment is so terminated [Proviso to Section 5 (2)].

4.9 Wages Must be Paid on a Working Day Only

It is provided in Section 5 (4) that all payments of wages must be made on a working day. Section 5 (4) is reproduced below:

"Save as otherwise provided in sub-section 2 of Section 5, all payments of wages shall be made on a working day".

4.10 Wages must be Paid in Currency Notes or Current Coins or in both

It is provided in Section 6 of this Act that all wages shall be paid in currency notes or in current coins or in both. It is also provided that the employer may, after obtaining the written authorisation of the employed person, pay him wages either by a cheque or by crediting the wages in his bank account.

This Section obviously makes it clear that no employer is permitted to pay wages in kinds. However, as the process of paying wages in cash may be cumbersome, if the number of persons employed is large, it is permitted that payment of wages can be made by issuing the cheques or crediting the bank accounts of the persons employed with their prior permission. This may also help to inculcate banking habits amongst the people whose bank accounts are thus opened.

4.11 Deductions from Wages

Unauthorised deductions are not allowed under this Act. However, certain deductions are authorised under this Act. The provisions have been made in this Act relating to authorised deductions, amount of deductions or limit on deductions. Now, consider these provisions.

4.12 Unauthorised Deductions not Allowed

One of the objectives of this Act is to regulate the payment of wages to persons employed in various factories, industrial and other establishments. The Act specifically authorises only certain deductions beyond which no employer, in any way, is authorised to make any deductions. Sections 7 to 13 of this Act deal with the deductions which may be made from wages. The various provisions related to the deductions which can be made from wages are as follows:

Section 7 (1) says that notwithstanding the provisions of Section 47 (2) of the Indian Railways Act, 1890, the wages of an employed person shall be paid to him without deductions of any kind except those authorised by or under this Act. These provisions of Section 7 are mandatory.

Every payment made by the employed person to his employer or to the agent of the employer shall, for the purposes of this Act, be deemed to be a deduction from wages. [Explanation I to Section 7 (1)].

4.13 What Shall not be a Deduction?

It is made clear in the explanation II to Section 7 (1) that any loss of wages resulting from the imposition, for good and sufficient cause, upon a person employed of any of the penalties mentioned below:

(1) the withholding of increment of promotion which may include the stoppage of increment at an efficiency bar,

(2) the reduction to a lower post of time-scale or to a lower stage in a time-scale as the case may be; or

(3) suspension

shall not be deemed to be a deduction from wages in any case where the rules made by the employer for the purposes of imposition of any such penalty are in confirmity with the requirements, if any, which may be specified in this behalf by the appropriate Government by the notification in the Official Gazette.

4.14 Authorised Deductions

Section 7 (2) states that the deductions from the wages of an employed person shall be made only in accordance with the provisions of this Act. The kinds of deductions from the wages of an employed person that are allowed according to various Sections of this Act are as follows:

(I) Deductions on Account of the Fines [Sections 7 (2) (a) and 8]

Deduction made on account of fines is legal, provided the provisions of Section 8 are observed. As a general rule, Section 8 does not permit any employer to impose any fine on any person employed by him. But certain exceptions are made to this rule which are embodied in Section 8 of this Act and Section 8 is reproduced below:

No fine shall be imposed on any employed person save in respect of such act and omissions on his part as the employer, with the previous approval of the appropriate Government or of the prescribed authority, may have specified by notice under sub-section (2) [Section 8 (1)].

A notice specifying such acts and omissions shall be exhibited in the prescribed manner of the premises in which the employment is carried on or in the case of persons employed upon a railway (otherwise than in a factory), at the prescribed place or places [Section 8 (2)].

No fine shall be imposed on any employed person until he has been given an opportunity of showing cause against the fine, or otherwise than in accordance with such procedure as may be prescribed for the imposition of fines [Section 8 (3)].

The total amount of fine which may be imposed in any wage-period on any employed person shall not exceed an amount equal to three per cent of the wages payable to him in respect of that wage-period [Section 8 (4)].

No fine shall be imposed on any employed person who is under the age of fifteen years [Section 8 (5)].

No fine imposed on any employed person shall be recovered from him by instalments or after the expiry of ninety days from the day on which it was imposed [Section 8 (6)].

Every fine shall be deemed to have been imposed on the day of the act or omission in respect of which it was imposed [Section 8 (7)].

All fines and all realisations thereof shall be recorded in a register to be kept by the person responsible for the payment or wages under Section 3 in such form as may be prescribed; and all such realisations shall be applied only to such purposes beneficial to the persons employed in the factory or establishment as are approved by the prescribed authority [Section 8 (8)].

When the persons employed upon or in any railway, factory or industrial or other establishment are part of a staff employed under the same management, all such realisations may be credited to a common fund maintained for the staff as a whole, provided that the fund shall be applied only to such purposes as are approved by the prescribed authority. [Explanation to Section 8 (8)].

(II) Deductions for Absence from Duty [Section 7 (2) (b) and 9]

An employer may deduct from the wages of a person employed by him on account of the absence of an employed person from duty [Section 7 (2) (b)]. Section 9 of this Act analyses the causes and extent of the deductions allowed on account of absence from duty. Section 9 is reproduced below.

Deductions may be made under clause (b) of sub-section (2) of Section 7 only on account of the absence of an employed person from the place or places where, by the terms of this employment, he is required to work, such absence being for the whole or any part of the period during which is so required to work [Section 9 (1)].

The amount of such deductions shall in no case bear to the wages payable to the employed person in respect of the wage-period for which the deduction is made a larger proportion than the period for which he was absent, bears to the total period, within such wage-period, during which by the terms of his employment, he was required to work [Section 9 (2)].

Provided that, subject to any rules made in this behalf by the Appropriate Government, if ten or more employed persons acting in concert absent themselves without due notice (that is to say without giving the notice which is required under the terms of their contracts of employment) and without reasonable cause, such deduction from wage of any such persons may include such amount not exceeding his wages for eight days as may by any such terms be due to the employer in lieu of due notice [Proviso to Section 9].

For the purposes of this action, an employed person shall be deemed to be absent from the place where he is required to work if, although present in such place, he refuses, in pursuance of a stay-in strike or for any other cause which is not reasonable in the circumstances, to carry out his work [Explanation to Section 9].

(III) Deductions for Damages or Losses [Section 7 (2) (c) (m) (n) (o) and 10]

Deductions for damages or losses on account of different reasons from the wages of a person employed are allowed under this Act and accordingly provisions are made which are as follows:

(1) Deductions for damages or loss of goods expressly entrusted to the employed person for custody; or for loss of money for which he is required to account, where such damages or losses are directly attributable to his neglect or default [Section 7 (2) (c)].

(2) Deductions for recovery of losses sustained by a railway administration on account of acceptance by the employed person of counterfeit or base coins mutilated or forged currency notes [Section 7 (2) (m)].

(3) Deductions for recovery of losses sustained by a railway administration on account of the failure of the person employed to invoice, to bill, to collect or to account for the appropriate charges due to that administration, whether in respect of fares, freight, demurrage, wharfage and cranage or in respect of sale of goods in catering establishments or in respect of commodities in grainshops or otherwise [Section 7 (2) (n)].

(4) Deductions for recovery of losses sustained by a railway administration on account of any rebates or refunds of incorrectly granted by the person employed where such losses are directly attributable to the neglect or default of the person employed [Section 7 (2) (o)].

Section 10 of the Payment of Wages Act, 1936 lays down the procedure and the extent to which the deductions are permissible.

A deduction under Section 7 (2) (c) or (o) lays down the procedure and the extent to which the deductions are permissible.

A deduction under Section 7 (2) (c) or (o) shall not exceed the amount of damages or losses caused to the employer by a result of the negligence or default of the person employed [Section 10 (1)].

Deductions shall not be made under Section 7 (2) (c) or (m) or (n) or (o) until the employed person has been given an opportunity of showing cause against the deduction, or otherwise than in accordance with such procedure as may be prescribed for making such deductions [Section 10 (1-A)]. It is further provided that all such deductions and realisations thereof shall be recorded properly in a register to be kept by the person responsible for making payment of wages under Section 3 of the Payment of Wages Act, 1936 in such form as may be prescribed [Section 10 (2)].

(IV) Deductions for Services Rendered or Supplied by the Employer [Sections 7 (2) (d), (e) and 11]

If house accommodations and other such amenities or other services are rendered by the employer and accepted by any person employed, deductions from wages of the employed person for those purposes are allowed under clauses (d) and (e) of sub-section 2 of Section 7 which are as follows:

Deductions for house-accommodation supplied by the employer or by the Government or any housing board set up under any law for the time being in force (whether the Government or the board is the employer or not) or any other authority engaged in the business of subsidising house-accommodation which may be specified in this behalf by the Appropriate Government by notification in the Official Gazette [Section 7 (2) (d)].

Deductions for such amenities and services supplied by the employer as the State Government or any officer specified by it in this behalf may, be general or special order, authorise [Section 7 (2) (e)].

However, the word 'services' in the above mentioned clause does not include the supply of tools and raw materials required for the purposes of employment;

Section 11 of this Act imposes certain conditions and also certain limits beyond which deductions for house accommodation, amenities etc. from wages are not allowed. Section 11 states that a deduction under clause (d) or (e) of sub-section (2) of Section 7 shall not be made from the wages of an employed person, unless the house accommodation, amenity of service has been accepted by him, as a term of employment or otherwise, and such deduction shall not exceed an amount equivalent to the value of the house accommodation amenity or service supplied and in the case of a deduction under the said clause (e), shall be subject to such conditions as the Appropriate Government may impose.

(V) Deductions for Recovery of Advances of Money [Sections 7 (2) (f) and 12]

Section 7 (2) (f) states that deductions are allowed to be made for the recovery of advances of whatever nature, including advances for travelling allowance or conveyance allowance, and the interest due in respect thereof or for adjustment of over-payments of wages. Section 12 of the Payment of Wages Act, 1936 specifies under what conditions these deductions are allowed to be made from the wages of an employed person. Section 12 is reproduced below.

Deductions under clause (f) of sub-section (2) of Section 7 shall be subject to the following conditions namely:

(a) Recovery of an advance of money given before employment began shall be made from the first payment of wages in respect of a complete wage-period; but no recovery shall be made of such advances given for travelling expenses.

(aa) Recovery of an advance of money given after employment began shall be subject to such conditions as the Appropriate Government may impose.

(b) Recovery of an advance made, not already earned shall be subject to any rules made by the Appropriate Government regulating the extent to which such advances may be given for the instalments by which they may be recovered.

(VI) Deductions for the Recovery of Loans given by an Employer to an Employed Person [Sections 7 (2) (ff), (fff) and 12-A]

Deductions for the recovery of loans given to the employed person from any fund constituted for the welfare of labour and also of loans granted for house building and other purposes approved by the appropriate Government. They are also allowed to be made from the wages of employed persons. Not only the recovery of loans but also interest on loans taken can be deducted from the wages of the employed person. Section 7 (2) (ff) states that deductions for the recovery of loans made from any fund constituted for the welfare of labour in accordance with the rules approved by the Appropriate Government and the interest due thereof and Section 7 (2) (fff) lays down that deductions for the recovery of loans granted for house building or for other purposes approved by the Appropriate Government and the interest due in respect thereof.

Deductions for the recovery of loans granted under the above mentioned clause (fff) of sub-section (2) of the Section 7 of this Act shall be subject to any rules made by the appropriate Government regulating the extent to which such loans may be granted and the rate of interest payable thereon [Section 12-A].

(VII) Deductions Allowed to be made for Payments to Co-operative Societies and Insurance Schemes [Sections 7 (2) (j) (k) and 13]

The deductions allowed to be made for the payments to co-operative societies and insurance schemes include the following:

(i) Deductions for the payment to co-operative societies approved by the Appropriate Government or any other officer specified in this behalf or to a scheme of insurance maintained by the Indian Post Office [Section 7 (2) (j)];

(ii) Deductions, made with the written authorisation of the person employed for the payment of any premium of Life Insurance Policy of the employed person to the L.I.C. of India established under L.I.C. Act, 1956 or for the purchase of securities of the Government of India or of any State Government or for being deposited in any Post Office Savings Bank in furtherance of any savings scheme of any such Government [Section 7 (2) (k)];

However, the deductions under clauses (j) and (k) of sub-clause (2) of Section 7 are subject to such conditions as the Appropriate Government may impose [Section 13].

(VIII) Other Deductions

Other deductions which are allowed to be made from the wages of the employed persons under this Act are as follows:

(1) Deductions of income-tax payable by the employed person [Section 7 (2) (g)].

(2) Deductions required to be made by order of any court or other authority competent to make such order [Section 7 (2) (h)].

(3) Deductions for payments to co-operative societies of advances from any Provident Fund to which the Provident Fund Act, 1925 applies or any recognised Provident

Fund as defined in Section 58-A of the Indian Income Tax Act, 1922 or any Provident Fund approved on the behalf by the Appropriate Government during the continuance of such approval [Section 7 (2) (i)].

(4) Deductions made, with written authorisation of the employed person for the payment of his contribution to any fund constituted by the employer or a trade union registered under the Trade Union Act, 1926 for due welfare of the employed persons or the members of their families, or both, and approved by the Appropriate Government or any officer specified by the appropriate Government in this behalf, during the continuance of such approval [Section 7 (2) (kk)].

(5) Deductions made, with the written authorisation of the employed person, for payment of fees payable by him for the membership of any trade union registered under the Trade Union Act, 1926 [Section 7 (2) (kkk)].

(6) Deductions for making payments of insurance premia of Fidelity Guarantee Bonds [Section 7 (2) (l)].

(7) Deductions made with the written authorisation of the employed person for contribution to the National Relief Fund of the Prime Minister or to any such other fund as the Central Government may specify by giving proper notification in the Official Gazette [Section 7 (2) (p)].

(8) Deductions for contribution to any insurance scheme framed by the Central Government for the benefit of its employees [Section 7 (2) (q)].

4.15 Amount of Deductions or Limit on Deductions [Section 7 (3)]

Section 7 (3) of this Act places certain limits on the amount of deductions which are allowed to be made from the wages of the employed persons. Section 7 (3) is as follows:

Notwithstanding anything contained in this Act, the total amount of deductions which may be made under sub-section (2) in any wage period from the wages of any employed person shall not exceed:

(1) in cases where such deductions are wholly or partly made for payments to co-operative societies under clause (j) of sub-section (2), seventy-five per cent of such wages, and

(2) in any other case, fifty per cent of such wages.

However, where the total deductions authorised under sub-section (2) of Section 7 exceed seventy five per cent or, as the case may be, fifty per cent of wages, the excess may be recovered in such manner as may be prescribed [Proviso to Section 7 (3)].

Nothing contained in this section shall be construed as precluding the employer from recovering from the wages of the employed person or otherwise any amount payable by such person under any law for the time being in force other than the Indian Railways Act, 1989 [Section 7 (4)].

4.16 Maintenance of Records [Section 13 A]

It is mandatory on the part of an employer to maintain necessary registers and records which show particulars of deductions made, wages paid, receipts given etc. of employed persons in his factory, industrial or other establishment, as the case may be, such registers and records are required to be maintained in such form as may be prescribed. All such records and registers, required to be maintained for the purposes of this Act, are required to be preserved for a period of three years after the date of the last entry made therein. The provisions relating to the maintenance of records and registers are made in Section 13 A of this Act. Section 13 A states that every employer shall maintain such registers and records giving such particulars of persons employed by him, the work performed by them, the wages paid to them, the deductions made from their wages, the receipts given by them and such other particulars and in such form as may be prescribed. It is further provided that every register and record required to be maintained under this section shall, for the purposes of this Act, be preserved for a period of three years after the date of the last entry made therein.

4.17 Enforcement of the Act

For supervising whether the payment of wage is done to the employed persons and whether only authorised deductions are made from the wages of employed persons, according to the provisions of this Act and for making necessary inquiries and examination for that purpose, Inspectors of Factories appointed under Factories Act, 1948 have to work as Inspectors for the purposes of this Act in respect of all factories within the local limits assigned to the Inspectors [Section 14 (1)].

Section 15 of the Payment of Wages Act, 1936 empowers the Appropriate Government to make an appointment of some person as the authority to hear and decide for any specified area all claims arising out of deductions from wages, or delay in payment of wages of the persons employed in various factories, establishments to which it is applicable. Such person who is appointed as the authority by the Appropriate Government can be a preceding officer of any Labour Court or Industrial Tribunal constituted under the Industrial Disputes Act of 1947 or under any corresponding law relating to the investigation and settlement of industrial disputes in force in the State or any Commissioner for Workmen's Compensation or any other officer with experience as a judge of Civil Court or as a stipendiary magistrate [Section 15 (1)]. However, it is also provided that where the Appropriate Government considers it necessary to do so, it may appoint more than one authority for any specified area and may, by general or special order, provide for the distribution or allocation of work to be performed by them under this Act [Proviso to Section 15 (1)].

Section 16 of this Act provides for the single application in respect of claims from unpaid group while in Section 17, the provision of making an appeal is made.

Section 18 provides that every authority appointed under Section 15 of this Act shall have all the powers of a Civil Court under the Civil Procedure Code, 1908 for:

(a) the purpose of taking evidence and enforcing the attendance of witnesses; and

(b) the purpose of compelling the production of documents.

4.18 Appointment of Inspectors, their Rights, Functions etc. under the Act for the Purposes of Enforcement of the Act

As already mentioned, an Inspector of Factories appointed under Section 8 (1) of the Factories Act of 1948 works as the Inspector for the purposes of the Payment of Wages Act in respect of factories within the legal limits assigned to him [Section 14 (1)].

The appropriate Government is empowered to appoint such other persons as it thinks fit and proper to the Inspectors for the purposes of this Act by giving notification in the Official Gazette and it may also define the local limits within which the class of factories and other industrial or other establishments in respect of which the Inspectors shall exercise their functions [Section 14 (3)].

The Appropriate Government may also appoint Inspectors for the purposes of this Act in respect of persons employed upon a Railway, otherwise in a factory, to whom this Act applies [Section 14 (2)].

Section 14 (4) throws light on the powers, functions, rights etc. of the Inspectors thus appointed for the purpose of enforcement of the Act which are as follows:

(1) An Inspector may make such examination and inquiries as he thinks fit and proper in order to ascertain whether the provisions of this Act or rules made thereunder are being observed or not.

(2) An Inspector may enter, inspect and search any premises of any railway, factory or industrial or any other establishment at any reasonable time for the purpose of carrying out the objects of the Act with such assistants, if any, as he thinks fit and proper.

(3) An Inspector is empowered to supervise the payment of wages to persons employed upon any railway or in any factory or industrial or other establishment.

(4) He may require by a written order the production of any register or record maintained in the pursuance of the Act at such place as may be prescribed. Moreover, he may also take on the spot or otherwise the statements of any persons which he may consider necessary for carrying out the purposes of the Act.

(5) An Inspector has the right to seize or take copies of registers or documents or portions thereof if he considers it relevant in respect of an offence under this Act which he has reason to believe has been committed by an employer.

(6) Such Inspector may exercise such other powers as may be prescribed.

However, it should be noted that no person shall be compelled under this Section 14 (4) to answer any question or make any statement tending to incriminate himself [Proviso to Section 14 (4)].

According to Section 14 (4-A), the provisions of the Code of Criminal Procedure of 1973 shall, so far as may be, apply to any search or seizure as they apply to any other search or seizure made under the authority of a warrant issued under Section 94 of the said code. The Inspectors thus appointed are deemed to be the public servants within the meaning of the Indian Penal Code [Section 14 (5)].

4.19 Penalties

Section 20 of this Act provides for the imposition of penalties for various offences which are as follows:

(1) Penalty for Contravening the Provisions of the Following Sections

Section 5 (1) (2) and (3) [Time of payment of wages], Section 7 [Deductions which may be made from wages of an employed person], Section 8 except sub-section (8) thereof [fines], Section 9 [Deduction for absence from duty], Section 10 (1) (1-A) [Deductions for damages or losses], Section 11 [Deductions for services rendered], Section 12 [Deductions for recovery of advances] and Section 13 [Deductions for payment to co-operative societies and Insurance schemes].

Whoever being responsible for the payment of wages to an employed person contravenes any of the provisions of any of the above mentioned sections shall be punishable with fine which shall not be less than One Thousand Five Hundred Rupees but which may be extended to Seven Thousand Five Hundred Rupees [Section 20 (1)].

(2) Penalty for Contravening the Provisions of the Following Sections

Section 4 [Fixation of Wage period], Section 5 (4) [Making all payments of Wages on working day only], Section 6 [Wages to be paid in currency notes and current coins] Section 8 (8) [Fine imposed must be recorded properly in the prescribed form etc.], Section 25 (10), [Display of abstract of the Act by notice].

Whoever contravenes the provisions of the above mentioned sections shall be punishable with a fine which may extend to Three Thousand Seven Hundred Fifty Rupees [Section 20 (2)].

(3) Penalty for not Maintaining Records, Registers or not Furnishing required Information etc.

Whoever being required or responsible under this Act to maintain any records or registers or to furnish any information or return;

    (a) fails to maintain such register or record; or

    (b) wilfully refuses or without lawful excuse neglects to furnish such information or return; or

    (c) wilfully furnishes or causes to be furnished any information or return which he knows to be false; or

(d) refuses to answer or wilfully gives a false answer to any question necessary for obtaining any information required to be furnished under this Act; shall, for each such offence, be punishable with fine which shall not be less than One Thousand Five Hundred Rupees but which may extend to Seven Thousand Five Hundred Rupees [Section 20 (3)].

(4) Penalty for Obstructing an Inspector etc.

Whoever –
  (a) wilfully obstructs an Inspector in the discharge of his duties under this Act; or
  (b) refuses or wilfully neglects to afford an Inspector any reasonable facility for making any entry, inspection, examination, supervision, or inquiry authorised by or under this Act in relation to any railway, factory or industrial or other establishment; or
  (c) wilfully refuses to produce on the demand of an Inspector any register or other document kept in pursuance of this Act; or
  (d) prevents or attempts to prevent or does anything which he has any reason to believe is likely to prevent any person from appearing before or being examined by an Inspector acting in pursuance of his duties under this Act; shall be punishable with a fine which shall not be less than One Thousand Five Hundred Rupees but which may be extended to Seven Thousand Five Hundred Rupees [Section 20 (4)].

(5) Penalty for Committing an offence Involving the Contravention of the same Provision for more than once

If any person who has been convicted of any offence punishable under this Act is again guilty of an offence involving contravention of the same provision, he shall be punishable on a subsequent conviction with imprisonment for a term which shall not be less than one month but which may extend to six months and with fine which shall not be less than ₹ Three Thousand Seven Hundred and Fifty but which may extend to ₹ Twenty Two Thousand Five Hundred [Section 20 (5)].

It is also provided that for the purpose of this sub-section, no cognizance shall be taken of any conviction made more than two years before the date on which the commission of the offence which is being punished came to the knowledge of the Inspector [Proviso to Section 20 (5)].

Additional Fine as a penalty for wilful negligence etc.

If any person fails or wilfully neglects to pay the wages of any employed person by the date fixed by the authority in this behalf, he shall, without prejudice to any other action that may be taken against him, be punishable with an additional fine which may extend to Seven Hundred Fifty rupees for each day for which such failure or neglect continues [Section 20 (6)].

The Minimum Wages Act, 1948

4.20 Introduction

Any discussion on the different methods of fixing wages has to take into consideration the concepts of a minimum wage, a living wage, and a fair wage. It is very important to consider these concepts while fixing wage rates in a developing country like India.

The government and the agencies connected with wage fixation have constantly been concerned with this problem. In India, various methods are employed while fixing wages. Different bodies such as pay commissions, wage boards, industrial tribunals, labour courts, high courts, the Supreme Court play a very important role in the process of wage fixation. Wages are also fixed through collective bargaining.

However, it is very essential to create conditions that make it possible for employees to enjoy a minimum standard of life. For that purpose, certain efforts must be carried out and fixation of the minimum rates of wages is one of the efforts in that direction. Of course, a minimum wage rate must ensure not merely physical needs of an employee which would keep him just above starvation but it must ensure for him not only his subsistence and that of his family but also preserve his efficiency as a workman.

Prima facie, it seems that the Minimum Wages Act of 1948 *ultra vires* Article 19 (1) (g) of the Constitution of India gives the right to all Indian citizens to practice any profession, or to carry on any occupation, trade or business, they desire.

While Article 19 (h) of the Indian Constitution assures that nothing in Article 19 (1) (g) shall affect the operation of any of the existing laws in so far as they impose or prevent the State from any law imposing, in the interest of the public, reasonable restrictions on the exercise of the right conferred by the sub-clause of the Article 19 of the Indian Constitution.

Further, the Article 43 of the Indian Constitution makes it clear that, "the State shall endeavour to secure by suitable legislation a living wage, a decent standard of life to the workers".

From this point of view, basically to protect the interest of the workers, to prevent their exploitation and to guarantee the workers working in industries, trade or business in respect of working conditions, payment of wages, compensation, various labour laws have been enacted. The Minimum Wages Act of 1948 is one such Act.

The Minimum Wages Act of 1948,

(1) Empowers the Government for fixing the minimum wages for employment mentioned in the Schedule of the Act.

(2) It provides that the appropriate Government shall fix or revise the minimum rates of wages by appointing committees or publishing its proposal by notification for the fixation or revision of wages.

(3) The provisions have been made in the Act for the fixation of minimum wages especially in those industries where there are inevitable chances of exploiting the workers and where there exists sweated labour.

Today, in India, it is found that workers are organised to a certain extent in some industries. But in the past, they were not organised and as their bargaining capacity was weak, they were exploited to a great extent. Therefore, there was a great need to take steps to fix minimum wages. But in spite of various efforts, no steps could be taken up to 1945.

It was only on 11th April 1946, that the Minimum Wages Bill was introduced in the Parliament. However, because of constitutional changes, it could not be passed immediately. *The Minimum Wages Act was ultimately passed in 1948 and came into operation on 15th March 1948.*

4.21 Objects, Scope and Application of the Act

The Minimum Wages Act, 1948 was basically passed to provide for fixing minimum rates of Wages in certain employments and it extends to the whole of India. The Minimum Wages Act of 1948 in totality states that *a minimum wage rate must ensure for an employee not only his subsistence and that of his family but also preserve his efficiency as a workman.*

(1) The Act enables the Central or the State Government, as the case may be, to fix the minimum rates of wages payable to employees in certain selected industries and trades. These industries and trades are those in which sweated labour exists and labour is exploited.

(2) The industries and trades to which this Act is made applicable are listed in the schedule appended to the Act and an Appropriate Government is authorised to extend the same to any employment in respect of which it is of the opinion that the minimum rates of wages should be fixed under this Act.

(3) The Appropriate Government is empowered to review the minimum rates of wages fixed under this Act at such intervals as it may think proper, but such intervals shall not exceed five years and the Government is also authorised to revise the same, if necessary.

(4) The Appropriate Government may refrain from fixing minimum rates of wages in respect of any of the scheduled employments in which there are in the whole state less than one thousand employees engaged in such employment. However, if it finds, at any time, that the number of employees in any scheduled employment has arisen to one thousand or more, it shall fix minimum rates of wages payable to employees in that employment immediately.

Thus, the scope of the Act seems to be narrow. It has excluded many regulated and un-regulated industries and trades where wages are extremely low and where sweating is common, e.g. coir, coir-mat manufacture, furniture making, potteries, bangle manufacture and so on.

The main object of the Act is to provide machinery and procedure for fixing the minimum rates of wages in certain employments. The other objects are given below:

(a) To prevent sweating in industry. This means that care must be taken so that the payments are not so low as to put the workers working in certain employments at a disadvantage.

(b) The wages must correspond to the toils the workers put in and they should not be exploited.

(c) To see that lock-outs, strikes etc. are rooted out by satisfying the workers through fair payments.

(d) To see that the unorganised workers do not suffer from unfair bargaining and their rights are protected.

(e) The Act also provides for the fixation of a minimum piece-rate, a guaranteed time-rate, an overtime-rate appropriate to different occupations, minimum time-rates etc.

(f) The Act does not only intend to protect male workers, but also women, children and adolescent workers and apprentices too.

It is quite possible that the employers may find it very difficult to bear the restrictions imposed on them by this Act in view of the economic conditions. Some people may charge the Act as unreasonable. But in Cotton Mills V/s Ajmer State, it has been held that the Act is not repugnant to Article 19 (1) (9) of the Indian Constitution. The restrictions imposed by the Act are neither unreasonable nor unrealistic within the meaning of Article 19 (6) of the Constitution.

The Minimum Wages Act does not cast any statutory obligation on the State Government to fix or revise the rates of minimum wages strictly according to the cost of living index. If the cost of living index in any particular locality is not strictly followed while either fixing or revising minimum wages rates, there is no breach committed of a statutory duty.

4.22 Outline of the Minimum Wages Act of 1948

There are in all only 31 sections included in the Act. Of these sections, Section 6 – Advisory Committees and sub-committees was omitted by Section 5 of Act 30 of 1957. There is one schedule appended to this Act. Besides these sections, in exercise of powers conferred by Section 30 of the Minimum Wages Act of 1948, the Central Government has also made the rules. i.e. The Minimum Wages (Central) Rules of 1950 for the purposes of the Act. In exercise of the powers conferred by Section 30 (1) and (2) of the Minimum Wages Act of 1948, the Maharashtra Government has passed the Maharashtra Minimum Wages Rules of 1963.

4.23 Definitions

The definitions of eleven words, terms and so on are given in this Act. Unless there is anything repugnant in the context or subject, the meanings, definitions of words, terms etc. given in Section 2 of the Act are as follows:

(1) Adolescent [Section 2 (a)]

'Adolescent' means a person who has completed his fourteenth year of age but not completed his eighteenth year.

(2) Adult [Section 2 (aa)]

'Adult' means a person who has completed his eighteenth year of age.

(3) Appropriate Government [Section 2 (b)]

'Appropriate Government' means

(i) in relation to any scheduled employment carried on by or under the authority of the Central Government or Railway Administration or in relation to a mine, oil-field or major port, or any corporation established by any Central Act, the Central Government; and

(ii) in relation to any other scheduled employment, the State Government.

(4) Child [Section 2 (bb)]

'Child' means a person who has not completed his fourteenth year of age.

(5) Competent Authority [Section 2 (c)]

'Competent authority' means the authority appointed by the Appropriate Government by notification in the Official Gazette to ascertain from time to time the cost of living index number applicable to the employees employed in the scheduled employments specified in such notification.

(6) Cost of Living Index Number [Section 2 (d)]

'Cost of living index number', in relation to employees in any scheduled employment in respect of which minimum rates of wages have been fixed, means 'the index number ascertained and declared by the competent authority by notification in the Official Gazette to be the cost of living index number applicable to employees in such employment.

(7) Employer [Section 2 (e)]

'Employer' means any person who employs, either directly or through another person, or whether on behalf of himself or any other person, one or more employees in any scheduled employment in respect of which minimum rates of wages have been fixed under this Act, and includes, except in sub-section 3 of Section 26.

(i) in a factory where there is carried on any scheduled employment in respect of which minimum rates of wages have been fixed under this Act, any person named under clause (f) of sub-section (1) of Section 7 of the Factories Act, 1948, as a manager of the factory.

(b) in any scheduled employment under the control of any Government in India in respect of which minimum rates of wages have been fixed under this Act, a person or an authority appointed by such Government for the supervision and control of employees or where no person or authority is so appointed, the head of the department;

(c) in any scheduled employment under any local authority in respect of which minimum rates of wages have been fixed under this Act, the person appointed by such authority for the supervision and control of employees or where no person is so appointed, the chief executive officer of the local authority,

(d) in any other case where there is carried on any scheduled employment in respect of which minimum rates of wages have been fixed under this Act, any person responsible to the owner for the supervision and control of the employees or for the payment of wages.

(8) Prescribed [Section 2 (f)]
'Prescribed' means prescribed by rules made under this Act.

(9) Scheduled Employment [Section 2 (g)]
'Scheduled employment means, an employment specified in the schedule, or any process or branch of work forming part of such employment.

Section 27 empowers the State Governments to add to the Schedule appended to the Act. Section 27 lays down that, *"The appropriate Government, after giving by notification in the Official Gazette not less than three month's notice of its intention to do so, may, by like notification, add to either part of the Schedule any employment in respect of which it is of the opinion that minimum rates of wages should be fixed under this Act, and thereupon the Schedule shall in its application to the State, be deemed to be amended accordingly."* Thus, the appropriate Government, according to the provisions of Section 27, can add to the Schedule appended to this Act.

The Schedule appended to this Act is given below:

	The Schedule – Part I
1.	Employment is any wollen carpet making or shawl weaving establishment.
2.	Employment in any rice mill, flour mill or dal mill.
3.	Employment in any tobacco (including bidi making) manufactory.
4.	Employment in any plantation, that is to say, any estate which is maintained for the purpose of growing cinchona, rubber, tea or coffee.
5.	Employment in any oil mill.
6.	Employment under any local authority.
7.	Employment on the construction or maintenance of roads or in building operations.
8.	Employment in stone breaking or stone crushing.
9.	Employment in any lac manufactory.
10.	Employment in any mica works.
11.	Employment in public motor transport.
12.	Employment in tanneries and leather manufactory.

	The Schedule – Part I
13.	Employment in gypsum mines.
14.	Employment in olfram mines.
15.	Employment in bauxite mines.
16.	Employment in manganese mines.
17.	Employment in the maintenance of building and construction and maintenance of runway.
18.	Employment in China clay mines.
19.	Employment in kyanite mines.
20.	Employment in copper mines.
21.	Employment in clay mines covered under the Mines Act, 1952.
22.	Employment in magnesite mines covered under the Mines Act, 1952.
23.	Employment in white clay mines.
24.	Employment in stone mines.
25.	Employment in steatite (including the mines producing olfram e and talc)
26.	Employment in ocher mines
27.	Employment in asbestos mines.
28.	Employment in fire clay mines.
29.	Employment in chromite mines.
30.	Employment in quartzite mines.
31.	Employment in silica mines.
32.	Employment in graphite mines.
33.	Employment in feldspar mines.
34.	Employment in laterite mines.
35.	Employment in dolomite mines.
36.	Employment in red-oxide mines.
37.	Employment in olfram mines.
38.	Employment in iron ore mines.
39.	Employment in granite mines.
40.	Employment in rock phosphate mines.
41.	Employment in haematite mines.
42.	Employment in loading and unloading in: (i) Railways, goods shed – (ii) Docks and ports.
43.	Employment in marble and calcite mines.
44.	Employment in uranium mines.

The Schedule – Part II
Employment in agriculture, that is to say, in any form of farming, including the cultivation, growing and harvesting of any agricultural or horticultural commodity, the raising of live stock, bees or poultry, and any practice performed by a farmer or on a farm as incidental to or in conjunction with farm operations including any forestry or timbering operations and the preparations for market and delivery to storage or to market or the carriage for transportation to market of farm produce.

(10) Wages [Section 2 (h)]

'Wages' means all remuneration, capable of being expressed in terms of money, which would, if the terms of the contract of employment, express or implied, were fulfilled, be payable to a person employed in respect of his employment or of work done in such employment, and includes house rent allowance, but does not include:

- (a) the value of:
    - (i) any house accommodation, supply of light, water, medical attendance, or
    - (ii) any other amenity or any service excluded by general or special order of the Appropriate Government.
- (b) any contribution paid by the employer to any Pension Fund or Provident Fund or under any scheme of social insurance;
- (c) any travelling allowance or the value of any travelling concession;
- (d) any sum paid to the person employed to defray special expenses entailed to him by the nature of his employment; or
- (e) any gratuity payable on discharge.

(11) Employee [Section 2 (i)]

'Employee' means any person who is employed for hire or reward to do any work, skilled or unskilled, manual or clerical, in a scheduled employment in respect of which minimum rates of wages have been fixed; and includes an out-worker to whom any articles or materials are given out by another person to be made up, cleaned, washed, altered, ornamented, finished, repaired, adapted or otherwise processed for sale for the purposes of the trade or business of that other person where the process is to be carried out either in the home of the out-worker or in some other premises not being premises under the control and management of that other person; and also includes an employee declared to be an employee by the Appropriate Government; but does not include any member of the Armed Forces of the Union.

If the minimum wages have not been fixed for any branch of work of any scheduled employment, the person employing workers in such branch is not an employer within the meaning of this Act.

If an out-worker produces goods at his place and thereafter supplies the same to his employer, he is treated as an employee for the purpose of this Act.

Provisions

4.24 Fixing of Minimum Rates of Wages

Sections 3, 4 and 5 pertain to fixing of minimum rates of wages, minimum rates of wages and procedure for fixing and revising minimum wages respectively. Let us now consider the provisions of these three Sections i.e. Section 3, Section 4 and Section 5.

Section 3 of the Act states the basic principles and procedure to be observed in fixing the minimum rates of wages payable to employees in an employment specified in Part I and Part II of the schedule. For the benefit of the students, Section 3 of the Act is reproduced as follows:

The Appropriate Government shall, in the manner hereinafter provided:

(1) fix the minimum rates of wages payable to employees employed in an employment specified in Part I or Part II of the schedule and in employment added to either part by notification under Section 27.

Provided that the appropriate government may in respect of employees employed in an employment specified in part II of the schedule, instead of fixing of minimum rates of wages under this clause for the whole state, such rates for a part of the State or for any specified class or classes of such employment in the whole State or part thereof;

(2) review at such intervals as it may think fit, such intervals not exceeding five years, the minimum rates of wages so fixed and revise the minimum rates, if necessary.

Provided that where for any reason the appropriate government has not reviewed the minimum rates of wages fixed by it in respect of any scheduled employment within any interval of five years, nothing contained in this clause shall be deemed to prevent it from reviewing the minimum rates after the expiry of the said period of five years and revising them, if necessary, and until they are so revised the minimum rates in force immediately before the expiry of the said period of five years shall continue in force [Section 3 (1)].

Notwithstanding anything contained in such-section (1) of Section 3 mentioned above, the Appropriate Government may refrain from fixing minimum rates of wages in respect of any scheduled employment in which there are in the whole State less than one thousand employees engaged in such employment, but if at any time; the Appropriate Government comes to a finding after such inquiry as it may make or cause to be made in this behalf that the number of employees in any scheduled employment in respect of which it has refrained from fixing minimum rates of wages, has risen to one thousand or more, it shall fix minimum rates of wages payable to employees in such employment as soon as may be after such finding [Section 3 (1-A)].

The Appropriate Government may fix:

(a) a minimum rate of wages for time work (Minimum time-rate).

(b) a minimum rate of wages for piece work (Minimum piece-rate).

(c) a minimum rate of remuneration to apply in the case of employees employed on piece work for the purpose of securing to such employees a minimum rates of wages on a time-rate basis (A guaranteed time-rate).

(d) a minimum rate (whether a time-rate or a piece-rate) to apply in substitution for the minimum rate which would otherwise be applicable, in respect of overtime work done by employees [Overtime rate] [Section 3 (2)].

Where in respect of an industrial dispute relating to the rates of wages payable to any of the employees employed in a scheduled employment, any proceeding is pending before a Tribunal or National Tribunal under Industrial Disputes Act, 1947 or before any like authority under any other law for the time being in force, or an award made by any Tribunal or National Tribunal or such authority is in operation, and a notification fixing or revising the minimum rates of wages in respect of the scheduled employment is issued during the pendency of such proceeding or the operation of the award, then, notwithstanding anything contained in this Act, the minimum rates of wages so fixed or so revised shall not apply to those employees during the period in which the proceeding is pending and the award made therein is in operation or, as the case may be, where the notification is issued during the period of operation of an award, during that period, and where such proceeding or award relates to the rates of wages payable to all the employees in the scheduled employment, no minimum rates of wages shall be fixed or revised in respect of that employment during the said period [Section 3 (2-A)].

In fixing or revising the minimum rates of wages under this section:
(a) different minimum rates of wages may be fixed for:
  (i) different scheduled employments;
  (ii) different classes of work in the same scheduled employment;
  (iii) adults, adolescents, children and apprentices;
  (iv) different localities.
(b) minimum rates of wages may be fixed by any one or more of the following wage periods, namely:
  (i) by the hour,
  (ii) by the day;
  (iii) by the month; or
  (iv) by such other larger wage-period as may be prescribed.

and where such rates are fixed by the day or by the month, the manner of calculating wages for a month or for a day, as the case may be, may be indicated.

Provided that where any wage-periods have been fixed under Section 4 of the Payment of Wages Act, 1936, minimum wages shall be fixed in accordance therewith [Section 3 (3)].

4.25 Minimum Rate of Wages

Any minimum rate of wages fixed or revised by the Appropriate Government in respect of any of the scheduled employments under Section 3 of this Act may consist of :
(1) a basic rate of wages and a special allowance at a rate to be adjusted at such intervals and in such manner as the Appropriate Government may direct, to accord

as nearly as practicable with the variation in the cost of living index number applicable to such workers (hereinafter referred to as the cost of living allowance); or

(2) a basic rate of wages with or without the cost of living allowance, and the cash value of the concessions in respect of supplies of essential commodities at concessional rates, where so authorised; or

(3) an all inclusive rate allowing for the basic rate, the cost of living allowance and the cash value of the concessions, if any [Section 4 (1)].

The cost of living allowance and also the cash value of the concessions in respect of supplies of essential commodities at concessional rates shall be computed by the competent authority at such intervals and in accordance with such directions as may be specified or given by the Appropriate Government [Section 4 (2)].

It must be remembered here that the basic wage is an integral part of the minimum wage. The question of dearness allowance arises only if the basic wage falls short of the minimum wage (State of Karnataka V/s. Karnataka Film Chambers, 1986). *Bhatta* is an extra payment over and above pay. The only extras that can be added to the pay under this Minimum Wages Act, 1948 are allowance and concessions contemplated in Section 4 (1) (i) and (ii).

4.26 Procedure for Fixing and Revising Minimum Wages

Section 5 of the Act lays down the procedure for fixing and revising the minimum rates of wages and according to it, the Appropriate Government shall adopt any of the following procedures while fixing minimum rates of wages in respect of scheduled employment for the first time under this Act or in revising minimum rates of wages so fixed:

(1) The Appropriate Government may appoint as many committees and sub-committees as it considers necessary to hold enquiries and advice it in respect of such fixation or revision, as the case may be [Section 5 (a)], or

(2) It may publish its proposals by notification in the Official Gazette for the information of persons likely to be affected thereby and specify a date, not less than two months from the date of the notification, on which the proposals will be taken into consideration [Section 5 (b)].

After considering the advice of the committees appointed and all representations received by it before the date specified in the Official Gazette; the Appropriate Government shall, by notification in the Official Gazette, fix or revise, as the case may be, revise the minimum rates of wages in respect of each scheduled employment, and unless such notification otherwise provides, it shall come into force on the expiry of three months from the date of its issue [Section 5 (2)].

It is further provided that where the Appropriate Government proposes to receive the minimum rates of wages by the mode specified in Section 5 (1) (b), the Appropriate Government shall also consult the Advisory Board.

It must be remembered that any committee or sub-committee appointed under Section 5 (1) (a) is only an advisory body and the advice of such committee or sub-committee is not binding on the Government. If no advice is given or if the inadequate advice is given by such committee, the Government has power to fix or revise the minimum rates of wages.

The provision has been made in Section 10 of this Act to correct the errors, if any. The Appropriate Government may, at any time, by the notification in the Official Gazette, correct clerical or arithmetical errors or mistakes in any order fixing or revising minimum rates of wages under this Act or arising therein from any accidental slip or omission and every such notification shall, as soon as may be, after it is issued, be placed before the Advisory Board for its information.

4.27 Wages in Kind

Section 11 (1) of the Act states *that the Minimum Wages payable under this Act shall be paid in cash.*

However, where it has been the custom to pay wages wholly or partly in kind, the Appropriate Government being of the opinion that it is necessary in the circumstances of the case may, by notification in the Official Gazette, authorise the payment of minimum wages either wholly or partly in Kind [Section 11 (2)].

If the Appropriate Government is of the opinion that the provision should be made for supplying the essential commodities at concessional rates, the Appropriate Government may, by notification in the Official Gazette, authorise the provision of such supplies at concessional rates [Section 11 (3)].

The cash value of wages in kind and of concessions in respect of supplies of essential commodities at concessional rates authorised under sub-section (2) and (3) of Section 11 shall be estimated in the manner prescribed for this purpose.

From these provisions of Section 11, it becomes clear that the minimum wages payable under this Act must be paid in cash. However, where it is a custom to pay wages wholly or partly in kind, it is permissible under this Act, subject to the following conditions.

(1) The Appropriate Government should be of the opinion that it is necessary in the specific circumstances to pay the wages in kind.

(2) It should, by notification in the Official Gazette, authorise the payment of minimum wage either wholly or partly in kind.

(3) If the Government is of the opinion that provision should be made for supply of essential commodities at concessional rates, it should do so by notification in the Official Gazette authorising such supplies.

(4) The cash value of wages in kind and of concessions in respect of supplies of essential commodities should be estimated in the prescribed manner.

4.28 Payment of Minimum Rate of Wages

The Minimum Wages Act, 1948 provides for the payment of minimum wages to all those employees who are covered by the Act. If the contract rate of payment of wages is higher than the minimum rate, the statutory rights and obligations do not come in the way. Thus, except the liability of paying the minimum, the contract between employer and his employees is left intact. Of course, payment of wages less than the minimum on the ground of less performance or output is not legal.

The employer can fix any reasonable norm specifying the quantity of work which he expects from his workmen during the day; but if any of the workmen or many of them do not produce in conformity with the norms fixed, the employer cannot pay anything less than the minimum wages. The employer may take any other disciplinary action for doing less work other than paying his workers less than the minimum wages.

Section 12 (1) of the Act states that, *"where in respect of any scheduled employment a notification under Section 5 of the Act is in force, the employer shall pay to every employee engaged in a scheduled employment under him, wages at a rate not less than the minimum rate of wages fixed by such notification for that class of employees in that employment, without any deductions except as may be authorised within such time and subject to such conditions as may be prescribed"*, while; Section 12 (2) lays down that, *"Nothing contained in this section shall affect the provisions of the Payment of Wages Act of 1936"*.

Thus, the provisions of Section 12 make it clear that when the minimum rates of wages are made enforceable by the notification vide Section 5 of the Act, the employer has to pay to every employee engaged in a scheduled employment under him, the wages at a rate not less than the minimum rate of wages fixed by such notification under this Act and such payments must be made without any deductions except as may be authorised within such time and subject to such conditions as has been prescribed. These provisions do not affect the provisions of the Payment of Wages Act of 1936.

4.29 Fixing the Hours for a Normal Working Day

In regard to any scheduled employment, minimum rates of wages in respect of which have been fixed under this Act, the Appropriate Government may –

(1) fix the number of hours of work which shall constitute a normal working day, inclusive of one or more specified intervals;

(2) provide for a day of rest in every period of seven days which shall be allowed to all employees or to any specified class of employees and provide for the payment of remuneration in respect of such day of rest;

(3) provide for payment for work on a day of rest at a rate not less than the overtime rate [Section 13 (1)].

Section 13 lays down the procedure for fixing the hours for a normal day working. The Appropriate Government, under this section, is authorised to take action or decision in respect of the number of hours of work as well as the classes of employees. So far as the number of hours of work is concerned, the Appropriate Government may –

(a) fix the number of hours of work which shall constitute a normal working day, inclusive of one or more specified intervals;

(b) provide for a day of rest in every period of seven days which shall be allowed to all employees or to any specified class of employees and provide for the payment of remuneration in respect of such days of rest;

(c) provide for payment for work on a day of rest at a rate not less than the overtime rate.

4.30 Provisions related to Overtime

Where an employee, whose minimum rate of wages is fixed under this Act by the hour, by the day or by such a longer wage-period as may be prescribed, works on any day in excess of the number of hours constituting a normal working day, the employer shall pay him for every hour or for part of an hour so worked in excess at the overtime rate fixed under this Act or under any law of the Appropriate Government for the time being in force, whichever is higher [Section 14 (1)].

And nothing in this Act shall prejudice the operation of the provisions of the Factories Act of 1948 in any case where those provisions are applicable.

It must be remembered that the minimum rate of wages for overtime work need not be confined to double the minimum rates of wages but they may be fixed at double the wages ordinarily received by the employees [Mamarde V/s. Authority under Minimum Wages Act case (1972) 2 Sec. 108].

Thus, over-time, in short, means wages for the work done in excess as prescribed 'under normal working day'. The rates of overtime are fixed under this Act or under any Law for the time being in force whichever are higher.

4.31 Wages of Workers who Work for Less than Normal Working Day

If any employee whose minimum rate of wages has been fixed under this Act by the day, works on any day on which he was employed for a period less than the requisite number of hours constituting a normal working day, he shall be entitled to receive wages in respect of work done by him on that day as if he had worked for a full normal working day [Section 15].

However, he shall not be entitled to receive wages for a full normal working day:

(1) in any case where his failure to work is caused by his unwillingness to work and not by the omission of the employer to provide him with work; and

(2) in such other cases and circumstances as may be prescribed [Proviso to Section 15].

4.32 Wages for Two or More Classes of Work

Where an employee does two or more classes of work to each of which a different minimum rate of wages is applicable, the employer shall pay to such an employee in respect of the time respectively occupied in each such class of work, wages at not less than the minimum rate in force in respect of each such class [Section 16].

4.33 Minimum Time-rate Wages for Piece Work

Where an employee is employed on piece work for which minimum time-rate and not a minimum piece-rate has been fixed under this Act, the employer shall pay to such employee wages at not less than the minimum time-rate [Section 17].

4.34 Maintenance of Registers and Records

The employer is responsible for maintaining the required registers, records and so on in the particular form according to the provisions of Section 18 of the Act and of rule 26 of the Minimum Wages (Central) Rules of 1950. These provisions and relating rules are as under:

(1) Every employer shall maintain such registers and records giving such particulars of employees employed by him, the work performed by them, the wages paid to them, the receipts given by them and such other particulars and in such forms as may be prescribed [Section 18 (1)].

(2) Every employer shall keep exhibited, in such manner, as may be prescribed in the factory, workshop or place where the employees in the scheduled employment may be employed, or in the case of out-workers, in such factory, workshop or place as may be used for giving out work to them, notices in the prescribed form containing prescribed particulars [Section 18 (2)].

(3) The Appropriate Government may, by rules made under this Act, provide for the issue of wage books or wage slips and attendance cards to employees employed in any scheduled employment in respect of which minimum rates of wages have been fixed and prescribed to manner in which entries shall be made and authenticated in such wage books or wage slips and attendance cards by the employer or his agent [Section 18 (3)].

4.35 Appointment of Inspectors and their Powers

Section 19 of the Act pertains to the appointments, powers etc. of the Inspectors. Section 19 is given below:

(1) The Appropriate Government may, by notification in the Official Gazette, appoint such persons as it thinks fit to be Inspectors for the purposes of this Act, and define the local limits within which they shall exercise their functions [Section 19 (1)].

(2) Subject to any rules made in this behalf, an Inspector may within the local limits for which he is appointed –

(a) enter at all reasonable hours with such assistants (if any), being persons in the service of the Government or any local or other public authority, as he thinks fit, any premises or place where employees are employed or work is given out to out-workers in any scheduled employment in respect of which minimum rates of wages have been fixed under this Act, for the purposes of examining any register, record of wages or notices required to be kept or exhibited by or under this Act or rules made thereunder, and require the production thereof for inspection;

(b) examine any person whom he finds in any such premises or place and who, he has reasonable cause to believe is an employee employed therein or an employee to whom work is given out therein;

(c) require any person giving out-work and any out-workers, to give any information which is in his power to give, with respect to the names and addresses of the persons to, for and from whom the work is given out or received and with respect to the payments to be made for the work;

(d) seize or take copies of such register, record of wages or notices or portion thereof as he may consider relevant in respect of an offence under this Act which he has reason to believe has been committed by an employer; and

(e) exercise such other powers as may be prescribed [Section 19 (2)].

(3) Every Inspector shall be deemed to be a public servant within the meaning of the Indian Penal Code, 1860 (Act XLV of 1860) [Section 19 (3)].

(4) Any person required to produce any document or thing or to give any information by an Inspector under sub-section (2) shall be deemed to be legally bound to do so within the meaning of Section 175 and Section 176 of the Indian Penal Code, 1860 (Act XLV of 1860) [Section 19 (4)].

From these provisions of Section 19, we come to know that the Appropriate Government has the right to appoint inspectors for the purposes of this Act and it may define the local limits within which they shall exercise their rights and perform the duties entrusted to them. Every inspector is deemed to be a public servant within the meaning of the Indian Penal Code. These inspectors have to see that the provisions of this Act are complied with. The powers given to inspectors appointed under this Act are as follows:

(a) To enter at all reasonable hours any premises with his assistants or any place where employees are employed in respect of which the minimum rates of wages have been fixed. The inspectors are empowered to examine any register, record of wages or notices required to be kept or exhibited under this Act and require the production thereof for the purpose of inspection.

(b) To examine any person whom an inspector finds in any such premises or place and who, he has reasonable cause to believe, is an employee.

(c) To require any person giving out-work and any out-worker to give any information he wants, which is in his powers to give, with respect to other persons to, for and from whom the work is given out or received, and with respect to the payments to be made for the work.

(d) To seize or to take copies of such register, record of wages or notices as he considers relevant in respect of an offence under the Act which he has reason to believe has been committed by an employer.

(e) To exercise all such other powers as may be prescribed [Section 19].

These provisions of Section 19 also make clear the functions of the Inspectors appointed under this Act. For example, to enter any premises where employees are employed in any scheduled employment for examining the records, registers etc. along with the assistants authorised for this purpose, to examine any person in such premises who is an employee for the purposes of the Act, to seize or to take copies of such registers, record of wages, notices etc. which the Inspectors or his assistance have reasons to believe has been committed by an employer etc.

4.36 Penalties

Provisions have been made in Section 22 for imposing certain penalties for certain offences. These provisions of Section 22 are as under.

Any employer who:

(a) pays to any of his employees less than the minimum rates of wages for that class of employee's or less than the amount due to him under any of the provisions of this Act, or

(b) contravenes any rule or any order made under Section 13 of this Act i.e. fixing hours of normal working day etc. is punishable with the imprisonment for a term which may extend to six months or with a fine which may extend to five hundred rupees or both [Section 22].

It is also provided that in imposing any fine for an offence under this Section, the Court shall take into consideration the amount of any compensation already awarded against the accused in any proceedings under Section 20. Section 20 is related to 'Claims'.

General Provision for Punishment of other Offences

Any employer who contravenes any provision of this Act or of any rule or any order made thereunder, if no other penalty is provided for such contravention by this Act, is punishable with a fine which may extend to five hundred rupees [Section 22-A].

Cognizance of Offences

No court shall take cognizance of a complaint against any person for an offence;

under clause A of Section 22 unless an application in respect of the fact constituting such offence has been presented under Section 20 (claims) and has been granted wholly or partly and the Appropriate Government or an officer authorised by it in this behalf has sanctioned making of the complaint [Section 22-B (1)], and no court shall take cognizance of an offence under clause A or clause B of Section 22, unless the complaint thereof is made within the period of one month of the grant of sanction under this section and under Section 22-A unless the complaint thereof is made within the period of six months from the date on which the offence is alleged to have been committed [Section 22-B (2)].

Offences by Companies

If the person committing any offence under this Act is a company, every person, who at the time the offence was committed, was incharge of and was responsible to the company for the conduct of the business of the company as well as the company shall be deemed to be guilty of the offence and shall be liable to be prosecuted against and punished accordingly [Section-22C (1)].

It is provided further that nothing contained in this sub-section shall render any such person liable to any punishment provided in the Act if he proves that the offence was committed without his knowledge or that he exercised all due diligence to prevent the commission of such offence [Proviso to Section 22-C (1)].

Notwithstanding anything contained in the sub-section (1) mentioned above, where an offence under this Act has been committed by a company and it is proved that the offence has been committed with the consent or connivance of, or is attributable to any neglect on the part of any director, manager, secretary or other officer of the company, such director, manager, secretary or any other officer of the company shall also be deemed to be guilty of that offence and shall be liable to be prosecuted against and punished accordingly [Section 22-C (2)].

For the purpose of this Section 22-C, a Company means any body corporate and includes a firm or other association of individuals and a director in relation to a firm means a partner in the firm.

RECENT AMENDMENTS IN THE MINIMUM WAGES ACT, 1948

- The Narendra Modi led BJP Government is considering a proposal to amend the Minimum Wages Act 1948.
- Under the provisions of Minimum Wages Act, 1948, both the Central and State governments are appropriate governments to fix, review and revise minimum wages of workers employed in the Scheduled employment under their respective jurisdiction.

- The appropriate governments have been empowered to notify any employment in the schedule where the number of employees is 1,000 or more in a state and fix rates of minimum wages in respect to employees employed therein.
- There are 45 scheduled employments under central sphere and the workers employed in various mini cement plants and petroleum products outlets are not included in the scheduled employment of central sphere.
- The rates of minimum wages fixed by Central government are applicable to establishments under its authority, railways administration, mines, oilfields, major ports and corporations created under Acts of Parliament.
- In the unskilled section of the agriculture sector, rates of wages including Variable Dearness Allowance per day w.e.f. April 1, 2014, are ₹ 215, ₹ 195 and ₹ 193 in Area A, Area B and Area C respectively. Similarly for the highly skilled in the same sector, it is ₹ 283, 262 and ₹ 235 for Areas A, B and C respectively.

Questions for Discussion

1. State the object and scope of the Payment of Wages Act, 1936.
2. Describe the various deductions from wages.
3. Explain the following (Payment of Wages Act, 1936).
    (A) Responsibility for Payment of Wages
    (B) Time of Payment of Wages
    (C) Penalties for Offences
4. State the objects and scope of the Minimum Rate of Wages, 1948.
5. State the Procedure for Fixing and Revising Minimum Wages.
6. State the various provisions relating to penalty (Minimum Wages Act, 1948)
7. Explain the following (Minimum Wages Act, 1948).
    (A) Wages in Kind
    (B) Maintenance of Registers and Records
    (C) Provisions related to Overtime
8. Write short notes on:
    (A) Factory (Payment of Wages Act, 1936)
    (B) Appointment of Inspectors (Payment of Wages Act, 1936)
    (C) Fixing Hours of a Normal Working Day (Minimum Wages Act, 1948).

***

Chapter 5...

Trade Union Laws

Contents ...

The Trade Union Act, 1926

- 5.1 Introduction
- 5.2 Objects of the Trade Unions Act, 1926
- 5.3 Definitions
- 5.4 Registration of Trade Union
- 5.5 Membership to a Trade Union
- 5.6 Registered Office of a Trade Union
- 5.7 Rights and Privileges of a Registered Trade Union
- 5.8 Duties and Liabilities of a Registered Trade Union
- 5.9 Amalgamation of Trade Unions
- 5.10 Dissolution of a Registered Trade Union

Maharashtra Recognition of Trade Union and Unfair Labour Practices Act

- 5.11 Introduction
- 5.12 Objects of the M.R.T.U. and P.U.L.P. Act, 1971
- 5.13 Definitions
- 5.14 Constitution of the Industrial Court and Qualifications of the Members of Industrial Court
- 5.15 Labour Court - Its Constitution, Duties and Powers
- 5.16 Investigating Officer - Their Appointment, Duties and Powers
- 5.17 Recognition of Unions
- 5.18 Cancellation of Recognition and Suspension of Rights [Section 13]
- 5.19 Recognition of Other Union [Section 14]
- 5.20 Obligation of Recognised Unions [Section 19]
- 5.21 Rights of Recognised Unions [Section 20]
- 5.22 Rights of Unrecognised Unions [Section 22]
- 5.23 Meaning of Unfair Labour Practices and Various Unfair Labour Practices [Section 26]
- 5.24 Provisions relating to Modifications of Schedules

5.25 The Procedure to be followed for Dealing with Complaints relating to Unfair Labour Practices [Section 28]

5.26 Penalties

5.27 Recovery of Money Due from Employer

5.28 Recovery of Fines

- Questions for Discussion
- Questions from Previous Pune University Examinations

The Trade Union Act, 1926

5.1 Introduction

The term 'Trade Union' is commonly used to refer to that body or organisation of workers, which is formed not only to protect their rights but also to enhance their welfare. According to India's former President, Late Shri V. V. Giri, "Trade Unions are voluntary organisations of workers formed to promote and protect their interests by collective action." A trade union must have definite aims, its members must be welded together as a unified front for the good of the whole class of workers. Trade Unions have a definite role to play in countries like India where workers are not yet properly organised. But up to the end of the First World War, there was no beginning of trade union movement in the real sense; though the first important step towards organising labour was taken by Mr. Lokhande, who was a factory worker in Bombay. He laid the foundation in 1890 of the first organisation of workers, viz., the Bombay Mill Hands' Association.

The First World War was responsible for a mass awakening in the sense that, situations like discrimination against Indian Workers, the growth of Indian National Movement, the revolution in Russia were some of the concurrent and yet colluding factors happening across the global landscape being responsible for giving a fillip to Indian Labour Movement.

The Indian Trade Union Act, which was passed in 1926, is a landmark in the history of trade union movement in India. This Act gave the Trade Unions legal status and immunity to its officers and members from civil and criminal liability for concerted actions. Subsequently, by Amendment 38 of Act, 1964, the word 'Indian' was deleted. The said Act has been amended many times to suit the circumstances since its enforcement.

In 1937, under provincial autonomy, the registered Trade Unions were given special representation in the provincial legislatures which further encouraged the registration of Trade Unions. Then, immediately after the Independence, the Trade Union Amendment Act, 1947, was passed which provided for the compulsory recognition of the Trade Unions by employers under the orders of a Labour Court. A new Trade Union Bill was introduced in May 1982 which aimed at reducing the multiplicity of unions. The Government introduced the Trade Union Bill on 13th May, 1988, to replace the earlier legislation. The Bill suggested comprehensive amendments in the Trade Union Act. Presently, the said Act requires a trade union to be registered within sixty days of the receipt of the application. Thus, the registration of the Trade Unions has become time-bound. Besides this, it is also provided for a statutorily recognised collective bargaining agent for a unit or for an industry and the term of such an agent is fixed for three years. Thus, by amending the Act from time to time, the efforts have been made to safeguard the interests of the workers.

5.2 Objects of the Trade Unions Act, 1926

The object of this Act is made clear in the preamble which states that it is to provide for the registration of trade unions and, in certain respects, to define the law relating to registered trade unions.

Thus, this Act besides aiming to make provisions for the registration of trade unions; goes further to mention the various objects on which general funds of a trade union can be spent. It also provides for the constitution of a separate fund for political purposes. Further, this Act confers certain rights on registered trade unions and makes clear their liabilities. That apart, it also provides for the protection of the members and officers of registered trade unions from various civil and criminal liabilities which may be incurred while promoting and safeguarding their legitimate interests.

This Act is intended to promote cordial relations between employers and their employees or workmen to facilitate the peaceful settlement of disputes between them by means of adjudication or arbitration [New Gujarat Cotton Mills vs. L.A.T. - AIR - 195 Bombay - 111].

In a sentence, it can be said that this Act has been passed to make provisions for the registration and regulation of trade unions for furthering the interests of the common workmen.

5.3 Definitions

In the Trade Union Act which came into force from 1st June, 1927, and extends to the whole of India, the definitions of certain words, concepts and expressions are given in Section 2 which is as follows:

Appropriate Government [Section 2]

In this Act, the Appropriate Government means in relation to trade unions whose objects are not confined to one state, the Central Government and, in relation to other Trade Unions, the State Government.

Thus, if the jurisdiction of a Trade Union is any particular state, then, in that case, the State Government concerned is the Appropriate Government and if the objects of a trade union are not confined to any one State, then, the Central Government, in that case is the Appropriate Government.

Executive [2(a)]

'Executive' means the body by whatever name called to which the management of affairs of a trade union is entrusted.

Office Bearer [2(b)]

'Office bearer' in the case of a Trade Union includes any member of the executive thereof but does not include an auditor.

Prescribed [2(c)]

"Prescribed' means prescribed by regulations made under this Act.

Registered Office [2(d)]

'Registered Office' means office of a Trade Union, which is registered under this Act as the Head Office thereof:

Registered Trade Union [2(e)]

Registered Trade Union means a Trade Union registered under this Act.

Registrar [2(f)]

'Registrar' means:
1. A Registrar of Trade Union is appointed by the Appropriate Government under Section 3 and includes an additional or Deputy Registrar of Trade Unions and
2. In relation to any Trade Union, the Registrar appointed for the State in which the head or registered office, as the case may be, of the situated Trade Union.

Trade Dispute and Workmen [2(g)]

'Trade dispute' means any dispute between employers and workmen, or between workmen and workmen or between employers and employers which is connected with the employment or non-employment or the terms of employment or the conditions of labour of any persons, and 'workmen' means all persons employed in trade or industry whether or not in the employment of the employer with whom the trade dispute arises.

For any trade dispute, there must be demand made by one of the parties and refusal to accept the same by the other party and so far as this Act is concerned, such trade disputes include any dispute between:
(a) Employers and employers; or
(b) Employers and workmen; or
(c) Workmen and workmen; and such disputes may be connected with
   1. The employment or non-employment; or
   2. The terms of employment; or
   3. Conditions of labour of any person.

Section 2(g) of this Act also defines the word 'workmen' and, accordingly, the definition of workmen includes any employee:
1. Employed in any trade or industry, or
2. Dismissed, discharged removed or retrenched.

This Act does not make any distinction between skilled and unskilled workmen; or clerical employees or officers; the only requirement being that the person concerned must be employed in some industry or trade.

Here, it must be remembered that the Trade Union Act is not in *Pari Materia* with the Industrial Disputes Act, 1948, and so the definition of an 'industry' as given in it has no application to the former Act. [Rangaswami vs. Registrar of Trade Unions - AR 1962 - Madras - 321]

Trade Union [2(h)]

'Trade Union' means any combination, whether temporary or permanent, formed primarily for the purpose of regulating the relations between workmen and employers or between workmen and workmen; or between employers and employers; or for imposing restrictive conditions on the conduct of any trade or business, and includes any federation of two or more trade unions.

Provided that this Act shall not affect -

(i) Any agreement between partners as to their own business.

(ii) Any agreement between any employer and those employed by him as to such employment; or

(iii) Any agreement in consideration of the sale of goodwill of a business or of instruction in any profession trade or handicraft.

From this definition of a 'trade union', we come to know that:

1. A Trade Union is any combination.
2. Such combination can be formed by -
    (a) Employers and employers; or
    (b) workmen and workmen; or
    (c) Employers and workmen.
3. The purposes of forming such combination are to regulate the relations between such persons who form the combination.
4. Such combination can either be temporary or permanent.
5. A Trade Union is formed for imposing certain restrictive conditions on the conduct of any trade or business.
6. A Trade Union may include any federation of two or more trade unions.
7. The Trade Union Act does not affect any agreement :
    (a) Between partners as to their own business,
    (b) Between employer and employees regarding their employment, and
    (c) Which is in consideration of sale of goodwill of a business or of instruction in any profession Trade or handicraft.

In ordinary parlance, trade union means an association of workmen formed to protect their own interest. But the expression 'trade union' includes both workers' and employers' organisations. The intention in covering organisations of employers under this Act is to put both the workers and employers' organisations on par in matters of rights and responsibilities.

5.4 Registration of Trade Unions

It has not been made compulsory under this Act that every trade union must be registered. Unregistered trade unions are not illegal. There are many unions which are not registered under this Act and have remained outside the purview of the provisions of this Act. But the registered Trade Unions get certain benefits because of their registration, which are as follows:

1. Upon registration, a trade union becomes a corporate body by the name under which it is registered. It gets the legal entity which is distinct from its members. It can acquire and hold all types of properties, enter into contracts with the third party, can sue and be sued.

2. The Office bearers and members of a registered trade union are given protection against criminal proceedings for conspiracy in respect of any agreement entered into between the members for furthering such objects of the trade union on which it funds can be spent.

3. No suit is maintainable in any civil court against a registered trade union or its office bearers or members in respect of any act done in contemplation or furtherance of any trade dispute to which a member of trade union is a party on the ground that such act induces some person to break any contract of employment or causes interference with the business or trade of any employer. Such protection is given to trade unions because many times, the activities of trade unions cause interference with the business or trade of the employers and if no such protection is given to the trade unions, the trade unions would be liable for damages under the general law.

4. It is expressly provided for in this Act that any agreement between the members of a registered trade union shall be valid and not void and voidable.

Thus, from the above discussion, it becomes clear that the registered trade unions enjoy certain advantages. Though the unregistered trade unions are not illegal but they run the risk of being held illegal. They do not possess corporate existence neither legal entity nor are they quasi corporations.

In this Act, the procedure has been laid down for registering a trade union. Now, let us study the various provisions related to the registration of a trade union.

(1) Appointment of Registrars

Various provisions have been made in Section 3 of this Act to appoint Registrar, Deputy Registrar and Additional Registrar. It is as follows:

Section 3(1): The Appropriate Government shall appoint a person to be the registrar of the trade unions for each state.

Section 3(2): The Appropriate Government may appoint as many Additional and Deputy Registrars of Trade Unions as it thinks fit for the purpose of the exercising and discharging, under the superintendence and direction of the Registrar, such powers and functions of the Registrar under this Act as it may by order specify and define the local limits within which any such Additional or Deputy Registrar shall exercise and discharge the powers and functions so specified.

Section 3(3): Subject to the provisions of any order under sub-section 3(2), where an Additional or Deputy Registrar exercises and discharges the powers and functions of a Registrar in an area within which the registered office of a trade union is situated, the Additional or Deputy Registrar shall be deemed to be the Registrar in relation to the trade union for the purposes of this Act.

Here, Registrar means a Registrar of Trade Unions appointed by the Appropriate Government under Section 3 and includes Deputy or Additional Registrar of Trade Union and in relation to any trade union, the Registrar appointed for the State in which the head or registered office of the trade union is situated [Section 2(f)]

Certain powers are given to the registrar, for example, he may call for necessary particulars in respect to the registration of the given trade union. If he is satisfied that the requirements in this Act have been complied with, the Registrar has to register such trade union. He may refuse to register the trade union until he gets necessary information. He has also the powers to ask to change the name of the trade union or he may cancel the registration of trade unions, if there are sufficient reasons to do so.

When there are any disputes between two rival factions, i.e., self-interested parties which claim to be the office bearers of a trade union, the Registrar has the powers to hold an enquiry for giving proper decision for the matters mentioned in Section 8. However, his decision in this respect, shall be to either confer any right on one person, or, a group of persons, as the case may be, nor deprive any person or a group of persons of any legal rights.

The Registrar has no powers to issue any directive or to give any direction to the Labour Department of the Government or the employer to recognise and treat any person or a group of persons as the duly elected office-bearers of the union in dealing with the union. The Registrar of Trade unions cannot direct, or has no power to direct the holding of election of the office bearers of a trade union under his own supervision or under any person nominated by him. In the absence of any provision made in the Trade Union Act, 1926, if any dispute of this kind arises, it can only be resolved by filing a suit before a Civil Court. [Bokaro Steel Workers Union vs. State of Bihar [1995 – II C.L.R. 723 (Pat – D.B.)] In Ratan Kumar Dey and Ors vs. Union of India and Ors case [1991 – II – C.L.R. 159 (Gan H.C)], it was held that the Registrar of Trade Unions has no power to decide a dispute between rival bearers of trade union under Section 28.

(2) Mode of Registration

Any seven or more members of a Trade Union may, subscribing their names to the rules of Trade Union and by otherwise complying with the provisions of this Act with respect to registration, apply for registration of the Trade Union under this Act [Section 4(1)] And where an application has been made under this sub-section (1) of Section 4 for the registration of a Trade Union, such application shall not be deemed to have become invalid merely by reason of the fact that, at any time after the date of application, but before the registration of the trade union, some of the applicants, but not exceeding half of the total number of persons who made the application, have ceased to be members of the Trade Union or have given notice in writing to the Registrar disassociating themselves from the application [Section 4(2)].

(3) Application for Registration of a Trade Union

An application for registering a Trade Union is made to the Registrar of Trade Unions and it must be accompanied by (1) a copy of its rules, and (2) a statement of the following particulars, namely - (a) the names, occupations and addresses of members making such application for the registration of the Trade Union, (b) the name of the Trade Union and the address of its head office, and (c) the titles, names, ages, addresses, occupations of the officers of the Trade Union [Section 5(1)].

And where a Trade Union has been in existence for more than one year before the making of an application for its registration, a general statement of assets and liabilities of such trade union prepared in the prescribed form and with other necessary information as required, must be submitted to the Registrar, together with the application of registration [Section 5(2)].

(4) Rules of Trade Union [Section 6]

Section 6 of this Act states the provisions to be continued in the rules of a Trade Union. A trade union cannot be registered under this Act unless the executive thereof is constituted in accordance with the provisions of this Act and the rules thereof provide for the following matters namely:

(a) The name of a Trade Union.

(b) The whole of the objects of the Trade Union for which it is established.

(c) The whole of the purposes for which the general funds of a Trade Union are lawfully applicable under this Act.

(d) The maintenance of a list of the members of the Trade Union and adequate facilities for the inspection thereof by the office bearers and members of the Trade Union.

(e) The admission of ordinary members who shall be persons actually engaged or employed in an industry with which the Trade Union is connected, and also the admission of the honorary or temporary members as office bearers required under Section 22 to form the executive of the Trade Union.

(f) The payment of a subscription by members of the Trade Union which shall not be less than Twenty-Five Naye Paise per month per member.
(g) The conditions under which any member shall be entitled to any benefit assured by the rules and under which any fine or forefeiture may be imposed on the members.
(h) The manner in which the rules shall be amended, varied or rescinded (repealed or cancelled).
(i) The manner in which the members of the executive and other office-bearers of the Trade Union shall be appointed, reappointed and removed.
(j) The safety custody of the funds of the Trade Union, and annual audit in the prescribed manner, of the accounts thereof, and adequate facilities for the inspection of the account books by the office-bearer and members of the Trade Union.
(k) The manner in which the Trade Union may be dissolved.

(5) Registration

Section 8 of this Act states that the Registrar, on being satisfied that the Trade Union concerned has complied with all the requirements of this Act regarding the registration of the Trade Union, shall register the Trade Union by making a proper entry in the register maintained for this purpose in such form as may be prescribed, particulars relating to the Trade Union contained in the statement accompanying the application for registration.

The register of Trade Union, referred to in Section 8 above is maintained in 'Form B', is as follows :

FORM B

Name of Trade Union Registration Number	Date of Registration Number of application form	Remarks :
Subsequent change of the address of the Head Office.		Names of Members making application
1.		1.
2.		2.
3.		3.
4.		4.
5.		5.
6.		6.
7.		7.
8.		8.
Officers (Transfers from one post to another count as relinquishment of appointment held.)							

Year of entering in office	Name	Office held in Union	Age on entry	Address	Occupation	Year of relinquishing Office	Other Offices held in addition to membership of executive with dates

Thus, if all the conditions of this Act are fulfilled and all necessary provisions are complied with, it is obligatory upon the Registrar of the Trade Union to register a Trade Union. He has no discretionary powers in this regard.

(6) Issue of the Certificate of Registration

The Registrar, after registering a Trade Union under Section 8 has to issue a certificate of registration in the prescribed form to serve as the conclusive evidence that a Trade Union is duly registered under this Act [Section 9]

Once a Trade Union is registered, it acquires the following characteristics:

(a) It becomes a body corporate by that name under which it is registered

(b) It becomes a legal entity distinct from its members.

(c) It has a common seal.

(d) It has a perpetual succession.

(e) It enjoys the powers to acquire and hold the property, movable as well as immovable.

(f) It gets the powers to enter into contracts.

(g) It can sue and can be sued in its own name.

The procedure of registering any Trade Union can be summarised in the following ways:

(a) Any seven or more members of a Trade Union can apply for the registration of the Trade Union.

(b) Such application is required to be made to the Registrar of the Trade Unions.

(c) Necessary information according to Section 5 of this Act is required to be given in the application.

(d) Every application of the registration is required to be accompanied with a copy of the rules of Trade Union as such rules must provide for various matters as specified in Section 6 of the Act.

(e) If the Trade Union is in existence for more than a year before the application for the registration is made, the application must be submitted to the Registrar of Trade Unions along with a general statement of its assets and liabilities in the prescribed form and other necessary particulars.

(f) After receiving an application with necessary information, if the Registrar is satisfied, he registers the name of the given Trade Union in the register maintained for that purpose and issues a Certificate of Registration.

(g) If all the terms of the Act are complied with, the Registrar has to register a Trade Union and issue the certificate of Registration which is the conclusive evidence of the Trade Union's registration.

The certificate of registration issued by the Registrar under Section 9 is in 'Form C', is as follows:

FORM C

Trade Unions Act, 1926

Certificate of Registration of Trade Unions

Name of Trade Union –

Registration Number

        Office of the Registrar of Trade Unions :

        Bombay.

It is hereby certified that the

    Union has been registered under the Trade Unions Act, 1926, this day of 19..

    Registrar of Trade Unions,

    Maharashtra State, Bombay

| Seal |

---

(7) Cancellation of Registration

Section 10 of this Act provides for the cancellation of Registration. It states that a certificate of registration can be withdrawn or cancelled by the Registrar of Trade Unions.

(a) On the application of the Trade Union to be verified in such a manner as may be prescribed or

(b) If the Registrar is satisfied that
  (i) The Certificate has been obtained by fraud or
  (ii) It is issued by mistake; or
  (iii) The Trade Union has ceased to exist; or
  (iv) The Trade Union has wilfully and after notice from the Registrar contravened any provision of the Act, or
  (v) It has allowed any rule to continue in force which is inconsistent with any such provision; or
  (vi) The Trade Union has rescinded any rule providing for any matter; provision for which is required by Section 6.

It is also provided in this section that if the cancellation is to be effected on account of clause (b) above, not less than two months prior notice in writing specifying the ground on which it is proposed to withdraw or cancel the certificate must be given by the Registrar to the Trade Union concerned before the certificate of registration is withdrawn or cancelled. [Proviso to Section 10].

Every application by a Trade Union for withdrawal or cancellation of its certificate of registration is required to be sent to the Registrar in Form 'D' which is as follows:

FORM 'D'
Trade Unions Act, 1926
Request to withdraw or cancel Certificate of Registration.

Name, of Trade Union –
Registration Number
        (Address) :
    Dated this .... day of 20
To
    The Registrar of Trade Unions,
    Mumbai, Maharashtra State.

The above mentioned Trade Union desires that its certificate of registration under the Trade Unions Act, 1926, may be withdrawn (or cancelled) and at a general meeting* duly held on the day of 19 it was resolved as follows :

      (Here give exact copy of Resolution)

      (Signed)

---
* If not at a general meeting, state in what manner the request has been determined upon.

The Registrar, on receiving an application for withdrawal or cancellation of registration and before granting such application, has to verify whether the application was properly approved in the general meeting of the Trade Union or, if it was not thus approved, that it has the approval of a majority of members of the trade union. For this purpose, the Registrar may call for such further particulars as he may deem necessary and he may examine any office at the trade union. The Registrar of Trade Unions has jurisdiction to cancel registration on being satisfied from legal points of view. It should be noted that a person who ceased to be a member at a Registered Trade Union has no *locus standi* to seek cancellation of registration of the trade union. [D. Munirathnam vs. Additional Registrar of Trade Union – I. – Madras – 6 – 1997 I L.L.J. 509 (Madras H. C.]

5.5 Membership to a Trade Union

In Section 21 of this Act, it is made clear that any one who has attained the age of fifteen years may become a member of a registered Trade Union. This is subject to any rules of the Trade Union to the contrary. Any such person, subject to the rules of the Trade Union, may enjoy all the rights of a member and execute all instruments and also give all acquaintance necessary to be executed or given under the rules. But one who has not attained the age of eighteen years he cannot become an office-bearer [Section 21(A)]

Any one, who has been convicted by any Indian Court of any offence involving moral turpitude and so sentenced to imprisonment, also cannot become an office bearer until a period of five years is elapsed since his or her release [Section 21(A)(ii)]

It must be remembered that only those persons who are engaged in trade or business which also includes an industry, can form a Trade Union. Therefore, the persons employed in a Raj Bhavan for domestic and other duties cannot form a Trade Union. The Government servants who are engaged in the task of sovereign and legal functions are also not allowed to form and register their Trade Union.

5.6 Registered Office of a Trade Union

Section 12 of this Act, requires that all communications and notices to a registered Trade Union must be addressed to its registered office. Notice of a change in the address of the head office shall be given within fourteen days of such change to the Registrar in writing and the changed address must be recorded in the register referred to in Section 8 of this Act.

Notice of any change in the address of the head office of a Registered Trade Union is required to be given to the Registrar of Trade Unions in the 'Form G,' as follows :

FORM 'G'

Trade Unions Act, 1926

Notice of a change of address of the Head Office of a Registered Trade Union

Name of Trade Union –

Registration Number :

        (Address) :

        Dated this .... day of 20

To

    The Registrar of Trade Unions.

    Mumbai, Maharashtra State.

Notice is hereby given that the Head Office of the above mentioned Trade Union has been removed from .... and is .... now situated at .... in .... City (or town or district)

                                                                                                    (Signed)

                                                                                                     Secretary

---

This part to be detached by the Registrar when the notice is registered, and returned to the Trade Union	Received this ..... day of 20 notice of removal of the Head Office of the Register No. .... to City (or town or district),
Seal	
	(Signed)
	Registrar of Trade Unions, Mumbai, Maharashtra State

5.7 Rights and Privileges of a Registered Trade Union

The following are the rights and privileges of a registered Trade Union and its members.

(1) Incorporation [Section 13]
(2) Separate fund for political purposes [Section 16]
(3) Immunity from punishment for criminal conspiracy [Section 17]
(4) Certain acts not to apply [Section 14]
(5) Immunity from civil suits in certain cases [Section 18]
(6) No Liability in respect of tortuous Act [Section 18(2)]
(7) Enforceability of agreements [Section 19]
(8) Right to inspect books of trade union [Section 20]
(9) Right of minors to be members [Section 21]
(10) Right to change its name [Sections 23, 25 and 26]
(11) Right of amalgamation of unions [Sections 24]

Now, let us discuss each of the above mentioned rights and privileges of a Trade Union.

(1) Incorporation

Once a Trade Union is registered, it becomes a body corporate by that name under which it is registered. Thereafter, it enjoys perpetual succession and common seal with power to acquire and hold property. As a logical corollary, it becomes empowered to enter into contract in its own name. A Registered Trade Union thus can sue and be sued in its registered name [Section 13]. Thus, thanks to registration, the registered Trade Unions enjoy certain rights and privileges.

(2) Separate fund for political purposes

A registered Trade Union has a right to constitute a separate fund, from the contributions separately levied for or made to that fund. The payments can be made from such fund for the promotion of the civic and political interests of its members. The fund can be utilised for achieving the objectives specified in sub-section 2 of Section 16 [Section 16(1)].

However, no member is compelled to contribute to the fund constituted under Section 16(1). A member who does not contribute to the said fund is not excluded from any of the benefits of Trade Union. Contribution to the said fund is not a pre-condition for admission to the Trade Union [Section 16(3)].

(3) Immunity from punishment for criminal conspiracy

Section 17 of the Trade Unions Act, 1926, clearly states that no office bearer or any registered Trade Union is liable to punishment under sub-section (2) of Section 120-B of the Indian Penal Code, in respect of any agreement made between the members for the purpose of furthering any such object of the Trade Union as is specified in Section 15 of this Act unless the agreement is an agreement to commit an offence or crime.

Thus, any agreement entered into for committing an offence or crime makes the members of the Trade Union liable for criminal conspiracy. In one case, where a strike was accompanied by violence, intimidation, threat, assault etc., this exemption was not available to the members of the Trade Union concerned. A union leader is not entitled to claim immunity from punishment for any breach of discipline.

(4) Certain Acts not to apply

It is already mentioned elsewhere in this chapter that certain Acts, namely, The Societies Registration Act, 1860; the Co-operative Societies Act, 1912; and the Companies Act, 1956, are not applicable to any registered trade unions. If the registration is done under any of these Acts, then, it would be void [Section 14].

(5) Immunity from civil suits in certain cases

According to sub-section (1) Section 18 of this Act, no suit or any other legal proceeding shall be maintainable in any Civil Court against any registered Trade Union or its office-bearers or members of any Registered Trade Union in respect of any act done in contemplation or furtherance of a trade dispute to which a member of a Trade Union is a party on the ground only that such act induces some other person or persons to break a contract of employment, or that it is in interference with the trade, business or employment of some other person to dispose off his capital or of his labour, as he wills.

(6) No liability in respect of act of torts

Section 18(2) says that a registered Trade Union shall not be liable in any suit or other legal proceeding in any Civil Court in respect of any act of torts done in contemplation or furtherance of a trade dispute by an agent of the Trade Union if it is proved that such person acted without the knowledge of, or contrary to express instructions given by the executive of the Trade Union.

This Section 18 grants certain protection to the members office-bearers of a Trade Union in respect of Civil suits in certain cases and of tortious act, but does not afford immunity to any trade union or its members or office-bearers for any act of deliberate trespass. The Trade Unions have rights to pursue their obligation by means of a strike, so long as it does not indulge in acts unlawful and tortious acts. Even the court concerned cannot prevent or interfere with the legitimate rights of the workers.

The conduct of workers in blocking the passage of men and materials of the plaintiff company was not justified in one case only because of the right of the trade union or a fundamental right under the Article 19 of the Constitution of India. [Simpson and Group Companies Workers and Staff Union vs. Amco Batteries Ltd. 1990 II CLR 832 (Kam H.C.)] Protection under Section 18 of the Trade Union Act, 1926, to the workers does not get enlarged or constricted depending upon the situation of strike or lockout. The consideration and principles are obviously ought to be one and the same for both the situations.

(7) Enforceability of agreements

The provision in respect of enforceability of agreements has been made in Section 19 of this Act as follows:

"Notwithstanding anything contained in any other law for time being in force, an agreement between the members of a registered trade union shall not be void or voidable merely by reason of the fact that any of the objects of the agreement are in restraint of trade."

It is further provided that nothing in Section 19 shall enable any of the Civil Courts to entertain any legal proceeding instituted for the express purpose of enforcing or recovering damages for the breach of any agreement concerning the conditions on which any members of a Trade Union shall or shall not sell their goods, transact business, work, employ or be employed.

(8) Right to inspect books of trade union

Section 20 of this Act provides for the inspection of books of Trade Union by the office-bearers or members of such Trade Union. Section 20 says that the account books of a registered trade union and the list of its members shall be open for inspection by any office-bearer or member of the Trade Union at such time as may be provided for in the rules of the Trade Union. The object of conferring this right is that the office-bearers and members of Trade Union should be satisfied as to the genuineness of members and of the accounts of the Trade Union.

(9) Right of minors to become members

Subject to any rule of the Trade Union to contrary, any one who has completed his fifteen years of age may become a member of a registered trade union and such person may enjoy all the rights and privileges of such membership [Section 21].

(10) Right to change the name

Any registered Trade Union has the right to change its name, if:

(a) Two-thirds of the total number of its member give consent to such change of name; [Section 23] and (b) the proposed new name is not identical with that of any other registered Trade Union in existence and in the opinion of the Registrar of Trade Unions, it does not resemble any such name so nearly as to be likely to deceive the public in general and members and office-bearers of either union. Such change in name of the Trade Union must be informed to the Registrar by sending him the notice in writing, signed by the secretary and any seven members of the Trade Union. The Registrar records the change in name of the Trade Union in the registrar if he is satisfied that the provisions of the Act have been complied with properly and such change in name takes effect from the date of registration [Section 25(2) and (3)].

However, the change in the name does not affect any right or obligation of the Trade Union or render defective any legal proceeding by or against such Trade Union. The change in the name does not even affect any legal proceeding which might have been continued or commenced by or against it by its former name may be continued or commenced by or against it by its new name [Section 26(1)].

(11) Right of amalgamation of Trade Unions

The registered Trade Unions have got the right under this Act to become amalgamated together as one Trade Union. Section 24 of the Act states that any two or more registered Trade Unions may become amalgamated together as one Trade Union with or without dissolution or division of funds of such Trade Unions or either or any of them, provided that the votes of at least one-half of the members of each or every such Trade Union entitled to vote are recorded and that at least sixty percent of the votes recorded are in favour of the proposal.

5.8 Duties and Liabilities of a Registered Trade Union

The Trade Union Act, 1926, imposes certain duties and liabilities on registered trade unions, which are as follows:

(1) Change in the address of registered office of a trade Union: It is the duty of a registered trade union to inform any change in the address of its head office by giving the notice of such change to the Registrar of Trade Unions in writing within fourteen days of such change [Section 12]. Thereafter, such change in the address of the registered office is recorded by the Registrar.

(2) Duties relating to the spending of general funds of a registered trade union: Section 15 provides that the general funds of a registered trade union shall not spend on any other objects than the following:

(a) The payment of salaries, allowances and expenses to office bearers of the Trade Union;

(b) The payments of expenses for the administration of the Trade Union, including audit of the accounts of the general funds of the Trade Union;

(c) The prosecution or defence of any legal proceeding to which the Trade Union or any member thereof if a party, when such prosecution or defence is undertaken for the purpose of securing or protecting any rights of the Trade Union as such or any rights arising out of the relations of any member with his employer or with a person whom the member employs;

(d) The conduct of trade dispute on behalf of the Trade Union or any member thereof;

(e) The compensation of members for loss arising out of trade disputes;

(f) Allowances to members or their dependents on account of death, old age, sickness, accidents or unemployment of such members;

(g) The issue of, or the undertaking of liability under, policies of assurance on the lives of members, or under policies insuring members against sickness, accident or unemployment;

(h) The provision of educational, social or religious benefit for members (including the payment of the expenses of funeral or religious ceremonies for deceased members) or for the dependants of members;

(i) The upkeep of a periodical published mainly for the purpose of discussing questions affecting employer's workmen as such;

(j) The payment in furtherance of any of the objects on which the general funds of the Trade Union may be spent, of contributions to any cause intended to benefit workmen in general, provided that the expenditure in respect of such contributions in any financial year shall not at any time during that year be in excess of one-fourth of the combined total of the gross income which has up to that time accrued to the general funds of the Trade Union during that year and of the balance at the credit of those funds at the commencement of that year; and

(k) Subject to any conditions contained in the notification any other object notified by the Appropriate Government in the Official Gazette.

Thus, it is the duty and responsibility of a registered trade union to spend its general funds strictly according to the provisions made in Section 15. If such funds are spent on any other objects other than enumerated in Section 15 of the Act, the expenditure incurred is considered unlawful and *ultra vires* the Act. If any trade union does so, it can be restrained by injunction from applying its general funds for any such object.

(3) The duty and responsibility of spending of the fund constituted for political purposes: Under Section 16(1), a registered trade union may constitute a separate fund, from contribution separately levied for or made, to that fund, from which payments may be made for the promotion of the civic and political interest of its members in furtherance of any of the objects specified in Section 16(2). The objects of using political funds mentioned in Section 16(2) are as follows:

(a) The payment of any expenses incurred either directly or indirectly, by a candidate or prospective candidate for election to a legislative body under the Constitution or to a local body. Such expenses might have been incurred before, after or during the election. or

(b) The holding of any meeting or the distribution of any literature or documents in support of such a candidate or prospective or a candidate.

(c) The maintenance of a person who is a member of a legislative body under the Constitution or of any local authority. or

(d) The registration of electors or the selection of a candidate for election to a legislative body under the Constitution or any local authority, or

(e) The holding of political meeting of any kind or the distribution of political literature or political documents of any kind.

Thus, it is the duty and the responsibility of a registered trade union to use the political fund for the above objects. In no case, expenditure for political purposes is allowed out of the general funds and even interest on investments of general funds must be credited to the general fund only. Moreover, while creating political fund, a registered trade union has to follow conditions, according to the provisions of Section 16 as mentioned below:

(a) Such fund can be created only from contributions separately levied or made to that fund [Section 16(1)].

(b) Members must be compelled to contribute to the fund.

(c) A member who does not contribute to the fund must not be excluded from any benefits of the Trade Union or even placed under any kind of disadvantage, disability etc., indirectly or directly.

(d) Contribution to the political fund must not be made a condition for admission to the Trade Union [Section 16(3)].

(4) Proportion of officers to be connected with the industry: Not less than one-half of the total number of the office bearers of every registered Trade Union shall be persons actually engaged or employed in an industry with which the Trade Union is connected [Section 22].

It is also provided that "the Appropriate Government may by special or general order, declare that the provisions of this section shall not apply to any Trade Union or class of Trade Unions as specified in the order." [Provision to Section 22]

The provisions of Section 22 imply that fifty per cent of the office bearers of a registered trade union may be social or political workers. It is also provided in the section that the Appropriate Government can exempt any trade union from the application of these provisions by special or general order. But it is the responsibility of every registered trade union to consider the provisions of this Section 22 while carrying out its functions.

(5) Duty and responsibility of a registered trade union relating to returns: The provisions relating to returns have been made in Section 28 as follows:

There shall be sent annually to the Registrar, on or before such date as may be prescribed, a general statement audited in the prescribed manner, of all receipts and expenditure of every registered Trade Union during the year ending on the 31st day of December next preceding such prescribed date, and of the assets and liabilities of the Trade Union existing on such 31st day of December. The statement shall be prepared in such form and shall comprise such particulars as may be prescribed [Section 28(1)].

Together with the general statement there shall be sent to the Registrar a statement showing all changes of office bearers made by the Trade Union during the year to which the general statement refers, together also with copy of the rules of the Trade Union corrected up to the date of the despatch thereof to the Registrar [Section 28(2)].

A copy of every alteration made in the rules of a registered Trade Union shall be sent to the Registrar within fifteen days of the making of the alternation [Section 28(3)].

For the purpose of examining the documents referred to in sub-sections (1), (2) and (3), the Registrar, or any officer authorised by him, by general or special order, may at all reasonable times inspect the certificate of registration, account books, registers and other documents, relating to Trade Union, at its registered office or may require their production at such place as he may specify in this behalf, but such place shall be at a distance of more than ten miles from the registered office of a Trade Union [Section 28(4)].

Every registered trade union has to comply with the provisions of Section 28.

(6) Responsibility of a registered trade union not to appoint office-bearers who are disqualified: Provision relating to disqualification of office bearers of a trade union has been made in Section 21-A. By taking into consideration these provisions, persons who are disqualified should not be appointed as office bearers of trade union.

A person shall be disqualified for being, chosen as and for being a member of the executive or any other office bearer of a registered Trade Union, if –
(i) he has not attained the age of eighteen years;
(ii) he has been convicted by a Court in India of any offence involving moral turpitude and sentenced to imprisonment, unless a period of five years has elapsed since his Release [Section 21-A(1)].

Any member of the executive or other office bearer of a registered Trade Union who, before the commencement of the Trade Unions (Amendment) Act, 1964, has been convicted of any offence involving moral turpitude and sentenced to imprisonment, shall on the date of such commencement cease to be such member or office bearer unless a period of five years has elapsed since his release before that date [Section 21-A(2)].

(7) Duty and responsibility relating to audit of accounts: The accounts of a registered trade union must be audited annually by an auditor authorised under the Companies Act, 1956. Thus, it is necessary for every trade union to get its accounts duly audited as per rules.

5.9 Amalgamation of Trade Unions

The provisions relating to amalgamation of Trade Unions have been made in Sections 24, 25 and 26 of this Act. Section 24 provides for the amalgamation of two or more Trade Unions. Section 25 makes provision for the issue of the notice of amalgamation to the Register of Trade Unions and Section 26 makes clear the effects of amalgamation. Now, let us study these provisions.

Any two or more registered Trade Unions may be amalgamated together as one Trade Union with or without dissolution or division of the funds of such Trade Unions or either or any of them. The amalgamation of Trade Unions shall be effective only when votes of at least one-half of the members [of each of the Trade Unions desiring to be amalgamated] entitled to vote are recorded at least sixty per cent of votes thus recorded are in favour of the proposal of amalgamation [Section 24].

It is very essential that the notice in writing of every amalgamation signed by the secretary and by seven members of each and every Trade Union which is the party thereto is required to be sent to the Registrar of Trade Unions. If the head office of the amalgamated Trade Union is situated in a different state, the notice in writing of every amalgamation must be sent to the Registrar of that State [Section 25(1)].

If the Registrar of the State in which the registered head office of the amalgamated trade union is situated is satisfied that all the necessary formalities are complied with and the Trade Union formed as a result is entitled to the registration under Section 6 of this Act, he registers the Trade Union in the manner as provided for in Section 8. The amalgamation becomes effective from the date of such registration [Section 25(4)].

An amalgamation of two or more registered Trade Unions shall not prejudice any right of any such Trade Unions or any right of a creditor of any of them [Section 26(2)].

5.10 Dissolution of a Registered Trade Union

Any registered Trade Union may be dissolved according to the rules of the Trade Union. When a registered Trade Union is dissolved, a notice of the dissolution signed by the Secretary and any seven members of the Trade Union is required to be sent to the Registrar of Trade Unions within fourteen days of the dissolution.

If the Registrar is satisfied that the dissolution has been effected in accordance with the rules of the Trade Union, he registers the dissolution of the Trade Union and such dissolution becomes effective from the date of such registration [Section 27(1)].

It is further provided in Section 27(2) of this Act that where the dissolution of any registered Trade Union has been registered and becomes effective and the rules of the Trade Union do not provide for the distribution of funds of the Trade Union on dissolution, the Registrar shall divide the funds of the Trade Union amongst the members in such a manner as may be prescribed by the rules framed under this Act.

When a registered trade union is dissolved, the notice of the dissolution is required to be sent to the Registrar of Trade Unions in 'Form H' as given below:

FORM 'H'
Trade Unions Act, 1926
Notice of Amalgamation of Trade Unions

Name of Trade Union -
Registration Number
(Address)
Dated the ..... day of .. of ...... 20.

To,
The Registrar of Trade Unions,
Mumbai, Maharashtra State.

Notice is hereby given that the above mentioned Trade Union was dissolved in pursuance of the rules thereof on the .... day of .... 20..

We have been duly authorised by the ....Union to forward this notice on its behalf, such authorisation consisting of a resolution passed at a general meeting on the* day of 20..

(Signed)
1.   Secretary

1
2
3
4
5
6
7
8

---

* Here, insert the date or, if there was no such resolution, state in what other way the authorisation was given.

Maharashtra Recognition of Trade Union and Prevention of Unfair Labour Practices Act

5.11 Introduction

One of the major and important pre-requisites for industrial progress is the prevalence of industrial peace i.e. a suitable climate in which the industries can thrive. Industrial peace broadly implies the absence of industrial unrest, labour problems or the existence of a harmonious cordial relationship or co-operation between workers and their employers. But the problem of industrial peace is common to almost all the industrially developed and developing countries of the world and ever since industrialisation began, every country is making various efforts to find out solutions for establishing industrial peace. However, the methods and ways used in solving the problem of industrial peace or industrial unrest differ from country to country depending upon its economic, social and political environment in existence. Still the problem has not been solved completely. On the contrary, with the advent of the industrial development, labour problems are becoming more and more complicated.

In India, the magnitude of labour problems has increased with the tempo of industrial activities and with industrial development. Problems of wages, strikes and lock-outs, industrial housing, unemployment, trade unions etc. confront the Government as well as social reformers. These labour problems apart from their economic impact, also have social and other repercussions. The welfare of the working class in industrial sector is important both to the industries as well as to the community at large. The Government concern for the welfare of the industrial workers in our country is evident from the fact that a large number of legislative enactments in this field have been passed or improved upon after 1947. Several labour enactments have been promulagated by the central as well as State Governments to safeguard the interests of the industrial workers. Payment of Wages Act, Minimum Wages Act, Industrial Disputes Act, Factories Act, Trade Unions Act, Workmen's Compensation Act, Payment of Bonus Act are some of such Acts.

So far as the Maharashtra State is concerned, previously, the Bombay Industrial Disputes Act, 1938 was passed. The provisions of this Act were availed extensively by the employers as well as the employees in the textile industry. But, with the passage of time and on the strength of the experience gained after passing the Bombay Industrial Disputes Act of 1938, the Government felt it necessary to build further on the same foundations and hence 'The Bombay Industrial Relations Act of 1946' was passed. That Act also was found to be ineffective to deal fully with the growing problems of the industrial workers and hence 'The Maharashtra Recognition of Trade Unions and Prevention of Unfair Labour Practices Act of 1971 was passed to deal with the problems of trade unions and also to provide for the recognition of trade unions for facilitating collective bargaining for certain undertakings, to make clear their rights and obligations, to confer certain powers on unrecognised unions, to provide for declaring certain strikes and lock-outs as illegal strikes and lock-outs, to define properly certain unfair labour practices and to provide for their prevention, to constitute certain courts as independent machinery for carrying out the purposes of the Act etc. The importance of this M.R.T.U. and P.U.L.P. Act is eminent from its title. Efforts have been made to cover many labour litigations under this Act.

Now let us study important provisions of the M.R.T.U. and P.U.L.P. Act of 1971. But before that let us first consider the important objects of passing the Act, its extent commencement and the definitions as given in sections 1, 2 and 3 of the Act.

5.12 Objects of the M.R.T.U. and P.U.L.P. Act of 1971

In the preamble of the Act, various objects of the Act are clearly mentioned. In the preamble, it is stated that –

"Act to provide for the recognition of trade unions for facilitating collective bargaining for certain undertakings, to state their rights and obligations; to confer certain powers on unrecognised unions; to provide for declaring certain strikes and lock-outs as illegal strikes and lock-outs; to define and provide for the prevention of certain unfair labour practices; to constitute courts (as independent machinery) for carrying out the purposes of according recognition to trade unions for enforcing the provisions relating to unfair practices; and to provide for matters connected with the purposes aforesaid.

Thus, from the preamble, we come to know the following objectives behind passing the Act.

1. To provide for the recognition of trade unions for facilitating collective bargaining for certain undertakings covered by the Act;
2. To state the rights and obligations of trade unions;
3. To provide for declaring certain strikes and lock-outs as illegal strikes and lock-outs;
4. To define certain unfair labour practices and to provide for their prevention;
5. To constitute courts as independent machinery for carrying out the purposes of according recognition to trade unions for enforcing the provisions relating to unfair practices.

5.13 Definitions

In this Act, unless the context requires otherwise, the definitions of eighteen words or terms are given in Section three which are as follows:

1. Bombay Act: "Bombay Act" means the Bombay Industrial Relations Act, 1946, Bombay XI of 1947 [Section 3 (1)].

2. Central Act: Central Act" means the Industrial Disputes Act, 1947, XIV of 1947 [Section 3 (2)].

3. Concern: "Concern" means any premises including the precincts thereof where any industry to which the Central Act applies is carried on [Section 3 (3)].

In the definition of 'concern', the words 'any premises' are used. But, they imply any one premise and not more than one. The word 'concern' as defined in this sub-section implies any premises including the precencts thereof where any industry to which the Central Act i.e. the Industrial Disputes Act of 1947 applies is carried on and the expression 'any' in this context should mean only one premise and not more than one premises.

4. Court: "Court" for the purposes of Chapter VI and VII means the Industrial Court, or as the case may be, the Labour Court [Section 3 (4)].

5. Employee: "Employee" in relation to an industry to which the Bombay Act for the time being applies, means an employee as defined in clause (13) of Section 3 of the Bombay Act; and in any other case, means a workman as defined in clause (s) of Section 2 of the Central Act [Section 3 (5)].

The Section 4 (5) is explanatory. It merely states that the term 'employee', in relation to an industry to which the Bombay Industrial Relations Act applies, means an employee as defined in Section 3 (13) of the Bombay Industrial Relations Act and in other cases, an employee means a workman as defined under Section 2 (s) of the Industrial Disputes Act of 1947. Therefore, let us consider the definitions of an employee and a workman as given in both Acts.

According to Section 3 (13) of the Bombay Industrial Relations Act of 1946, "employee means any person employed to do any skilled or unskilled work for hire or reward in any industry, an includes:

(a) A person employed by a contractor to do any work for him in the execution of a contract with an employer within the meaning of sub-clause (e) of clause (14);

(b) A person who has been dismissed, discharged or retrenched or whose services have been terminated from employment on account of any dispute relating to change in respect of which notice is given or an application made under Section 42 whether before or after his dismissal, discharge, retrenchment or, as the case may be, termination from employment.

but does not include –

(i) A person primarily employed in a managerial, administrative, supervisory, or technical capacity drawing basic pay (excluding allowances) exceeding one thousand rupees per month;

(ii) Any other person or class of persons employed in the same capacity as those specified in clause (i) above irrespective of the amount of pay drawn by such persons which the State Government may, by notification in the Official Gazette, specify in this behalf.

6. Employer: "Employer" in relation to an industry to which the Bombay Act applies, means an employer as defined in clause (14) of Section 3 of the Bombay Act; and in any other case, means an employer as defined in clause (g) of Section 2 of the Central Act [Section 3 (6)].

Section 3 (14) of the Bombay Industrial Relations Act of 1946 defines the term 'Employer' as follows:

"Employer" includes –

(a) An association or a group of employer;

(b) Any agent of employers;

(c) Where an industry is conducted or carried on by a department of the State Government, the authority prescribed in that behalf, and where no such authority is prescribed, the head of the department;

(d) Where an industry is conducted or carried on by or on behalf of a local authority, the Chief Executive Officer of the authority;

(e) Where the owner of any undertaking in the course of or for the purpose of conducting the undertaking contracts with any person for the execution by or under the contractor of the whole or any part of any work which is ordinarily part of the undertaking, the owner of the undertaking.

7. Industry: "Industry" in relation to an industry to which the Bombay Act applies means an industry as defined in clause (19) of Section 3 of the Bombay Act, and in any other case, means an industry as defined in clause (j) of Section 2 of the Central Act [Section 3 (7)].

In the M.R.T. and P.U.L.P. Act of 1971, the term 'Industry' has not been defined. But, the Act merely states that in relation to an industry to which the Bombay Industrial Relation Act applies, means an industry as defined in section 3 (19) of Bombay I. R. Act and in other cases, an industry means an industry as defined in Section 2 (J) of the Industrial Disputes Act of 1947. Thus, an industry covers all the industries included in these two Acts. Therefore, let us consider the definitions of an industry as given in both the Acts.

The definition of 'Industry' as given in Section 3 (19) of the Bombay Industrial Relations Act of 1946 is as follows:

"industry" means –

(a) Any business, trade, manufacture of undertaking or calling of employers;

(b) Any calling, service employment, handicraft, or industrial occupation or avocation of employees;

and includes –

(i) Agriculture and agricultural operations;

(ii) Any branch of an industry or group of industries which the [State] Government may be notification in the Official Gazette declare to be an industry for the purposes of this Act.

8. Industrial Court: "Industrial Court" means on Industrial Court constituted under Section 4 of the M.R.T.U. and P.U.L.P. Act of 1971 [Section 3 (8)].

9. Investigating Officer: "Investigating Officer" means an officer appointed under Section 8 of the M.R.T.U. and P.U.L.P. Act of 1971 [Section 3 (9)].

10. Labour Court: 'Labour Court' means a Labour Court constituted under Section 6 of the M.R.T.U. and P.U.L.P. Act of 1971 [Section 3 (10)].

11. Member: 'Member' means a person who is an ordinary member of a union, and has paid a subscription to the union of not less than 50 *paise* per calendar month;

It is also provided that, no person shall at any time be deemed to be a member, if his subscription is in arrears for a period of more than three calendar months during the period of six months immediately preceding such time, and the expression "membership" shall be construed, accordingly [Proviso to the clause 11 of Section 3].

Explanation: A subscription for a particular calendar month shall, for the purpose of this clause, be deemed to be in arrears, if such subscription is not paid within three months after the end of the calendar month in respect of which it is due.

12. Orders: "order" means an order of the Industrial or Labour Court" [Section 3 (12)].

13. Recognised Union: "Recognised union" means a union which has been issued a certificate of recognition under Chapter III [Section 3 (13)].

14. Schedule: "Schedule" means a Schedule to this Act [Section 3 (14)]

15. Undertaking: "Undertaking" for the purposes of Chapter III, means any concern in industry to be one undertaking for the purpose of that Chapter [Section 3 (15)].

16. Unfair Labour Practices: "Unfair labour practices" means unfair labour practices as defined in Section 26 [Section 3 (16)].

17. Union: "Union" means a trade union of employee, which is registered under the Trade Unions Act, 1926 [Section 3 (17)].

It is made clear in clause 18 of Section 3 that "words and expressions used in this Act and not defined therein, but defined in the Bombay Act, shall, in relation to an industry to which the provisions of the Bombay Act apply, have the meanings assigned to them by the Bombay Act; and in any other case, shall have the meanings assigned to them by the Central Act.

5.14 Constitution of the Industrial Court and Qualifications of the Members of the Industrial Court

The State Government is empowered under this Act to constitute the Industrial Court, Provisions relating to the constitution and qualifications of the members of the Industrial Court have been made in Section 4 of the Act which are as follows –

1. The State Government shall by notification in the *Official Gazette*, constitute an Industrial Court.

2. The Industrial Court shall consists of not less than three members, one of whom shall be the President [Section 4 (2)].

3. Every member of the Industrial Court shall be a person who is not connected with the complaint referred to that Court, or with any industry directly affected by such complaint [Section 4 (3)].

It is also provided that, every member shall be deemed to be connected with a complaint or with an industry by reason of his having shares in a company which is connected with, or likely to be affected by, such complaint, unless he discloses to the State Government the nature and extent of the shares held by him in such company and in the opinion of the State Government recorded in writing such member is not connected with the complaint, or the industry [Proviso to Section 4 (3)].

4. Every member of the Industrial Court, shall be a person who is or has been a Judge of a High Court or is eligible for being appointed a Judge of such Court [Section 4 (4)].

It is further provided that one member may be a person who is not so eligible if he possesses in the opinion of the State Government expert knowledge of labour or industrial matters" [Proviso to Section 4 (4)].

Thus, by the notification in the Official Gazette, the State Government has constituted the Industrial Court. The Industrial Court consists of three members and one of them works as the President. Sub-section (3) and (4) of Section 4 throw light on the qualifications of the members of the Industrial Court and also make clear certain restrictions on the State Government to appoint these members. Section 2 (4) provides that every member of the Industrial Court must be person who is or has been a Judge of the High Court or he must be such person who is eligible for being a Judge of the High Court. But it is also provided in clause 4 of Section 4 that there can be one member who is not so qualified. However, such member, in the opinion of the State Government, must have the expert knowledge of labour or industrial matters.

It is also provided in Section 2 (3) that any member of the Industrial Court must not be person who is connected with the complaint referred to that court or with any industry directly affected by such complaint.

Every member is considered to be connected with a complaint or with an industry by reason of his having shares in a company which is connected with or likely to be affected by, such complaint, unless such member discloses to the State Government the nature and the extent of his share holding in such company and in the opinion of the State Government recorded in writing such member is not connected with the complaint, or the industry [Proviso to Section 4 (3)].

Duties of the Industrial Court

There are certain duties entrusted to the Industrial Court under this Act. These duties are enumerated in Section 5 of this Act which are as follows:

Section 5 states that it shall be the duty of the Industrial Court:

(a) To decide an application by a union for grant of recognition to it;

(b) To decide an application by a union for grant of recognition to it in place of a union which has already been recognised under this Act;

(c) To decide an application from another union or an employer for withdrawal or cancellation of the recognition of a union;

(d) To decide complaints relating to unfair labour practices excess unfair labour practice falling in item 1 of Schedule IV;

(e) To assign work and to give directions to the Investigating Officers in matters of verification of membership of unions and investigation of complaints relating to unfair labour practices;

(f) To decide references made to it on any point of law either by any civil or criminal court; and

(g) To decide appeals under Section 42.

5.15 Labour Court – Its Constitution, Duties and Powers

(1) Constitution of Labour Court

The State Government is empowered under this Act to constitute one or more Labour Courts and to appoint persons to preside over such Courts. The provisions relating to the constitution of Labour Courts and to the appointment of persons to preside over such Courts, their qualifications have been made in Section 6 which are as follows:

The State Government shall by notification in the *Official Gazette,* constitute one or more Labour Courts, having jurisdiction in such local areas, as may be specified in such notification, and shall appoint persons having the prescribed qualifications to preside over such Courts".

So far as qualifications of persons to be appointed to preside over Labour Courts under this Act, it is provided that, "no person shall be so appointed, unless he possesses qualifications (other than the qualification of age), prescribed under Article 234 of the Constitution for being eligible to enter the judicial service of the State of Maharashtra; and is not more than sixty years of age" [Proviso to Section 6].

(2) Duties of Labour Court

Following duties have been entrusted to the Labour Court or Labour Courts constituted under this Act.

(a) To decide complaints relating to unfair labour practices which are mentioned or described in item 1 of the Schedule IV; and

(b) To try offences punishable under the Act.

Section 7 lays down that, "It shall be the duty of the Labour Court to decide complaints relating to unfair labour practices described in item 1 of Schedule IV and to try offences punishable under this Act".

Thus, the jurisdiction of the Labour Courts appointed under this Act is limited to give decisions in respect of the complaints relating to unfair labour practices described in item 1 of the Schedule IV appended to this Act and also to try offences punishable under this Act.

In Schedule IV appended to this Act, various general unfair labour practices on the part of employers are given. But the duty of the Labour Courts constituted under this Act is to decide complaints only relating to unfair labour practices described in item 1 of this schedule IV. This item 1 of the said schedule provides that the discharge or dismissal of employees by the employer shall amount to an unfair labour practice if such discharge or dismissal is

(a) By way of victimisation;

(b) Not in good faith, but in the colourable exercise of the employer's rights;

(c) By falsely implicating an employee in a criminal case on the false evidence or on concocted evidence;

(d) For patently false reasons;

(e) On unture or trumped up allegations of absence without leave.

(f) In utter disregard of the principles of natural justice in the conduct of domestic enquiry or with undue haste;

(g) For misconduct of a minor or technical character, without having any regard to the nature of the particular misconduct, so as to amount to a shockingly disproportionate punishment.

5.16 Investigating Officers – Their Appointment, Duties and Powers

(1) Appointment of the Investigation Officers

The Investigating Officers are appointed by the State Government to assist the Industrial Court and Labour Courts in discharge their duties. Such Investigating Officers are appointed for different areas as the State Government considers necessary. The provision relating to the appointment to Investigating Officers are made in Section 8 which is as follows.

"The State Government may, by notification in *Official Gazette,* appoint such number of Investigating Officers for any area as it may consider necessary, to assist the Industrial Courts and Labour Courts in the discharge of their duties".

(2) Duties of Investigating Officers

(a) The Investigating Officer shall be under the control of the Industrial Court, and shall exercise powers and perform duties imposed on him by the Industrial Court [Section 9 (1)].

(b) It shall be the duty of an Investigating Officer to assist the Industrial Court in matters of verification of membership of unions, and assist the Industrial and Labour Courts for investigating into complaints relating to unfair labour practices [Section 9 (2)].

(c) It shall also be the duty of an Investigating Officer to report to the Industrial Court, or as the case may be, the Labour Court the existence of any unfair labour practices in any industry or undertaking, and the names and addresses of the persons said to be engaged in unfair labour practices and any other information which the Investigating Officer may deem fit to report to the Industrial Court, or as the case may be, the Labour Court [Section 9 (3)].

The Investigation Officers work under the control of the Industrial Court and they exercise various powers and perform certain duties as imposed on them by the Industrial Court. Their important duties are as follows:

(a) The Investigation Officers have to assist the Industrial Court in the matters which are mentioned below:

(i) Verification of membership of unions.

(ii) Investigation into complaints relating to unfair labour practices in order to assist the Industrial as well as Labour Courts [Section 9 (2)].

(b) The duty of the Investigating Officers is to report to the Industrial Court or the Labour Court, as the case may be, relating to the following matters:

(i) The existence of any unfair labour practices in any industry or undertaking;

(ii) Information relating to the names and addresses of persons said to be engaged in unfair labour practices; and

(iii) Any other information which the Investigation Officers deem fit to report to the Industrial Court or the Labour Court, as the case may be [Section 9 (3)].

5.17 Recognition of Unions

Provisions relating to the recognition of unions have been made in Chapter III of M.R.T.U. and P.U.L.P. Act. Section 10 throws light on the conditions under which the provisions of Sections 11 and 18 included in Chapter III are made applicable to the undertakings covered by this Act.

Section 10 (1) states that, "Subject to the provisions of sub-sections (2) and (3), the provisions of this Chapter shall apply to every undertaking, wherein fifty or more employees are employed, or were employed on any day of the proceeding twelve months".

It is further provided that, "the State Government may, after giving not less than sixty days' notice of its intention so to do, by notification in the *Official Gazette*, apply the provisions of this Chapter to any undertaking, employing such number of employees less than fifty as may be specified in the notification". [Proviso to Section 10 (1)].

Thus, subject to the provisions of sub-sections (2) and (3) of Section 10, the provisions of Sections 11 to 18 of Chapter III are applicable to every undertaking wherein fifty or more employees are employed or were employed on any day of the preceding twelve months. It is also provided that the State Government, after giving sixty day' notice and by giving notification in the Official Gazette, may apply to provisions of Chapter III to any undertaking even though the number of employees employed is less than fifty.

It is further made clear that, "The provisions of this Chapter shall not apply to undertakings in industries to which the provisions of the Bombay Act for the time being apply" [Section 10 (2)]

Thus, the provisions of this Chapter III are not applicable to undertakings in industries to which the provisions of the Bombay Industrial Relations Act is applicable.

"If the number of employees employed in any undertaking to which the provisions of this Chapter apply at any time falls below fifty continuously for a period of one year, those provisions shall cease to apply to such undertaking" [Section 10 (3)].

The provisions of Section 10 (3) clearly indicate that any undertaking to which the provisions of Chapter III apply; if in such undertaking, the number of employees employed falls below fifty continuously for a period of one year, then the provisions of this Chapter III shall not apply to such undertaking. Thus, the provisions of Section 10 makes clear the scope of Chapter III.

5.18 Cancellation of Recognition and Suspension of Rights [Section 13]

Provisions have been made in Section 13 of this Act relating to cancellation of recognition and suspension by empowering and Industrial Court either to cancel the recognition of a union or to suspend any or all of its rights under certain circumstances. The grounds for cancellation of recognition and suspension of rights of a union are given in Section 13 (1). This Section 13 also lays down the procedure and the manner in which the

Industrial Court and exercises its power in that respect. The provisions of Section 13 are given below:

Section 13 Cancellation of Recognition and Suspension of Rights: The Industrial Court shall cancel the recognition of a union if after giving notice to such union to show cause why its recognition should not be cancelled and after holding an inquiry, it is satisfied.

1. That it was recognised under mistake misrepresentation or fraud; or
2. That the membership of the union has, for a continuous period of six calendar months, fallen below the minimum required under Section 11 for its recognition:

Provided that, where a strike (not being an illegal strike under the Central Act) has extended to a period exceeding fourteen days in any calendar month, such month shall be excluded in computing the said period of six months:

Provided further that, the recognition of a union shall not be cancelled under the provisions of this sub-clause, unless its membership for the calendar month in which show cause notice under this section was issued was less than such minimum; or

3. That the recognised union has, after its recognition, failed to observe any of the conditions specified in Section 19; or
4. That the recognised union is not being conducted *bona fide* in the interest of employees, but in the interest of employer to the prejudice of the interest of employees; or
5. That it has instigated, aided, or assisted the commencement or continuation of a strike which is deemed to be illegal under this Act, XVI of 1926; or
6. That its registration under the Trade Union Act, 1926, is cancelled; or
7. That another union has been recognised in place of a union recognised under this Chapter.

Thus, from the provisions of Section 13 (1), we come to know the following seven grounds on which the Industrial Court is empowered to cancel the recognition of a union even after giving the notice to such union to show cause as to why its recognition should not be cancelled.

After holding an inquiry, if the Industrial Court is satisfied that the Union –

1. Was recognised under mistake misrepresentation or fraud, or
2. Its membership has fallen below the minimum required under Section 11, or
3. It failed to observe any of the conditions specified in Section 19, or
4. It acted against the interest of the employees and in the interest of the employer, or
5. It has instigated, aided or assisted the commencement or continuation of a strike deemed to be illegal, or
6. Its registration is cancelled under the Trade Unions Act, 1926 or
7. Another union has been recognised in its place under this chapter. However, the proviso to sub-section (1) lays down that (a) where a strike extends for more than

fourteen days in any calendar month such month shall be excluded in computing the period of six months, or (b) its recognition shall be cancelled its membership falls down for the calendar month in which show cause notice under this section was issued, the Industrial Court is empowered to cancel the recognition of such union. Section 13 (2) states that, "The Industrial Court may cancel the recognition of a union if, after giving notice to such union to show cause why its recognition should not be cancelled, and after holding an inquiry, it is satisfied, that it has committed any practice which is, or has been declared as, an unfair labour practice under this Act".

It is further provided that, in having regard to the circumstances in which such practice has been committed, the Industrial Court is of opinion that instead of cancellation of the recognition of the union, it may suspend all or any of its rights under sub-section (1) of Section 20 or under Section 23, the Industrial Court may pass an order accordingly, and specify the period for which such suspension may remain in force [Proviso to Section 13 (2)].

Thus, section 13 (2) provides that the recognition can also be cancelled if the union has committed any practice which is, or has been declared as an unfair labour practice under this Act.

However, considering the circumstances, if the Industrial Court is of the opinion that there is no need of cancellation of the recognition of the union, it may suspend all or any of its rights under section 20 (1) or 23 by passing the necessary orders and specifying the period for which such suspension shall remain in force.

5.19 Recognition of Other Union [Section 14]

Section 14 provides for granting the status of a recognised union to other union in place of a recognised union which is already registered as such subject to certain essential conditions. These conditions are laid down in Section 14 in clauses (1) to (4). In brief, these conditions are as follows:

1. Applicant union must have largest membership of employees;
2. A period of two years must have elapsed since the date of registration of recognised union, or/and;
3. A period of one year has elapsed since the date of disposal of the provisions application of that union;
4. The applicant union complies with the conditions necessary for recognition, as specified in Section 11 and 19 of this Act;
5. Its membership during the whole period of six months, (immediately preceding the calendar month in which it made application was larger than the membership of the recognised union.

Section 14 also lays down the procedure to be followed by the Industrial while taking action in respect of recognition of other union. Section 14 is reproduced below in order to understand fully the essential conditions and the procedure to be followed while giving recognition to other union.

5.20 Obligations of Recognised Unions [Section 19]

According to the provisions of Section 19 which relates to the obligations of recognised union, "The rules of a union seeking recognition under this Act shall provide for the following matters, and the provisions thereof shall be duly observed by the union, namely:

1. The membership subscription shall be not less than fifty paise per month;
2. The Executive committee shall meet at intervals of not more than three months;
3. All resolutions passed, whether by Executive Committee or the General Body of the union, shall be recorded in a minute book kept for the purpose;
4. An auditor appointed by the State Government may audit its account at least once in each financial year".

Above mentioned four conditions have been imposed upon a union seeking recognition under this Act. But so far as last condition i.e. an auditor appointed by the State Government may audit its account at least once in each financial year, is concerned this condition is not within the control of the union as it is the State Government to appoint the auditor for the purpose of auditing its accounts. If the State Government appoints any auditor, it is obligatory on the part of a union seeking recognition under this Act to get its account duly audited. Section 13 (1) (iii) empowers the Industrial Court to cancel the recognition or to suspend the rights of a recognised union if it fails to observe the conditions mentioned in Section 19. Thus, a recognised union or any union seeking recognition must comply with the conditions as are laid down in Section 19. Besides these conditions, a union seeking recognition has to fulfil the conditions mentioned in section 12 of this Act. Provisions of Section 12 have been already discussed.

5.21 Rights of Recognised Unions [Section 20]

Recognised unions enjoy certain rights. The provisions relating to such rights have been made in Section 20 of the Act. Section 20 lays down that –

(1) Such officers, members of the office staff and members of a recognised union as may be authorised by or under rules made in this behalf by the State Government shall, in such manner and subject to such conditions as may be prescribed have a right:

(a) To collect sums payable by members to the union on the premises, where wages are paid to them;

(b) To put up or cause to be put up a notice board on the premises of the undertaking in which its members are employed and affix or cause to be affixed notice thereon;

(c) For the purpose of the prevention or settlement of an industrial dispute:

(i) To hold discussion on the premises of the undertaking with the employees concerned, who are the members of the union but so as not to interfere with the due working of the undertaking;

(ii) To meet and discuss, with an employer or any person appointed by him in that behalf, the grievances of employees employed in this undertaking;

(iii) To inspect, if necessary, in an undertaking any place where any employee of the undertaking is employed;

(d) To appear on behalf of any employee or employees in any domestic or departmental inquiry held by the employer [Section 20 (1)].

(2) Where there is a recognised union for any undertaking:

(a) That union alone shall have the right to appoint its nominees to represent workmen on the Works Committee constituted under Section 3 of the Central Act;

(b) No employee shall be allowed to appear or act or be allowed to be represented in any proceedings under the Central Act (not being a proceedings in which the legality or propriety of an order to dismissal, discharge, removal retrenchment, termination of service, or suspension of an employee is under consideration), except through recognised union and the decision arrived at, or order made, in such proceeding shall be binding on all the employees in such undertaking; and accordingly, the provisions of the Central Act, that is to say, the Industrial Disputes Act, 1947, XIV of 1947, shall stand amended in the manner and to the extent specified in Schedule I [Section 20 (2)].

5.22 Rights of Unrecognised Unions [Section 22]

Unrecognised unions also enjoy certain rights under this Act. Such rights are given in Section 22 where are as follows:

"Such officers, members of the office staff and members of any union (other than a recognised union) as may be authorised by or under the rules made in this behalf by the State Government shall, in such manner and subject to such conditions as may be prescribed, have a right –

(1) To meet and discuss with an employer or any person appointed by him in that behalf, the grievances of any individual member relating to his discharge, removal, retrenchment, termination of service and suspension;

(2) To appear on behalf of any of its members employed in the undertaking in any domestic or departmental inquiry held by the employer" [Section 22].

Thus, the officers, members of the office staff and members of a recognised union have a right to (1) discuss with an employer in the matters related to discharge, removal, retrenchment, termination of service and suspension of any individual member, and (2) to appear an behalf of its members in any domestic or departmental inquiry held by the employer under Section 22.

5.23 Meaning of Unfair Labour Practices and Various Unfair Labour Practices [Section 26]

In this Act, unless the context requires otherwise, unfair labour practices mean any of the practices listed in Schedules II, III and IV [Section 26]. It is laid down in Section 27 that "no employer or union and no employee shall engage in any unfair labour practice".

Various unfair labour practices on the part of the employers are given in Schedule II.

SCHEDULE II
Unfair Labour Practices on the part of the employers

1. To interfere with, restrain or coerce employees in the exercise of their right to organise, form, join or assist a trade union and to engage in concerted activities for the purposes of collective bargaining or other mutual aid or protection, that is to say –
   (a) Threatening employees with discharge or dismissal, if they join a union;
   (b) Threatening a lock-out or closure, if a union should be organised;
   (c) Granting wage increase to employees at crucial periods of union organisation, with a view to undermining the efforts of the union at organisation.

2. To dominate, interfere with, or contribute, support - financial or otherwise - to any union, that is to say –
   (a) An employer taking an active interest in organising a union of his employees; and
   (b) An employer showing partiality or granting favour to one of several unions attempting to organise his employees or to its members, where such a union is not a recognised union.

3. To establish employer sponsored unions.

4. To encourage or discourage membership in any union by discriminating against any employee, that is to say -
   (a) Discharging or punishing an employee because he urged other employees to join or organise a union;
   (b) Discharging or dismissing an employee for taking part in any strike (not being a strike which is deemed to be an illegal strike under this Act);
   (c) Changing seniority rating of employee because of union activities;
   (d) Refusing to promote employees to higher posts on account of their union activities;
   (e) Giving unmerited promotions to certain employees, with a view to show discord amongst the other employees, or to undermine the strength of their union;
   (f) Discharging office-bearers or active union members, on account of their union activities.

5. To refuse to bargain collectively, in good faith, with the recognised union.

6. Proposing or continuing a lock-out deemed to be illegal under this Act.

Various unfair labour practices on the part of trade unions are given in Schedule III.

SCHEDULE III

Unfair Labour Practices on the part of Trade Unions

1. To advise or actively support or instigate any strike deemed to be illegal under this Act.
2. To coerce employees in the exercise of their right to self-organisation or to join unions or refrain from joining any union, that is to say –
(a) for a union or its members to picketing in such a manner that non-striking employees are physically debarred from entering the workplace;
(b) to indulge in acts of force or violence or to hold out threats of intimidation in connection with a strike against non-striking employees or against managerial staff.
3. For a recognised union to refuse to bargain collectively in good faith with the employer.
4. To indulge in coercive activities against certification of a bargaining representative.
5. To stage, encourage or instigate such forms of coercive actions as willful "go-slow" squatting on the work premises after working hours or of "gherao" of any of the members of the managerial staff.
6. To stage demonstrations at the residence of the employers or the managerial or other staff members.

In schedule IV, the general unfair labour practises on the part of employers are given.

SCHEDULE IV

General Unfair Labour Practices on the Part of employers

1. To discharge or dismiss employees –
(a) By way of victimisation;
(b) Not in good faith, but in the colourable exercise of the employer's rights;
(c) By falsely implicating an employee in a criminal case on false evidence or on concocted evidence;
(d) For patently false reasons;
(e) On untrue or trumped up allegations of absence without leave;
(f) In utter disregard of the principles of natural justice in the conduct of domestic enquiry or with undue haste;
(g) For misconduct of a minor or technical character, without having any regard to the nature of the particular misconduct or the past record of service of the employee, so as to amount to a shockingly disproportionate punishment.
2. To abolish the work of a regular nature being done by employees, and to give such work to contractors as a measure of breaking a strike.
3. To transfer an employee *mala fide* from one place to another place, under the guise following management policy.

4. To insist upon individual employees, who were on legal strike, to sign a good conduct-bond, as a pre-condition to allowing them to resume work.
5. To show favouritism or partiality to one set of workers, regardless of merits.
6. To employ employees as "badlis", casuals or temporaries and to continue them as such for years, with the object of depriving them of the status and privileges of permanent employees.
7. To discharge or discriminate against any employee for filing charges or testifying against an employer in any enquiry or proceeding relating to any industrial dispute.
8. To recruit employees during a strike which is not an illegal strike.
9. Failure to implement award, settlement or agreement.
10. To indulge in act of force or violence.

5.24 Provisions Relating to Modification of Schedules

Provisions relating to modifications of various schedules appended to this Act have been done in Section 53 of the Act. These provisions are as under:

1. The State Government may, after obtaining the opinion of the Industrial Court, by notification in the *Official Gazette*, at any time make any addition to, or alteration, in any Schedule II, III or IV and may, in the like manner, delete any item therefrom [Section 53 (1)].

It is also provided that, before making any such addition, alteration or deletion, a draft of such addition, alternation or deletion shall be published for the information of all persons likely to be affected thereby, and the State Government shall consider any objections or suggestions that may be received by it from any person with respect thereto [Proviso to Section 53 (1)].

2. Every such notification shall, as soon as possible after its issue, be laid by the State Government before the Legislature of the State [Section 53 (2)].

5.25 The Procedure to be followed for Dealing with Complaints relating to Unfair Labour Practices [Section 28]

While dealing with the complaints relating to unfair labour practices, following procedure is to be followed according to the provisions of Section 28 of the Act.

1. Where any person has engaged in or is engaging in any unfair labour practice, then any union or any employee or any employer or any Investigating Office may, within ninety days of the occurrence of such unfair labour practice, file a complaint before the Court competent to deal with such complaint either under section 5, or as the case may be, under section 7, of this Act;

Provided that, the Court may entertain a complaint after the period of ninety days from the date of the alleged occurrence, if good and sufficient reasons are shown by the complainant for the late filing of the complaint.

2. The Court shall take a decision on every such complaint as far as possible within a period of six months from the ate of receipt of the complaint.

3. On receipt of a complaint under sub-section (1), the Court may, if it so considers necessary, first cause an investigation into the said complaint to be made by the Investigating Officer, and direct that a report in the matter may be submitted by him to the Court, within the period specified in this direction.

4. While investigating into any such complaint, the Investigating Officer may visit the undertaking, where the practice alleged is said to have occurred, and make such enquiries as he considers necessary. He may also make efforts to promote settlement of the complaint.

5. The Investigating Officer shall, after investigating into the complaint under sub-section (4) submit his report to the Court, within the time specified by it, setting out the full facts and circumstances of the case, and the efforts made by him in settling the complaint. The Court shall, on demand and on payment of such fee as may be prescribed by rules, supply a copy of the report to the complainant and the person complained against.

6. If, on receipt of the report of the Investigating Officer, the Court finds that the complaint has not been settled satisfactorily, and that facts and circumstances of the case require, that the matter should be further considered by it, the Court shall proceed to consider it, and give its decision.

7. The decision of the Court, which shall be in writing, shall be in the form of an order. The order of the Court shall be final and shall not be called in question in any civil or criminal court.

8. The Court shall cause its order to be published in such manner as may be prescribed. The order of the Court shall become enforceable from the date specified in the order.

9. The Court shall forward a copy of its order to the State Government and such officers of the Stage Government as may be prescribed.

5.26 Penalties

Provision relating to penalties for (1) disclosure of confidential information, (2) contempts of the Industrial or Labour Courts and (3) obstructing officers from carrying out their duties and for failure to produce documents or the compliance with requision or order have been made in Section 47, 48 and 49 respectively. These sections are given below:

(1) Penalty for Disclosure of Confidential Information:

If an Investigating Officer or any person present at, or concerned, in any proceeding under this Act wilfully discloses any information or the contents of any document in contravention of provisions of this Act, he shall, on conviction, on a complaint made by the party who gave the information or produced the document in such proceeding, be punished with fine which may extend to one thousand rupees [Section 47].

(2) Penalty for contempts of the Industrial or Labour Courts [Section 48]:

The main object of Section 48 is to impose certain legal obligations upon the concerned persons or parties to comply with the orders of the Industrial or Labour Courts, as the case may be. If the persons or parties do not comply with the orders of the Industrial or Labour Courts, that leads to the contempt of the Court punishable under this Act. The punishments for contempts of the Industrial or Labour Courts according to the provisions of section 48 are as under.

(a) Any person who fails to comply with any other of the Court under clause (b) of sub-section (1) or sub-section (2) of section 30 of this Act shall, on conviction, be punished with imprisonment which may extend to three months or with fine which may extend to five thousand rupees.

(b) If any person,

(i) When ordered by the Industrial Court or a Labour Court to produce or deliver up any document or to furnish information being legally bound so to do, intentionally omits to do so; or

(ii) When required by the Industrial Court or a Labour Court to bind himself by an oath or affirmation to state the truth refuse to do so;

(iii) Being legally bound to state the truth on any subject to the Industrial Court or a Labour Court refuses to answer any question demanded of him touching such subject by such Court; or

(iv) Intentionally offers any insult or causes any interruption to the Industrial Court or a Labour Court at any stage of its judicial proceeding, he shall, on conviction, be punished with imprisonment for a term which may extend to six months or with fine which may extend to one thousand rupees or with both.

(v) If any person refuses to sign any statement made by him, when required to do so by the Industrial Court or a Labour Court, he shall, on conviction, be punished with imprisonment for term which may extend to three months or with fine which may extend to five hundred rupees or with both.

(vi) If any offence under sub-section (2) or (3) is committed in the view or presence of the Industrial Court or as the case may be, a Labour Court, such Court may, after recording the facts constituting the offence and the statement of the accused as provided in the Code of Criminal Procedure, 1898, V of 1898 forward the case to a Magistrate having jurisdiction to try the same, and may require security to be given for the appearance of the accused person before such Magistrate or, if sufficient security is not given, shall forward such person in custody to such Magistrate. The magistrate to whom any case is so forwarded shall proceed to hear the complaint against the accused person in the manner provided in the said Code or Criminal Procedure.

(vii) If any person commits any act or publishes any writing which is calculated improperly influence the Industrial Court, or a Labour Court or to bring such Court or a member of a Judge thereof into disrepute or contempt or to its or his authority, or to interfere with the lawful process of any such Court, such person shall be deemed to be guilty of contempt of such Court.

(viii) In the case of contempt of itself, the Industrial Court shall record the facts constituting such contempt, and make a report in that behalf to the High Court.

(ix) In the case of contempt of a Labour Court, such Court shall record the facts constituting such contempt, and make a report in that behalf to the Industrial Court; and thereupon, the Industrial Court may, if it considers it expedient to do so, forward the report to the High Court.

(x) When any intimation or report in respect of any contempt is received by the High Court under sub-sections (6) or (7), the High Court shall deal with such contempt as if it were contempt of itself, and shall have and exercise in respect of it the same jurisdiction, powers and authority in accordance with the same procedure and practice as it has and exercises in respect of contempt of itself.

(3) Penalty for Obstructing Officers from Carrying out their Duties and for Failure to Produce Documents or to Comply with Requisition or Order [Section 49]

Any person who wilfully:

(a) Prevents or obstructs officers, members of the office staff, or members of any union from exercising any of their rights conferred by this Act;

(b) Refuses entry to an Investigating Officer to any place which he is entitled to enter;

(c) Fails to produce any document which he is required to produce; or

(d) Fails to comply with any requisition or order issued by him or under the provisions of this Act or the rules made thereunder;

shall, on conviction, be punished with fine which may extend to five hundred rupees.

5.27 Recovery of Money due from Employer

Where any money is due to an employee from an employer under an order passed by the Court under Chapter VI, the employee himself or any other person authorised by him in writing in this behalf, or in the case of death of the employee, his assignee or heirs may, without prejudice to any other mode of recovery, make an application to the Court for the recovery of money due to him, and if the Court is satisfied that any money is so due, it shall issue a certificate for that amount to the Collector, who shall, proceed to recover the same in the same manner as an arrear of land revenue [Section 50].

It is provided that, every such application shall be made within one year from the date on which money became due to the employee from the employer [Proviso 1 to Section 50].

It is further provided further that, any such application may be entertained after the expiry of the said period of one year, if the Court is satisfied that the applicant had sufficient cause for not making the application within the said period [Proviso 2 to Section 50].

5.28 Recovery of Fines

The amount of any fine imposed under this Chapter shall be recoverable as arrears of land revenue [Section 51].

Questions for Discussion

1. State the objects of Trade Union Act, 1926.
2. Explain the procedure for registration of Trade Union.
3. State the various penalties under the Trade Union Act, 1926.
4. Explain the constitution and duties of Industrial Court (M.R.T.U. and P.U.L.P. Act, 1971).
5. Explain the constitution and powers of Labour Court (M.R.T.U. and P.U.L.P. Act, 1971).
6. Explain the various Penalties (under M.R.T.U. and P.U.L.P. Act, 1971).
7. Explain:
   (A) Cancellation of Registration of Trade Union
   (B) Amalgamation of Trade Unions
   (C) Investigation Officer (M.R.T.U. and P.U.L.P. Act, 1971)
   (D) Recognition of Union (M.R.T.U. and P.U.L.P. Act, 1971)
   (E) Rights of Recognised Unions (M.R.T.U. and P.U.L.P. Act, 1971)
   (F) Employee (M.R.T.U. and P.U.L.P. Act, 1971)
   (H) Unfair Labour Practices (M.R.T.U. and P.U.L.P. Act, 1971)
8. Write Short Notes:
   (A) Rules of Trade Union
   (B) Rights of Registered Trade Union
   (C) Dissolution of Trade Union
   (D) Rights of Recognised Unions (M.R.T.U. and P.U.L.P. Act, 1971)

Questions from Previous Pune University BBA Examinations

1. Write Short Notes:
   (A) Unfair Labour Practices. **April 2011**

Ans.: Refer to Article 5.23 of this Chapter.

   (B) Authorities under M.R.T.U. and P.U.L.P. Act, 1971. **October 2011**

Ans.: Refer to Articles 5.14, 5.15 and 5.16 of this Chapter.

2. Describe various powers of Industrial Court under the Maharashtra Recognition of Trade Union and Prevention of Unfair Labour Practices Act, 1971. **October 2012**

Ans.: Refer to Article 5.14 of this Chapter.

✱✱✱

April 2015

402: Industrial Relations And Labour Laws

(New 2013 Pattern) (Semester - IV)

Time: 3 Hours   Max. Marks: 80

Instructions to the candidates:
1. All questions are compulsory.
2. Figures to the right indicate full marks.

1. Discuss the various approaches towards the study of Industrial Relations.   [15]

   OR

   Discuss the concept of Trade union and its functions in detail.

2. Define "Industrial Dispute". What are its causes?   [15]

   OR

   What is conflict? Discuss the conflict Resolution Method of conciliation and Arbitration in detail.

3. Discuss the provisions related to Health under the factories Act, 1948.   [15]

   OR

   Discuss the concept of
   (a) Strikes and lay outs
   (b) Lay-off
   (c) Retrenchament

4. Define Trade union. Discuss the provisions relating to Registration of Trade union.

   [15]

   OR

   What is Worker's participation in Management? (WPM). Discuss its meaning, Advantages and Disadvantages.

5. Write Short notes on (Any four):   [20]
   (a) Features of collective Bargaining.
   (b) Provisions Relating to leave with wages.
   (c) Powers of labour court and Industrial court.
   (d) Concept of Employee Engagement.
   (e) Meaning of Wages under Minimum wages Act, 1948.
   (f) Mediation.

   ***

www.ingramcontent.com/pod-product-compliance
Lightning Source LLC
Chambersburg PA
CBHW062133160426
43191CB00013B/2292